PRAISE F[
CHOKEPOINT C[

"Are you a writer, a musician, an artist? Is Big Tech eating your brain and sucking your financial blood? Rebecca Giblin and Cory Doctorow's *Chokepoint Capitalism* tells us how the vampires crashed the party and provides protective garlic. Your brain must remain your own concern, however."

—MARGARET ATWOOD, author of *The Handmaid's Tale*

"The story of how a few giant corporations are strangling the life out of our media ecosystem is one of the most important of the decade, and Giblin and Doctorow tell it better than anyone. Searing, essential, and incredibly readable."

—ADAM CONOVER, comedian and host of *The G Word*

"This book is an absolute must-read for anyone who senses that the predominant economic mythology is a lie, who wants to know what's really happening in this economy—and who is ready to finally start fixing the problem."

—DAVID SIROTA, writer of *Don't Look Up* and founder of The Lever

"Rather than simply lamenting the problem, or falling back on clichés about starving artists, what Rebecca Giblin and Cory Doctorow do in *Chokepoint Capitalism* is make clear the overall pattern that drives exploitation of artists. . . . Every creator will find inspiration here."

—ANIL DASH, CEO of Glitch

"Capitalism doesn't work without competition. Giblin and Doctorow impressively show the extent to which that's been lost throughout the creative industries and how this pattern threatens every other worker."

—CRAIG NEWMARK, founder of Craigslist

"Instead of just complaining about the corporate stranglehold over production and exchange, Giblin and Doctorow show us why this happened, how it works, and what we can do about it. . . . An infuriating yet inspiring call to collective action."

—DOUGLAS RUSHKOFF, author of *Throwing Rocks at the Google Bus* and *Survival of the Richest*

"Rebecca Giblin and Cory Doctorow lay out their case in plain and powerful prose, offering a grand tour of the blighted cultural landscape and how our arts and artists have been chickenized, choked, and cheated."

—KAISER KUO, host and cofounder of *The Sinica Podcast*

CHOKEPOINT CAPITALISM

Rebecca Giblin is a professor at Melbourne Law School, where she works at the intersection of law and culture, leading interdisciplinary teams researching issues around creators' rights, access to knowledge, and technology regulation. She is director of the Intellectual Property Research Institute of Australia (IPRIA) and heads up the Author's Interest and eLending projects, as well as Untapped: The Australian Literary Heritage Project. Follow her on Twitter (@rgibli).

Cory Doctorow is a bestselling science fiction writer and activist. He is a special advisor to the Electronic Frontier Foundation, with whom he has worked for twenty years. He is also a visiting professor of computer science at the Open University (UK) and of library science at the University of North Carolina, and is an MIT Media Lab research affiliate. He cofounded the UK Open Rights Group and co-owns the website Boing Boing. Follow him on Twitter (@doctorow).

CHOKE POINT CAPITALISM

Rebecca Giblin &
Cory Doctorow

SCRIBE
Melbourne • London

Scribe Publications
18–20 Edward St, Brunswick, Victoria 3056, Australia
2 John St, Clerkenwell, London, WC1N 2ES, United Kingdom

First published by Beacon Press, Boston, Massachusetts 2022
Published by Scribe 2022

Internal pages designed by Kim Arney
Illustrations by Lauren Kinnard

Printed and bound in Australia by Griffin Press

Scribe is committed to the sustainable use of natural resources
and the use of paper products made responsibly from those
resources.

Scribe acknowledges Australia's First Nations peoples as the
traditional owners and custodians of this country, and we pay
our respects to their elders, past and present.

978 1 761380 07 5 (Australian edition)
978 1 915590 01 5 (UK edition)
978 1 922586 83 4 (ebook)

Catalogue records for this book are available from the National
Library of Australia and the British Library.

scribepublications.com.au
scribepublications.co.uk

For Joan Robinson,
who understood and explained
monopsony first.

If only we'd listened to her.

CONTENTS

PART 1

CULTURE HAS BEEN CAPTURED

CHAPTER 1

BIG BUSINESS CAPTURED CULTURE

Culture has been captured. Three massive conglomerates own the three record labels and three music publishers that control most of the world's music. They designed the streaming industry, dominated by Spotify, which itself is (or was) partly owned by those same three labels. When Disney swallowed 21st Century Fox, a single company assumed control of 35 percent of the US box office. Google and Facebook have a lock on the digital ads that are wrapped around music, videos, and news online. Google, along with Apple, is the gatekeeper of everything mobile, giving it a massive cut on games, books, music, and movies. Via YouTube, it controls video streaming. Live Nation has sewn up ticketing and concerts. In the US, one company dominates terrestrial radio, and another satellite. Amazon has an iron grip on book, ebook, and audiobook sales, and dominates ebook and audiobook production. The only publisher that might be able to hold its own is Penguin Random House, and then only by gulping down as many other big publishers as it possibly can. The Big Six trade book publishers had become the Big Five by the time we started writing this book, and are making moves to become the Big Four by the time it's published.

Between them, these corporations are generating enormous wealth. Some of the creators they distribute are too, but headlines about Jay-Z's billion-dollar fortune or the juicy advance paid to the debut author of a hot new thriller disguise the reality: precious little of the vast wealth generated by art and culture is shared with the people who actually make it.

Culture markets are winner-takes-all: a handful of people take almost all the rewards. This has long been the case, but now there's less and less to share between everyone else. For book authors, advances have been cut by more than half since the Great Financial Crisis of 2007–8. News publishers once got almost all the money from ads on their content, but that's fallen to as little as thirty cents on the dollar. Songwriters report royalty statements have become "four times as thick for a quarter of the money."[1] Fiona Bevan, who cowrote the hit track "Unstoppable" with Kylie Minogue, reported receiving just a hundred pounds in streaming royalties, despite its featuring on an album that topped the British charts.[2] Rebecca Gates, who surveyed musicians for the Future of Music Coalition, says even well-known artists are struggling. "I've seen hard data for people who are in successful bands, quote unquote, festival headlining bands, who would make more money in a good retail job."[3] Guitarist and producer Melvin Gibbs, who has been featured on almost two hundred albums, knows the system isn't working. "One of the principles of having a healthy ecosystem is that every level of the ecosystem has to be operating at maximum efficiency. The plankton have to be healthy for the blue whales to survive." But the music business (and arts industries more broadly), are "based on *starving* the plankton so that the whales can survive."[4]

The reason creative workers are receiving a declining share of the wealth generated by their work is the same reason all workers are receiving a smaller share—we have structured society to make rich people richer at everyone else's expense. The playing field has been tilted so far that a growing number of people are falling off the edge, beset by precarious employment, stagnating wages, high costs for education, housing and healthcare, and economic policies that prize shareholders over people and communities.

This great tilting of the playing field, away from workers and toward owners, has a variety of causes, but the biggest is a radical theory of antitrust, driven by jurist and far-right cult-of-personality darling Robert Bork and exported by his disciples at the Chicago school of economics.

During the glory years of antitrust—after the New Deal, before Bork—governments set themselves the task of shrinking monopolies on the grounds that they were *bad*. Very large companies were able to exert undue influence on governments, bribing or coercing them into enacting policies that were good for those companies' shareholders and harmful to their workers, customers, and the rest of society. These unelected titans were able to crush competitors, hold back entire industries, and reorder the economy and civilization according to their whims. Monopoly was viewed as a threat to the very idea of democratic citizenship. After all, firms making huge profits thanks to a lack of competition can launder that money into policy, with the result that policymakers make decisions based on the needs of the few, not the many.

Then the Chicago School pulled off a brilliant coup. They promoted an antitrust theory that dispensed with the idea of citizenship altogether; instead, they insisted anti-monopoly regulators should limit themselves to thinking about "consumer welfare," forgetting all that high-minded stuff about "democracy" and "citizenship." Bork's version of antitrust concerned itself primarily with maximizing *short-term* consumer welfare—mostly in the form of lower prices—rather than promoting competition as an end in and of itself. (We emphasize "short-term" because it turns out that once fields are cleared of competitors, consumer benefits like lower prices evaporate fast.)[5]

Putting the focus on consumer welfare changed the calculus completely. So long as prices went down (or at least, didn't go up), companies more or less stopped having to worry about antitrust enforcers showing up with subpoenas. That meant they could use predatory pricing to squeeze smaller rivals out of markets. It also meant they could dangle the promise of new efficiencies and lower prices to persuade regulators to let them buy up competitors that were previously out of bounds.

This new theory unleashed a powerful, slow-moving glacier of monopolization upon the world in the Reagan years, and it has now scraped away nearly all the beautiful and lively things in its path.

Capitalism is supposed to be based on free markets, but markets have a natural tendency "toward monopoly, destructive extraction, and rent-seeking," and so "require vigilant stewardship precisely to ensure they remain sufficiently marketlike."[6] That vigilance has been AWOL during the fifty-odd years of the Chicago School's hands-off approach, and, as a result, competition in the US was virtually eliminated in an astonishing variety of industries. Just a handful of firms—or sometimes only one—now control everything from the arts (publishing, movies, music, streaming, comics, bookselling, movie theaters, talent agencies, games, wrestling, radio stations) to finance (banks, investment funds, auditors, bond-rating agencies) to agribusiness (seeds, livestock, tractors, fertilizer, pesticides, precision agriculture, and the production of meat, eggs, grain, and produce) and everything in between (cruise lines, cheerleader uniforms, groceries, pharmaceuticals, glass bottles, medical devices, airlines, eyeglasses, athletic shoes, fast food, food delivery, and pet food).

Some of this increased concentration is courtesy of a tsunami of mergers: the number of US publicly traded companies dropped by half even as they increased by 50 percent in other developed nations.[7] Companies always pinkie swear their mergers will result in lower prices, but analyses done after the fact show again and again that prices actually go up—especially when the merger is in an already concentrated market.[8] Regulators keep accepting those promises, and their credulity sometimes appears to work in their favor: one FCC Commissioner joined Comcast as "senior vice president for government affairs" just four months after voting in favor of its mega-merger with NBC Universal.[9]

If the consumer welfare standard really were working out for us, wealth equality would be improving. In fact, it's going backwards, with the top 1 percent's net worth increasing by 650 percent in the thirty years from 1989, thanks largely to their holdings of corporate stock.[10] That outstrips the gains of the bottom half by almost four times. Of course, it's those Chicago School policies that made that stock skyrocket in value. Corporations in concentrated industries have higher margins—not because those companies are more efficient or particularly well-managed, but because they can keep competition at bay.[11]

If investors and corporations are the winners in all this, workers are the losers. When excessive corporate power saps workers' power to bargain for improved pay and conditions, we share less and less in the returns from our work. That's been happening for the last forty years—not just for creative workers, but for almost all of us. Between 1940 and 1980, US wage growth tracked closely with the increased value workers produced: as we became more productive, we got more pay. In the forty years since, however, we've been cut off from those gains. Productivity rose by more than 75 percent, but average pay by just 5 percent. In other words, labor's share of gross domestic product or GDP is declining as more and more of the value we create flows into other people's pockets. That's directly linked to increased corporate concentration,[12] with highly concentrated job markets associated with up to 25 percent lower wages than very competitive ones.[13] The decline in labor's share has been accompanied by a shift of risk to workers (particularly with the rise of precarious work). As corporations have come to wield more power, executives have been the only worker class to thrive: their pay has increased nearly 1,000 percent.[14]

Lina Khan, a leading antitrust scholar and now chair of the Federal Trade Commission, says the decline in competition is "so consistent across markets that excessive concentration and undue market power now look to be not an isolated issue but rather a systemic feature of America's political economy."[15]

While competition is supposed to be central to capitalism, the wealthiest people alive today have gotten rich by suppressing it.[16] They're brazen about it too. Peter Thiel famously announced in 2014 that "competition is for losers" and counseled companies to monopolize their domains. Business schools teach baby MBAs the same lessons: to avoid industries with high competition, to do what it takes to keep potential competitors out, and, if all else fails, to buy them up.[17] Warren Buffett explains that, in business, he looks "for economic castles protected by unbreachable moats,"[18] because "the products or services that have wide, sustainable moats around them are the ones that deliver rewards to investors."[19]

That language disguises what's *really* going on here. When Buffett talks about moats, he means the kind of barriers that lock in customers and suppliers and make markets inhospitable to new entrants. These corporations are not protecting castles from marauders. They are creating chokepoints that separate producers from consumers so they can capture a disproportionate share of the value from other people's work.

Moats have many different forms. Cost moats give companies cost advantages over their competition (perhaps because they have unbeatable economies of scale, or because it's expensive for customers or suppliers to switch elsewhere). Data moats arise where companies use information they've collected over time to give them an advantage over rivals. Network effect moats take advantage of the phenomenon whereby some products and services get more valuable as more people use them. A phone network is the classic example: it's useless if only one person has access, because there's no one to call, but its value increases rapidly with each new subscriber.

Powerful businesses typically have multiple moats. Facebook, for example, combines tremendously strong network effects (thanks to its almost three billion monthly active users) with a data advantage (the dossiers it has collected on you from its years-long surveillance are valued more by advertisers than anything a start-up could offer) *and* high switching costs (the fact that leaving makes it harder to communicate with your family, community, and friends). Google has a similar armory, but it doesn't want you to think it's relying on moats at all. That's why it has a blanket ban on its staff using phrases like "network effects" and "barriers to entry."[20]

Amazon is the master of moats, which it uses to ensure customers and suppliers are thoroughly cemented in. It attributes its success to its "flywheel." Flywheels are heavy revolving wheels, used in machines to increase momentum. Because they're so heavy, it takes a lot to get them spinning, but once they're going, it also takes a lot to stop them. Amazon describes its flywheel as a "virtuous cycle" that makes the business bigger, better, and faster: lower cost structures lead to lower prices, which create better customer experiences, which translates to more traffic and more sellers and thus better selection.

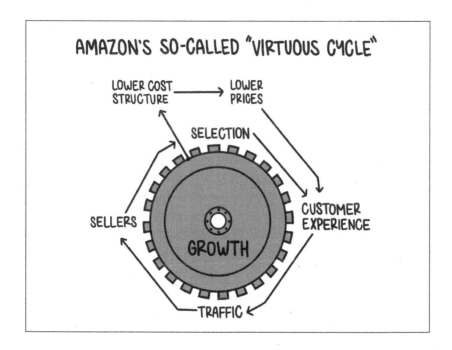

But this cycle is anything but virtuous. "Lower cost structure" is essentially a euphemism for shaking down suppliers and workers. The more customers Amazon gets, the more concessions it wrings from its suppliers (including publishers, wholesalers, and shippers). Since it passes many of these on to customers via lower prices and ever cheaper shipping, that feeds into the cycle too, as shoppers increasingly default to buying on Amazon. Once those shoppers are making a few purchases each year, it makes sense for them to pay the small yearly fee to join Amazon's Prime member program and get unlimited shipping plus all the other benefits it comes with, like book rentals and video streaming.

When Bezos decided to create Prime, he was very clear about his intentions: "I want to draw a moat around our best customers."[21] He succeeded. One in two American households are now members, and they're practically welded to the site: a recent study found just 1 percent of paid Prime members are likely to comparison shop elsewhere before making a purchase.[22]

Since they've pre-paid for their shipping, Prime members naturally prefer marketplace sellers who offer Prime fulfilment, and Amazon's algorithm gives those sellers priority in the ordering process, nudging buyers away from sellers who haven't given Amazon total control over their businesses.[23] Many vendors now have no choice but to use Amazon fulfillment services in order to reach those customers, even though this can be much more expensive than serving customers directly.

Using Amazon fulfillment requires businesses to pass even more control over to Amazon—which is dangerous, because Amazon has proved itself an untrustworthy business partner.[24] Among other dubious practices, Amazon uses its inside knowledge to track the sales of third-party vendors to identify the most profitable products, then clones those products and puts them up for sale, undercutting the vendors whose vision and investment built the markets for them in the first place. One study examined 850 clothing products initially sold on Amazon by third-party vendors and found that Amazon began selling a full quarter of its business customers' best sellers within just twelve weeks of the original listing.[25] Vendors know Amazon is scheming to clone their most successful products, but they can't stop selling via that platform because, without it, they can't reach their customers. After all, a whopping 66 percent of online shoppers bypass search engines and search for products directly from the Amazon search box. For customers who already know what product they want, the figure rises to 74 percent.[26] Third-party sellers pay dearly for Amazon's predations: Amazon's cut of their income has risen to an average of 40 percent—tripling in just a few years.[27]

Amazon's strategy is to lock in users and suppliers and make its markets hostile to new entrants: in other words, to create chokepoints that will force workers and suppliers to accept unsustainably low prices. That flywheel isn't virtuous—it's anticompetitive.

In chokepoint capitalism, the aim is to create enduring barriers to competition that enable corporations to monopolize or monopsonize their markets. We learn about monopolies from the first time we "pass go" as kids. Eventually, in every game, someone acquires enough properties to squeeze the other players dry. Monopolies form when a single seller controls the supply of some good or service to everyone else. The word *oligopoly* is used when a small number of companies control an industry, but *monopoly* is colloquially used in those situations too, and we use it to refer to both. What's less examined or understood is how chokepoints create *monopsony* power. While monopolies occur when sellers

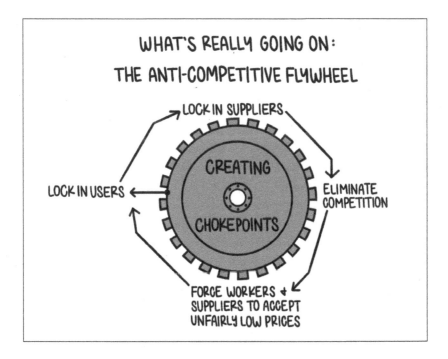

have power over buyers, monopsonies are when buyers have power over sellers. This is a less familiar concept—there's no board game for this one!—but it's even more important for understanding the plight of suppliers and workers.

In a monopsony,[28] the buyer has power over sellers instead of the other way around. Google and Amazon aren't just powerful sellers; they're powerful buyers too. Amazon's reach in the book market gives it enormous power over publishers. Google's monopsonies over search, ads, and video translate into dominance over numerous cultural domains, most directly affecting recording artists, record labels, songwriters, music publishers, journalists, and news publishers. As William Deresiewicz points out in *The Death of the Artist*, "If you can only sell your product to a single entity, it's not your customer; it's your boss."[29]

The hazard of monopsony was first noticed—and named—by economist Joan Robinson, working at the University of Cambridge in the 1930s. In her groundbreaking book *The Economics of Imperfect Competition*, she argued that monopsony endangered workers most, since it was employers who were the most likely to have monopsonistic levels of power. However, other suppliers could be affected too. Indeed, the original US antitrust laws were in large part a response to monopsony power, created after farmers got fed up with being exploited by grain elevator operators and meat-packers.[30]

Although we were clearly warned about monopsony's dangers, excessive buyer power has been largely neglected by economists and regulators during the Chicago School era.[31] Peter Carstensen—whose 2017 book digs into monopsony's unique characteristics—says monopsony is at least as serious as monopoly, but for reasons we'll come back to, "its abuse is inherently more difficult to control."[32]

Since monopsonists are such powerful buyers, they're able to drive the amount that goes to workers and suppliers below what they would be paid in a competitive market.[33] For corporate shareholders, this has the same benefits as raising consumer prices—fatter margins!—while being far less likely to attract unwanted scrutiny from regulators. In fact, Chicago School thinking practically *invites* corporations to turn the screws on suppliers and workers. A corporation that does so drives down the cost of inputs, which can lead (at least temporarily) to lower prices and thus appear to promote consumer welfare. Jeff Bezos perfectly understands this—it's right there in his famous aphorism: "Your margin is my opportunity."[34] Of course, this ignores the fact that those workers and suppliers will then have less money to spend, which ultimately has the same effect as prices going up, in that people are less able to afford the services and goods they need. After spending billions on the vanity project of blasting himself into space, Bezos thanked Amazon's employees and customers, noting that they "paid for all of this."[35] He was right, and many of them no doubt suffered from food, housing, and healthcare precarity as a result.

Trampling competition can be a long game. Chokepoint businesses invest profits into widening and deepening their fortifications against competition. Amazon didn't turn an annual profit until ten years after it started up, and even now its margins are razor thin. Spotify has lost money every year since its launch. But their stock prices have rocketed all the same because investors see how cleverly they're capturing their markets. Once competition has been sufficiently quashed, those margins will fatten and be used to persuade lawmakers to look the other way or pass regulations that enshrine their dominance.

After a generation-long drought, antitrust is finally back on the agenda—in a *big* way. The public is increasingly enraged about how the richest people and corporations are blocking action on society's most urgent problems, including the climate emergency, police brutality, wealth inequality, weakened democracy, and regulatory capture. For the first time, Congress has begun seriously investigating the dominance of Big Tech, particularly its power over suppliers. But we're still only just beginning to comprehend the fix we're in.

There's a lot of arguing over what does (and should) count as a monopoly or a monopsony for the purposes of antitrust law. Antitrust enforcement currently relies on highly technical infractions that are very difficult to prove until long after a corporation has wreaked terrible harms, at which point the company is likely so powerful the law can be difficult to actually enforce!

A growing coalition of interests opposed to concentrated corporate power is making the case that we should move away from the consumer welfare standard and return instead to antitrust's roots, interpreting the law to encompass broader public interest goals, such as dispersing economic power and promoting fairness. President Biden came down on this side when he issued an executive order charging the FTC with policing corporate concentration so as to protect "consumer autonomy and consumer privacy"—explicitly linking antitrust to concerns beyond ensuring prices stay low.[36] Critics fired back, saying that moving away from the consumer welfare standard will break more things than it fixes, by reducing certainty and making the law more difficult to administer.[37]

We agree there is an urgent need to reform antitrust law and enforcement and certainly criticize existing approaches in the pages that follow. But antitrust should not be relied upon to do *all* the heavy lifting. In this book, we explore how the chokepoints enabling corporations to extract more than their fair share of value are formed in the first place. Very often, as we will show, legal structures outside of antitrust contribute substantially to the accumulation of vast corporate power. For example, Amazon chokes publishers by chaining audiobook and ebook titles with digital locks that are illegal to remove. (This might sound like it's to the benefit of authors and publishers, but as we show in the next chapter, it has been crucial to stripping away their power.) Spotify does it to recording artists and labels through playlistification, which trains us to let it decide what we listen to, and by relying on fiendishly complex music licensing arrangements to keep competitors out of the market. Apple and Google get the power to squeeze game developers from their ability to control where we get our mobile phone software. Facebook and Google captured the market for news advertising by controlling all sides of the market for ads.

Chicago School economists view monopolies as inherently self-destructive, claiming monopoly conditions always rapidly attract new entrants who will chip away at that dominance.[38] After all, if a massive office complex offered just a single café at which to buy lunch, taco trucks would inevitably begin to congregate downstairs.

But it's not always that simple. What if regulators passed new food safety regulations that the café could comply with, thanks to its fancy kitchen, but that the trucks could not? (Big Business prefers power without responsibility but will take power *with* responsibility as a second choice.) What if the café proprietor could turn the elevators off at lunchtime, making it so inconvenient to get downstairs that most people stayed put? What if they bought up the trucks with the most interesting food just to shut them down? And what if the café could make it illegal for trucks to park there?

In effect, that's what's happening in the culture industries. Antitrust's failures are ultimately why we've ended up with such dangerously powerful corporations, but all kinds of other legal supports enable this accumulation of concentrated corporate power along the way. While the companies that control the culture industries often paint themselves as innovative disruptors, they owe their dominance to complex webs of legal rights, corporate bullying, and regulatory capture. Of course, corporations will try to create chokepoints to defeat competition, as that is demanded by the supposed duty of corporate executives to serve shareholders' interests over all else, including social justice, economic dignity, and the environment. But we should be demanding a pro-worker, pro–small business environment focused on removing the legal supports that enable corporations to capture an unfair share of value, even if they don't reach the high thresholds that justify antitrust intervention.

Capitalism without competition isn't capitalism at all; it's a "command economy" structured around the whims of corporate boardrooms. Of course, capitalism's inability to maintain the essential conditions required for its functioning raises questions about whether it should be replaced altogether. But while capitalism *does* remain the dominant economic and political system, we should be doing everything we can to promote competitive conditions—not just allowing those who already have wealth and power to extract ever more.

This notion opens up new pathways for reform. One reason antitrust has such high thresholds (including a definition of "market power" that is so hard to satisfy that merely holding the majority of the market isn't always enough to qualify!) is because regulators are keen to avoid "false positives"—that is, interventions that might make markets work less well. Regulators worry they might deter corporations who dominate simply because they're more efficient, benefiting rivals who are less skillfully managed, and thus driving up the prices consumers have to pay. Antitrust regulators also have to be cautious because, as we'll get into later, their remedies can be incredibly time-consuming and expensive to enforce, making it critical not to impose them lightly.

But since we're interested in identifying and clearing away the other legal supports for chokepoints, we can afford a more expansive reading of "power." The good practice of antitrust law may require that corporate power be concentrated until it reaches some stratospheric level of harm (although we have strong doubts that this is true!), but that doesn't mean we shouldn't intervene against other pathologies that lead to concentration. After all, the law should further the public interest—not be used to subvert it. And, critically, even when the chokepoint's origin looks like something that falls squarely in antitrust's realm—like the kind of horizontal and vertical integration that has allowed corporations like Google, Facebook, and Live Nation to take so much power—there's still scope for remedies *outside* of antitrust's limited toolkit to address it.

Chokepoints are by no means unique to the culture industries. Everywhere you look, corporations are trying to create the conditions that will secure them a disproportionate share of the value of other people's labor—Uber, Facebook, Monsanto, Google, Perdue Farms, and John Deere among them. But they are especially pervasive in creative labor markets, where corporations have demonstrated particular ingenuity in finding ways of burrowing between audiences and culture producers to capture the value that flows between them. That makes the culture industries an ideal microcosm from which to explore this phenomenon.

It's the right lens for other reasons too. Most obviously, culture enriches us by interpreting the human experience and the world we inhabit. And information and culture are the foundations on which the Big Tech edifice is built. "It's striking, when one pauses to think about it, how essential art and culture remain to the digital economy even as most of the money floating around goes to multibillion-dollar businesses that don't invest much in either," Astra Taylor points out in *The People's Platform*. "Art and culture are the stuff that ads are sold around, the bait that causes users to divulge their preferences by clicking so their data can be mined."[39] Billions in profits flow to companies like Google, Amazon, and Apple every year off the backs of creative workers. We can't understand their dominance without understanding how they came to achieve it.

Some insist the "platforms" themselves are the problem—and the fact we've pointed to Google, Amazon, and Apple above might add to that impression. But simply blaming "platforms" misunderstands the problem and obscures its real causes. There is no single accepted definition of "platform," and there are big differences between, for example, multi-sided marketplaces that sell different products to different groups of customers (as when Amazon sells books to consumers, while also selling access to premium display space and advertising to publishers) and those that predominantly aggregate listings (as, for example, Google does with search). Even if we focus specifically on those multi-sided marketplaces, it doesn't much help us identify what it is about that structure that is problematic. After all, as Orla Lynskey points out, subscription television and newspapers are "multi-sided" in the same way.[40] It can't simply be the fact these platforms are online that makes the difference.

In fact, we know it's not. Platforms are often distinguished from traditional "pipeline" businesses, which have producers at one end and consumers at the other.[41] But these create chokepoints too: as when record labels and music publishers accrue vast reservoirs of copyrights and use them to extract maximum value for themselves while simultaneously preventing creators from getting better deals. The problem lies not in the type of business, but in the ability to create hourglass-shaped markets, with customers paying money at one end, suppliers and workers creating value at the other, and a small number of predatory rentiers controlling access in the middle. Creators earn little from the culture they produce not because of platforms per se—even if tech platforms *are* the major culprits right now—but because their supply chains are colonized by powerful corporations who co-opt most of its value.

Creative workers should also be on our radars because they're the canaries in the coal mine. There has been a lot of media-fanned fear about robots taking blue-collar jobs. But have you ever watched a video of a robot attempting even a simple physical task like opening a door or climbing stairs? Not many manual jobs yet lend themselves to robot replacements. White-collar workers, on the other hand, *should* be feeling nervous. In 2020, hundreds of millions of the highest paid people on the planet demonstrated, in a sudden radical experiment, that their jobs could perfectly well be done from home. That's set the clock ticking on a social atom bomb.

If those jobs can be done from home, they can be done from the Philippines, or Estonia, or anywhere else with a reasonably reliable connection to the internet. All that sets this top level of workers apart is twenty years of socialization and skill development. Now that we've begun acquiring those online, the transition to an almost farcically large labor market has already begun.

Will increasingly gigantic corporations let us keep our pay, conditions, and jobs when the job market becomes geographically unbound?
Of course not. We have organized society around the principle that corporate executives' sole duties are to their investors, which means that
where there's a chance to make an investor richer while making a worker
or customer miserable, managers claim they are legally required to side
with the investor (so long as the misery doesn't backfire to the point
where it harms the investor's quarterly return). Combine the Borkian
focus on consumer welfare with the neoliberal dogma that a company's
only purpose is to maximize shareholder value and you get a toxic combination that pits large corporations against their workers in pursuit of
short-term investor value. Getting a fancy college degree doesn't exempt
you from fighting in the war of capital against labor. If your job can be
done well enough and cheaply enough by someone else, it will be.

Today's creative labor markets give us a glimpse of what a geographically unbound labor market might look like. Monopsonies are always
bad for workers, but creative workers have proved especially vulnerable.
Neoclassical economic theory assumes that when wages fall relative to
what's available elsewhere, workers move to other jobs (or even physi-
cally migrate) in search of better opportunities, which eventually leads to
an undersupply of labor that drives labor prices back up.

However, despite endemic low payments, arts industries are instead
characterized by an *oversupply* of labor.[42] That's because people are willing to supply creative labor for a lower price than they'd charge for other
kinds of work. That's why the Screen Actors Guild has to formally prohibit
members from taking work that doesn't comply with union minimums:
"The only way actors can overcome the temptation to work for below
scale is to enter into a group pledge to punish one another for doing so."[43]

Few people are willing to spend twelve hours on an assembly line or
grappling with bookkeeping without being paid for their trouble. However, humans *are* driven to create, even when there's no prospect of any
financial return. Cultural economist and professor Ruth Towse, who
spent her career analyzing creative labor markets, has documented how
corporations "free ride" on the human desire to create, exploiting the
oversupply of labor and precarious work conditions endemic to artistic
labor markets to secure most of the financial benefit for themselves.[44]
And it's not just writers, musicians, and artists they exploit: editors, ac-

countants, marketers, and administrators in every creative field are similarly passion-driven, making them willing to contribute their labor for less than they might get elsewhere. This isn't necessarily because they work for predatory businesses. But when Amazon squeezes publishers, for example, those publishers have to find savings somewhere. Naturally, they find most of them in labor costs—"that most bendy and squishable portion of an enterprise's expenditure."[45]

Creative workers have worked cheaply for decades because they have no other choice. The path we're on, in the direction of ever-increasing corporate concentration, will similarly eradicate choice for more and more workers. The chokepoint economy is already squeezing farmers and gig workers and college students. Unless we take urgent action, more and more of us will join them.

Creative workers know the culture industries are in trouble. They're told, variously, that the solution is more copyright protection, or internet filters to prevent infringement, or stronger locks on digital content. Many have thrown their energy into campaigning for all three, often incited by wealthy industry lobby groups who are primarily concerned with promoting the interests of powerful copyright owners over those of the people who actually create stuff.

Almost every fight that creators have backed as they try to get a fairer share has led to more of the same: ever fewer entertainment companies, selling to ever fewer distributors (increasingly controlled by Big Tech), with lots of money flowing up to investors and very little trickling down to them.

What if all this is just making things worse? What if excessive power over workers and suppliers, the kind of power that comes about when a small number of powerful corporations control crucial chokepoints, is actually the core problem faced by creative workers today?

We think it is. If we're right, it makes sense that tools like more copyright, internet filters, and better locks would make no meaningful difference to creators' abilities to share in the proceeds of their work. In fact, giving more copyright to creators who are struggling against powerful buyers is like giving more lunch money to your bullied kid. The bullies who were taking his money every day will just take that too. The upshot? The bullies now have enough money to pay the principal to look the other way, and your kid still goes hungry.

Before we can fix a problem, we need to understand its causes. To that end, the first half of this book digs into some of the many ways competition gets smothered within culture markets. We focus on the most successful value extractors—Amazon for books, Google and Facebook for news, YouTube for online video, iHeartMedia for radio, Live Nation for ticketing and live events, the Big Three record labels and Spotify for streaming, the Big Three Hollywood talent agencies for screenwriting and Apple and Google for everything mobile.

Each of these corporations has its own anticompetitive flywheel, designed to create chokepoints enabling them to capture an undue share of value. Their tools differ—with a reliance on combinations of network effects, licensing mazes, regulatory capture, horizontal and vertical integration, high switching costs, self-preferencing, and the industrial aggregation of copyrights—but they all seek to achieve the same things: to lock in users, lock in suppliers, make markets hostile to new entrants, and, ultimately, use the resulting lack of choice to force workers and suppliers to accept unsustainably low prices. Like Amazon, their aim is to force markets to take on that hourglass shape: workers and suppliers at one end, consumers at the other, and predatory corporations squeezing away at the neck.

Once we've pulled back the curtain on the strategies these corporations use to take over cultural markets, the second half of the book is about what we can do to *take them back*. Of course, that's going to include strengthening antitrust law and actually enforcing the law that's already on the books. On top of that, though, we propose a theory of change grounded in solidarity and systemic action, focusing on the distinctive tools available to creative workers—like interoperability, minimum wages for creative work, contractual protections, collective action and ownership, and transparency rights—that can help remove those chokepoints and help bring the playing field closer to level.

While Rebecca is Australian and Cory is from Canada, we focus much of our discussion on the situation in the United States, where most (though not all) of the world's biggest traders in culture are based. Having been left to grow there unchecked, they now pose a serious problem for the whole world. But we also bring in perspectives from elsewhere, especially in thinking about how the playing field might be leveled. While our focus is squarely on the creative industries, we hope activists and academics in other fields will engage with this conversation, raising awareness about the ways in which chokepoints are enabling workers in other fields to be shaken down as well.

For those who work within, or are concerned about, the future of culture, this book is intended to inspire new alliances and modes of thinking. Left unchecked, Big Tech and Big Content will come up with positions that keep both industries' shareholders happy at everyone else's expense. Instead of lending our support to whichever variety of Big Business looks like it'll throw us more crumbs, we need to be thinking about how to fight their dominance. That means analyzing who has power, where it comes from, how it's exercised, and how the effects ripple across each cultural ecosystem. And, critically, it means creative workers forging new coalitions—including with each other; with workers in other sectors; with libraries, museums, galleries, and archives; and with the audiences who love their creations. But before we get to that, we first have to persuade you that it's the chokepoints that are the problem. Here goes.

CHAPTER 2

HOW AMAZON TOOK OVER BOOKS

Amazon dominates *all* of online retail, which makes it easy to forget that it started with books. When Amazon launched in 1994, it was the kind of business Warren Buffett wouldn't have even glanced at. It had no moats to keep competitors at bay. It just sold books online, competing with neighborhood shops and brick-and-mortar superstores. Its method, which was to take orders and fulfill them via two wholesale distributors, was the same as other online sellers who were already in the market. Network effects were weak—you didn't get more value from shopping on Amazon just because your sister or friends did, and since books are the same wherever you get them, there was no particular reason for you to buy there instead of somewhere else.

It had no economies of scale, either. In fact, early on Amazon couldn't even meet the ten-book minimum order the distributors required for shipping. Jeff Bezos boasts of getting around that by ordering the book they wanted plus nine copies of an obscure out-of-print book on lichens, tricking the distributors into shipping it anyway.[1] That's right—Amazon's business was based on whittling down other people's margins to boost their own from the get-go. Today, Amazon enjoys a lock on the trade book market, selling more than 50 percent of physical copies in the US, and even more ebooks and audiobooks. As of 2020, the Authors Guild says, it controls more than 80 percent of sales for some publishers.[2]

From the very beginning it was planned that Amazon would be an "everything" store, but Bezos had good reasons to start with books.[3] The set-up of the industry gave it scope to expand quickly: customers would pay as soon as they ordered, but Amazon only had to settle its bills with distributors every couple of months. Its plan was to sell books at close to cost, "get big fast," and figure the rest out from there.

It worked. Its wide range and low prices meant it quickly took market share and was propelled to being one of trade publishing's most important buyers.

Publishers initially viewed Amazon as a welcome counterbalance to a dangerously consolidated book market. Barnes & Noble and Borders had snapped up most of the smaller chains and were wringing ever steeper discounts out of the publishing sector. Meanwhile, the "mass market"— grocery stores, pharmacies, and other non-bookstore retailers that used to sell the majority of popular fiction and other genres—were undergoing a mass extinction event, as big box retailers like Walmart and Costco drove many independent retailers under. Add to this a similar concentration in wholesaling, as hundreds of local book distributors were boiled down to three national companies (it's now just one!), and you had an industry whose sell-side was being gathered into fewer and fewer hands.

As Amazon expanded, however, it became increasingly clear that it was capable of all the cruelties of the distributors and mega-stores—and then some. One of the first big clues to Amazon's attitude toward the publishing industry was the Gazelle Project, a scheme designed to shake down small publishers for better and better terms. Brad Stone, author of *The Everything Store*, explains the name came from a Bezos suggestion "that Amazon should approach these small publishers the way a cheetah would pursue a sickly gazelle."[4] The company used its sales data to figure out which of them were most dependent on Amazon and then opened negotiations about the terms on which the giant might permit them to survive.

It demanded co-op payments—product placement fees for being featured prominently on the site and for priority from its recommendation algorithms. Amazon's recommendations don't promote the books readers are most likely to buy, but those whose publishers have paid up: "Publishers knew that they would stop being favored by the site's recommendation algorithms if they didn't comply."[5]

Dennis Johnson, founder of Melville House Publishing, fought back. After Amazon demanded co-op payments without even revealing how many of Melville House's titles had been sold on the site, Johnson took the story to the media. Retribution followed just hours after it went public: the BUY buttons had been removed from every Melville House book on Amazon.[6]

One important and under-recognized characteristic of monopsony power is that it can arise at much lower concentrations than monopoly does: a buyer responsible for just 10 or 20 percent of a producer's sales can have substantial power.[7] At the time of this shakedown, Amazon made up just 8 percent of Melville House's sales, but that was enough to force Johnson to give in. "I paid the bribe, and the books reappeared."[8] He had no choice because, if Amazon wouldn't buy those books, there was no other buyer who could step in to make up the shortfall. To be workably competitive, producers typically need access to *at least* five significant buyers.[9] As we'll show throughout this book, creative industries are now so heavily concentrated that few producers have that kind of choice.

Amazon's bully tactics brought the gazelles meekly into line, eventually enabling Amazon to raise the effective discount it receives on small publishers' books to about 60 percent.[10] Smashwords founder Mark Coker says there's no reason to think they'll stop there. "Once they've got control over you, they force you to stretch out your arm and give up more blood every year."[11] Today, these same tactics have been deployed across Amazon's entire business. Advertising added a massive $22 billion to Amazon's bottom line in 2020 alone, something that's only possible because it sits at the chokepoint between buyers and sellers. As journalist and antitrust expert Barry Lynn put it, "Amazon gets to sell both access to the market and protection from its own thuggish behavior."[12]

As publishers' margins were squeezed, so too were the most atomized parts of the supply chain: writers, independent booksellers, and of course the publishing employees, like editors, who found themselves laid off and recast as freelancers.

It also accelerated a trend toward consolidation that had already been in motion. Starting in the 1980s, virtually every mid-sized trade publisher in the US got absorbed by larger firms, which kept merging and merging until the field was dominated by a handful of megapublishers. But even gargantuan size turned out to be no bulwark against Amazon's power, with even the very biggest struggling to resist its predations. One of the most public and protracted battles was fought in 2014, when

Hachette's supply agreement came up for renewal. Over six months of negotiations, Amazon removed preorder capability from Hachette's major upcoming releases, took weeks to ship in-stock books, raised prices, and even recommended books from other publishers instead. With no alternatives, Hachette was forced to give in.

Don't feel *too* sorry for the largest publishers, though. They already have the biggest backlists and economies of scale, both of which beef up their profitability relative to other publishers. And they have more negotiating power too, which means they manage to hold onto a precious few more percentage points of margin than their smaller rivals. Thus, Amazon's tactics don't just extract an ever growing share of the proceeds from books; they actively tilt the competitive playing field in favor of the biggest firms.

Small publishers can be left with as little as 40 percent after Amazon extracts its cut, and that has to pay for almost everything: the author, publisher, and editor, but also the administrators who handle the metadata, accountants who process the royalties, salespeople who get the books into stores, staff who sell the rights overseas, the cover designers and marketing crew, and of course printing, shipping, and keeping the lights on in the office. Some of these costs are fixed. So what's going to give? As monopsony expert Carstensen explains, when companies are forced to give greater discounts to their most powerful buyers, they tend to find the money by "exercis[ing] their power over their workers to further depress wages and other workplace investments."[13] In other words, ultimately it's authors and other culture workers who pay for Amazon's fatter margins.

We see this in advances, which have plummeted by as much as half since 2007's global financial crisis. And we also see it in the growing role of literary agents, to whom publishers shift more and more of their costs of doing business. Agents are increasingly tasked with work that used to be the realm of publishers and editors, including the initial selection of manuscripts, working with authors to refine them, and providing support through the editorial process. They're paid for by authors—15 percent of their own declining share.

In other words, Amazon shakes down publishers, and, in turn, publishers shake down their workers and authors. It's easier to pull off this kind of heist in the creative industries than in some others, since authors and other arts workers are so powerfully motivated by nonfinancial considerations. People's passions are weaponized to facilitate their exploitation. This is why simply giving creators more copyright doesn't actually help, *unless it also comes with ways of holding on to the value of those rights.* The more authors have to give, the more there is for publishers—and, ultimately, *Amazon*—to take.

Of course, the more Amazon takes, the harder it is for anyone else to compete. As it leverages bigger discounts, it is able to attract more customers by offering lower prices and then to use those customers to wring out ever more concessions. This is the anticompetitive flywheel in action. Its ruthlessness shouldn't come as a surprise. Bezos signaled his intentions early on when he toyed with calling his company Relentless. Even today, navigating to relentless.com takes you to Amazon's site.

PUBLISHERS GAVE AWAY THE KEYS TO THEIR CASTLES

Amazon's control over the physical book market would not be such a big deal if publishers had been able to keep hold of the emerging ebook and audiobook markets. These have huge potential for profit, because after the production and editorial costs have been earned back on the print book, digital delivery has almost no manufacturing costs. There's no printing or shipping, and there's no risk of booksellers expensively returning unsold copies for a full refund—a longstanding feature of the physical book market, where it was also common practice for "mass market" paperbacks to be destroyed rather than returned, with their ripped off ("stripped") covers returned for a full credit from the publishers. But publishers were outmaneuvered. Ebook and audiobook sales were also captured by Amazon, whose tolls suck up much of that margin today.

In the early 2000s, Amazon's CD-selling business was eviscerated by Apple's iPod and iTunes, which created and then dominated the music download market. Recognizing the power of this play, it set out to create a device that would let it take over the book business in the way Apple's iPod let it dominate music. The mission was clear: Bezos told the executive in charge of developing its ebook reader to "proceed as if your goal is to put everyone selling physical books out of a job."[14]

The key to achieving this is anticircumvention rules, which were first mandated in 1996 via a pair of international copyright treaties.[15] Developed in response to fears from rights holders that the easy copying and distribution facilitated by the internet might destroy their business models, the treaties require member countries to prohibit the bypass of technological measures that are designed to protect against copyright infringement. Such measures, usually called "digital rights management" (DRM), are supposed to guard against unauthorized copying, and indeed the treaty drafters carefully limited the scope of the obligation to just that, with the WIPO Copyright Treaty expressly specifying that the obligation didn't "go further than the scope of copyright."[16] But that limitation was almost universally ignored by countries that implemented the treaty. The US version, contained in section 1201 of the Digital Millennium Copyright Act (DMCA), makes it a crime—punishable by a five-year prison sentence and a $500,000 fine for a first offense—to tamper with a software-based lock that restricts access to a copyrighted work. This is broader than what was required, as it does not distinguish between tampering with locks for legal or illegal purposes. Instead, once there's a lock in place that controls access to a copyrighted work, the lock itself becomes sacrosanct.

This overbroad implementation radically shifted the balance of power in the entertainment industry. It meant that any company who made an entertainment platform became the sole arbiter of whether and how customers, competitors, *and even the copyright owner* could alter the locks' functioning.

We can see the power of this shift in Apple's takeover of the music download market. The major record labels had insisted that Apple apply DRM to music downloads from the get-go. Scarred by the peer-to-peer file sharing free-for-all that began with Napster, they wanted guarantees that lawfully downloaded music would not make it onto the black market. But DRM was never actually going to prevent music piracy: in part because music could be easily ripped and shared from CDs, and partly because any lock can be unlocked. However, it did have another effect: it locked customers in to listening to their music with products made or authorized by Apple.

Apple refused to license its DRM technology to potential competitors, which meant people who bought songs on iTunes could only play them on Apple devices.[17] That was of course thanks to section 1201 of the DMCA, which prohibited people from removing the DRM wrapper to play them on other devices. For those who had built up iTunes libraries, this raised the cost of switching to an alternative brand, since they would have to repurchase all their content, making them more inclined to stay put (to be clear, copyright law permits you to play your music on devices other than the one it was originally sold for, but because Apple wouldn't license its DRM technology its customers were stuck). When RealMedia released software that let people play DRM–wrapped music from a different store on iPods, Apple accused it of hacker tactics, threatened litigation under the DMCA, and shut the software down. These strategies paid off. Within five years, Apple controlled 88 percent of the legal download market,[18] and quickly became the number one music retailer US-wide, outselling even Walmart.[19] By insisting on DRM, the record labels made Steve Jobs a powerful gatekeeper between themselves and their customers.

The only way to wrest back that control was through competition, and the only way competitors would be able to sell music to Apple users was if it didn't have DRM. So that's what happened. Belatedly recognizing that when consumers buy a slice of bread they want to be able to "put it in any toaster,"[20] the record industry threw its weight behind a new DRM–free music download store to be launched in September 2007 by none other than Amazon—which trumpeted its commitment to liberating the music world by distributing T-shirts emblazoned with the slogan *DRM: DON'T RESTRICT ME.*[21] Soon after, DRM was dropped by all the major music sellers, including Apple. By then, though, the playbook had been written, showing how DRM could convert a temporary market advantage (which lasts only so long as you're the best option) into one that endures even if your customers would rather go elsewhere.

Book publishers would be in a very different position today if they'd been paying attention when all this was going down. Unfortunately, they weren't. They told Amazon they were willing to let it sell their titles as ebooks, but only on the condition that they be wrapped in DRM. With that, they handed Amazon the keys to their castles.

Amazon understood that even though DRM is the enemy when you're trying to break someone else's monopoly, it's the best friend you can have when you're trying to create your own. The Kindle ebook store, launched mere weeks after Amazon launched its Apple-busting DRM-free music, featured exactly the same kind of DRM that enabled Apple to become so powerful in the music download space. Every book was shackled to Amazon's platform. Amazon wouldn't even permit publishers who *wanted* to release their titles without DRM to do so. Holdouts like the tech publisher O'Reilly, which understood the danger, weren't permitted to release their titles as DRM–free ebooks on Amazon's platform until Kindle's supremacy was safely established.[22]

Publishers also made another critical mistake at the outset. Amazon was pressuring them to digitize large parts of their catalogs, and do it quickly, or else risk demotion in search results and customer recommendations.[23] Publishers jumped to make the demanded investments from their biggest buyer, but in the rush there was one thing they forgot to ask—how much did Amazon intend to sell those digitized titles *for*? They didn't find out until seventeen minutes into the Kindle launch, in November 2007, when Bezos announced that the most popular ebooks and new releases would be $9.99—barely a third of the regular hardcover price.[24] That explained the urgency: Amazon needed publishers to digitize and license their catalogs before discovering its intention.

The publishers were as appalled as Amazon had anticipated they would be. Their most profitable sales were hardcovers that retailed for around $26, and they feared $9.99 ebooks would both cannibalize those sales and drive down customer perceptions of what books were worth. They were worried, too, that cheap ebooks would lure customers away from physical copies, threatening the ongoing viability of physical bookstores and giving Amazon even more power than it already had.

At $9.99 a pop, Amazon was actually losing money most times it sold a book, but it was willing to do so to lock in the market. Literary agent Andrew Wylie unpacks the strategy: "What Bezos wants is to drag the retail price down as low as he can get it—a dollar-ninety-nine, even ninety-nine cents. That's the Apple play—'What we want is traffic through our device, and we'll do anything to get there.'"[25] Antitrust's consumer welfare standard encourages such tactics, since in the short term they bring down prices. It's not concerned with what might happen later, when publishers and authors can't pay their bills.

These gambits paid off. Within two years, fully 90 percent of the ebook market was under Amazon's control. Publishers discovered that readers who had built up libraries of their favorite books weren't interested in moving to competing platforms that would be unable to read them. They had to keep buying from Amazon to keep their libraries intact.[26]

In other words, by wrapping those books in DRM, Amazon was able to convert a temporary market advantage to an enduring chokepoint.

Section 1201 of the DMCA ensures Amazon is the only one with the right to remove its software locks. Although the anticircumvention provision is part of copyright law, and was ostensibly created to protect copyright owners, those same owners have no right to remove the locks from their own content. If Hachette, for example, were to bypass the DRM attached to its own books to migrate its readers to a less abusive platform, it would face existential civil and criminal liability for doing so. Even if Hachette could persuade a court that it should have the right to remove Amazon's locks on its own books, the key would fit the lock on every other publisher's content too—and that would certainly be unlawful. And if it wanted to scan readers' Kindle accounts to find its own books in order to deliver fresh copies to a different app, it would face fierce resistance from Amazon, backed by force of law: Amazon's terms of service prohibit the sharing of passwords that would make this possible, and big companies forcefully argue that such breaches violate the Computer Fraud and Abuse Act, an ambiguously drafted Reagan-era statute. Even without that, Hachette might not dare to take such an action. Although it's one of the biggest publishers in the world, it's nonetheless reliant on Amazon for its survival. As we showed in the previous pages, Hachette has learned the painful lesson that Amazon will retaliate forcefully against any threat to its interests.

By using DRM to raise the switching costs to a point where few readers are interested in moving elsewhere, Amazon keeps publishers locked in too. The elegance of this moat is that it's self-digging: the more ebooks readers buy, the wider and more difficult to bridge it becomes. The strategy was obvious to writers like Charlie Stross as far back as 2012: "By foolishly insisting on DRM, and then selling to Amazon on a wholesale basis, the publishers handed Amazon a monopoly on their customers— and thereby empowered a predatory monopsony."[27]

Once publishers saw the trap they'd fallen into, they became desperate to get out. Amazon had already been demanding ever greater concessions as its grip over the physical book market grew tighter, and publishers knew it would do the same with ebooks. They also feared that Amazon might "disintermediate" them from the equation altogether, by negotiating directly with authors and agents for rights and selling books directly to the public.[28] Indeed, as we'll show, this is exactly what happened!

Publishers became fixated on raising prices from $9.99, which they thought was devaluing their products, undercutting physical sales, and threatening the viability of their non-Amazon sellers. At this point independent bookstores were disappearing fast, worn down by decades of fighting first the big box stores, and now the online giant.

Salvation (or so publishers thought!) came from Apple, about to launch its iPad and keen to create an accompanying bookstore. Working together, the tech giant and five of the then–Big Six (Hachette, Harper-Collins, Macmillan, Penguin, and Simon & Schuster—but not Random House, the largest) came up with a different model. Instead of selling ebooks wholesale, publishers would set their own prices, and Apple would take a 30 percent commission on whatever that happened to be. This is called "agency pricing," a model to which Amazon was vehemently opposed, because it would strip Amazon of its power to set prices. While Apple too insisted on price caps, it was willing to allow most books to be sold for up to $14.99—50 percent more than Amazon's price. Publishers hoped this would reinflate books' value in consumers' eyes and take some of the pressure off physical bookstores.

The terms of the deal show just how desperate publishers had become. On the old model, they had been selling ebooks to Amazon for the same wholesale price as hardcovers, pocketing about $13.00 without having to incur the costs of print production and distribution. Under the agency model, publishers could make consumers pay $14.99, but after paying 30 percent commission they'd end up with just $10.50. In other words, publishers were so determined to make the consumer price rise they were willing to accept substantially less themselves. That they colluded to make *less money* shows the depth of their fear about the consequences if Amazon's discounting were to persist.

While Apple had no problem with consumers paying higher prices, it wasn't willing to be undersold. So it made publishers guarantee that Apple could sell their books at the lowest retail price on the market. If Amazon continued selling them for $9.99, Apple could sell them for $9.99 too—and still take its 30 percent commission off the top.

Apple loved this arrangement because it guaranteed a fat margin while eliminating price competition. For publishers, it meant they had no choice but to move all of their ebook retailers to agency agreements. That was because, if Amazon continued selling at the same prices and Apple matched Amazon's prices (as their contract entitled it to), publishers would end up with less than seven dollars a sale—barely half what they'd been getting from Amazon. By entering into the pact together, the major publishers ensured they'd present Amazon with the united front necessary to force it to shift to the new model. That was integral to the plan. Not even the biggest publisher thought it could force Amazon's hand alone.

Amazon got wind of the deal shortly before the Apple agreements were actually signed. It retaliated straight away, announcing that authors who self-published via Kindle would now get 70 percent royalties in the US market, about double their previous cut.[29] This was the disintermediation push publishers had feared. Traditional publishing usually pays authors about 10 percent on physical copies and 25 percent on ebooks, and they knew 70 percent royalties would lure away some of their most profitable authors.

Nonetheless, those five of the Big Six publishers went ahead and signed agency agreements with Apple. Macmillan's CEO John Sargent was the first to admit the move, and Amazon retaliated immediately, pulling the "buy" buttons for every Macmillan title—print and Kindle—severing Macmillan's main source of sales.[30]

But once it became clear that almost all the major publishers had acted together, Amazon had to admit defeat. Soon after, Amazon reluctantly entered into the agency agreements the publishers had demanded. They'd been right: by acting in concert, they were strong enough to overcome Amazon's dominance. The era of $9.99 bestsellers was over.

The publishers' jubilation was short lived, however. In their eagerness to wriggle out from under Amazon's thumb, they had missed an important detail. US antitrust law has been largely neutered but colluding to raise consumer prices is still a textbook violation. Indeed, under the consumer welfare standard, it has become the main one that's ever actually enforced. Amazon complained to the Federal Trade Commission, and the Department of Justice took action against the conspirators.

The publishers were affronted: How could *they* be liable for anticompetitive conduct when they only did what they did to counteract Amazon's own bullying? But that's how it currently works. In fact, the most unusual thing about this dispute was that the defendants were powerful corporations in their own right. Chicago School antitrust theory doesn't just allow firms to get very big; it simultaneously clobbers independent workers who seek to band together to collectively enforce their rights. The law has an exemption that protects employees from liability for most kinds of organizing, but it doesn't apply to gig workers and other independent contractors. If such workers try to band together against a powerful buyer to collectively enforce their rights, they'll be liable for violating antitrust but the company squeezing them will not. Port of Los Angeles truckers found this out the hard way when they tried to unionize, only for regulators to accuse them of unlawfully colluding to fix the price of their labor.[31]

These rules are why US organizations like the Authors Guild can't unionize independent writers. They ensure that the more atomized labor becomes—and thus the more in need of collective action to protect it—the greater the likelihood that banding together to demand better treatment is against the law. (We develop this further in the chapter on collective action.)

The judge wasn't interested in the publishers' protestations that they were just trying to level the playing field with Amazon: "Another company's alleged violation of antitrust laws is not an excuse for engaging in your own violations of law."[32] The publishers were ultimately obliged to settle for $166 million. Apple was on the hook for $450 million more.

In one view, the publishers' mistake was to explicitly fix prices, instead of quietly engaging in strategic noncompetition. "Nod-and-wink" collusion, whereby firms coordinate behavior by watching and responding to their competitors' actions, can have the same outcomes as outright price-fixing but is almost never prosecuted.[33] Tacit collusion isn't effective for organizing large groups, but works well in highly concentrated markets where the finite number of players make it easy to track what the others are planning to do. This gives monopsonists yet another advantage: when their suppliers and workers coordinate to improve their outcomes they'll be threatened with prosecution, but when they tacitly coordinate with their massive competitors it will almost certainly be okay.

Had Penguin, say, publicly signaled to the market that it was considering switching to an agency model and kept an ear out for its competitors' (public) responses, it could have achieved the same end without the enormous expense and public humiliation that accompanied its own maneuver.

The court's sanctions against the publishers and Apple resulted in a brief modification to the agency model, but once the court orders expired, the agency model was back for good. Random House, the one major publisher to have balked at joining the conspiracy, initially stayed on wholesale terms with Amazon, and sought a similar deal with Apple. But Apple was only willing to enter into an agency deal, effectively locking Random House out of the lucrative and fast-growing market of iPhone and iPad readers. Random House tried to create its own app, but Apple refused to approve it. Just as Amazon made itself a gatekeeper between publishers and readers, Apple became a gatekeeper between app developers and its users. That forced Random House to finally reach its own agency agreement with Apple in 2011, about a year after the other major players.[34]

While the publishing industry eventually succeeded in pulling off its shift to agency terms, that did little to reduce Amazon's market power. As of 2018, Bloomberg estimates that Amazon controls 89 percent of the ebook market, with Apple taking just 6.3 percent and less than 5 percent being doled out between everyone else.[35] We have to rely on such estimates because Amazon refuses to release ebook sales data, as part of its well-documented mania for secrecy.

Amazon also refuses to disclose the size of the self-publishing market, although the market has exploded since Amazon increased royalties to 70 percent. We do know that about half of the best-selling books across the romance, fantasy, and science fiction genres are now self-published,[36] and by one estimate self-published titles comprise up to two-thirds of US consumer ebook purchases by volume.[37] Occasionally, however, Amazon throws out tantalizing clues: for example, that over a thousand indie authors earned over $100,000 in royalties in 2020, and "thousands more" made at least $50,000.[38] Some self-published writers, like LJ Ross and Hugh Howey, have sold millions of copies without publisher involvement. Howey was able to leverage these sales into a traditional publishing deal while also holding on to his ebook rights, giving him a best-of-both-worlds outcome. He's a rare exception: it's all but unheard-of for authors to retain their ebook rights in a deal with any publisher, let alone one of the majors.

Self-published books tend to sell for far less than traditionally published titles—often in the range of $3 to $5. This is driven by Amazon's policies, which only permit those fat 70 percent royalties for books priced between $2.99 and $9.99.

Despite everything the publishers attempted to drive up the price of ebooks, then, Amazon still succeeded in driving them down. That's good news for price-sensitive readers, and undoubtedly helps democratize reading and access to books. And it's terrific for authors who can find an audience on the platform, including the thousands of writers making the kind of middle-class living traditional publishing finds it increasingly hard to deliver.[39] But of course, this phenomenon will be temporary: Amazon's management doesn't give writers such a big share because it cares about them, but as a way of weakening traditional publishers. Once they've done so and those authors have no other options, they'll be shaken down too.

We've already had the first glimpse of this, when Amazon tried to monopolize the print-on-demand market by mandating that its self-published authors use its in-house service. In a rare example of US antitrust law actually serving to help a small company against a big one, Amazon was forced to abandon the ploy after a small publisher launched a class action against it.[40]

DRM didn't just let Amazon take an iron grip over ebooks but audiobooks too. Audio has been the fastest growing publishing format of the last decade and is now a multibillion-dollar market that's become as important to trade publishers as hardcover.

The leading producer and distributor of audiobooks has long been Audible, which Amazon bought up just three months after launching its Kindle store. At the time Audible had its own DRM, and Amazon promised it would get rid of it if customers complained.[41] But its audiobook DRM remains in place today, despite loud, consistent protests. Apple's audiobooks are DRMed too.

Who is the beneficiary of that protection? It's not publishers and authors. Random House abandoned mandatory DRM in 2008, but when it published the audiobook of Cory's novel *Little Brother*, both Amazon (Audible) and Apple refused to carry it without DRM.[42] Since he wouldn't permit DRM to be applied, the book simply could not be made available to the millions of audiobook users who were tethered to those two major audiobook providers. It's impossible to say exactly what this cost Cory, but his agent says it's enough to have paid off the mortgage on his Los Angeles home—a figure arrived at by comparing Cory's books to other authors his agent represents.

Random House isn't the only publisher to recognize DRM for the trap it is. In 2018 a huge coalition of publishers licensed Google to launch a DRM–free audiobook store with a range almost as comprehensive as Audible's.[43] That showed they no longer saw DRM as serving their interests, even though protecting their copyrights was the whole purpose of making circumvention illegal in the first place. But Amazon and Apple both still insist on DRM because it helps maintain their power over the very copyright owners it was supposed to protect.

Critically, Amazon is not just a powerful buyer of books. It's a direct competitor to publishers too, courtesy of its own publishing imprints, the self-publishing market, and its Audible productions. The data it collects from competitors gives it a massive edge. It has real-time information on the physical, digital, and audiobook titles of virtually every publisher on the planet and can see exactly how each of them is performing on every Amazon-owned platform. By contrast, individual publishers have only limited, delayed information about their own titles' sales, an increasingly incomplete picture of what's happening in the ebook space, and almost no information on audio. Without intervention, it's hard to imagine Amazon's flywheel ever slowing down.

GET BIG FAST

Bezos came up with the slogan "Get Big Fast" because he knew size was crucial to exacting ever lower prices from suppliers.[44] Publishers have tried to respond to Amazon's power by doing the exact same thing, accelerating their decades-long campaign of mergers and acquisitions to consolidate into an ever smaller number of bigger firms all trying to publish ever bigger books (like the memoirs of Barack and Michelle Obama, for which Penguin Random House advanced an astonishing $65 million). The push towards "big" explains Penguin Random House's play to absorb Simon & Schuster. Matt Stoller describes the merger as "defensive, an attempt to gain bargaining power against a monopolist bookseller." This kind of producer integration is an understandable response to overly powerful buyers, especially since antitrust law prevents separate companies from banding together to create countervailing power. But it causes knock-on problems for suppliers and workers downstream. As Stoller puts it, "it's not fair that authors must sell on the terms laid down by increasingly powerful publishers, but this dynamic is driven by the far more unfair situation whereby publishers are dealing with the utterly ruthless trillion dollar powerhouse Amazon."[45]

An increasing "bestseller" mentality contributes to the vulnerability of independent presses to being absorbed. Mass-market retailers only stock the titles they predict will be hits, and online marketplaces amplify the books that are shifting fastest. This results in "a cycle so self-fulfilling it's nearly tautological: Best sellers sell the best because they are best sellers."[46] As a result, according to book analyst Mike Shatzkin, "The medium-sized publishers can't sustain themselves anymore. They can't compete for the really big titles, so they get bought."[47]

Even the very biggest publishers are merging with one another. Incredibly, Penguin and Random House (the world's two biggest trade publishers) were permitted to merge in 2013, creating a behemoth of unimaginable scale, now fully owned by private German conglomerate Bertelsmann. That giant is now persuading regulators to let it gulp down Simon & Schuster, one of the world's biggest remaining publishers.

As publishers go around gobbling up others and being gobbled up themselves, they have sought to recover losses to Amazon with gains exacted from writers and libraries. Writers have found themselves with less power to negotiate the terms of their contracts than perhaps ever before, regularly being obliged to sign away their worldwide English-language rights, audio rights, even graphic novel rights all in one go. Libraries, meanwhile, have seen mounting costs and onerous conditions for the electronic materials they buy from major publishers, even as electronic materials account for an ever larger share of their collections. Amazon long refused to license the titles it publishes to libraries on any terms at all. In 2020, however, as the COVID-19 pandemic spotlighted the crucial importance of remote access to books, some US states passed legislation to require publishers to license titles to libraries on reasonable terms, and Amazon was finally forced to bend. Some publishers, like Hachette, make their books available to North American libraries but refuse to license them to libraries throughout the UK, Australia, and New Zealand on any terms at all. In other words, as more and more value gets siphoned further up the food chain, there's less and less for everyone else.

While Amazon started with books, that was never its main game. Right from the beginning it planned to use books we searched for and bought to gather data on us in order to sell us more stuff and, ideally, take over the world.[48] Ebooks were a perfect fit for Amazon's extractive mindset, because they cost us more in terms of privacy than physical titles ever could. Amazon knows what we search for, what we read, and what we listen to—when and for how long. This "actionable market intelligence" allows it to poach authors, market its own titles to readers, and cross-sell non-book items to readers. The combination of surveillance and vertical integration means that Amazon vastly outpowers both publishers and other retailers, cementing its dominance, and giving it more opportunities to spy on readers.

This is the true heart of "surveillance capitalism"—not the idea that Big Tech uses data-mining and machine learning to create mind-control systems that bypass our critical faculties and trick us into buying whatever they want to sell us. Rather, Big Tech abuses monopoly power to deprive us of choice by limiting what we can buy, redirecting our searches to hide rivals' products, and locking us into its ecosystem with technologies we can't alter without risking a lengthy prison sentence.[49]

Amazon tracks the phrases we highlight, the words we look up, who else is reading from the same address. All this allows it to deduce the most intimate information about our lives: whether we're struggling with our gender identity or sexual orientation, if we think our partner is cheating or that we might be depressed, if we're having money problems or struggling to get pregnant or considering leaving our jobs. Public libraries have some of this same information, and they guard it fiercely. But Amazon feeds it into an insatiable machine designed to extract maximum profit. If you, as a reader, feel uncomfortable with this, that's too bad: DRM makes it illegal for you to read or listen to the books you've purchased on surveillance-free platforms.

But our individual exposure and commoditization is just the beginning of the harm that was wrought. Amazon used books to extract data on consumers and used that data to slowly subsume all else. The data that came out of physical books and later ebooks and audiobooks all fed into that flywheel that gave it ever more information, which enabled it to attract ever more customers and ever more products, and which has ultimately ended up giving it the power to squeeze its suppliers and workers to near asphyxiation.

There's no reason to believe this flywheel will slow down without intervention. The money Amazon squeezes out all along the supply chain funds its famous "kill zone." Anyone who enters Amazon's territory (or that of Facebook, Google, and other giants) knows they'll be bought or destroyed. Amazon threw away $200 million in a single month when it went after the company behind diapers.com, first weakening it by bribing away its customers with impossibly low prices, then acquiring it for a fraction of its previous value. At that point Amazon shut down its new acquisition and put its own prices back up.[50]

That was an expensive way of capturing the diaper market but a cheap way of teaching everyone else to stay out of Amazon's path. Nobody has forgotten the lesson. Venture capitalists routinely refuse to fund companies that might impinge on the giants' territory,[51] resulting in provably less innovation in those spaces.[52] Amazon's web services division (AWS), which controls almost half the world's public cloud infrastructure, also gives it a bird's-eye view of emerging start-ups, which enables it to detect threats early and makes it even harder for potential competitors to reach the scale they need to compete.

We know by now that the story of the frog in the pot of boiling water is apocryphal: they actually jump out as soon as they get uncomfortably warm.[53] Publishers would have jumped out too if Amazon hadn't been able to use its DRM over books and audiobooks and its copyright licenses over reviews as a lid to keep them in. Without this power, Amazon might never have reached the dominance that made it so essential for so many third parties to sell via its platform, that made Prime so attractive, and that fueled a massive kill zone from which competitors had to steer clear.

Today, most publishers still require DRM be applied to their Kindle books, although this doesn't prevent piracy any more than did the DRM on the original iTunes music downloads. Widely available software tools can strip it off in microseconds. Amazon now lets publishers and self-published authors individually opt out, because there's no longer any risk to its position: so long as most books are locked in, most of its customers will be too. Now the lid is locked in place, Amazon is growing stronger as its competitors, suppliers, and workers weaken. This is not how it's supposed to work. The supracompetitive profits created by monopolies and monopsonies are supposed to attract new entrants who will compete them away. But that doesn't work when we gift powerful companies with ways of converting their temporary market advantages into enduring law-backed defenses.

DRM isn't just being used by Amazon. Computers are shrunk so small that they are woven into the fabric of every gadget, tool, and technology in our lives, and all of them run software, which is restricted by copyright and to which the DMCA applies. Because the law doesn't distinguish between lock-breaking for legal and illegal purposes, all companies need to do is add a thin skin of DRM that has to be bypassed for a customer to do anything that might lower their profits. General Motors uses DRM to prevent independent mechanics from diagnosing problems with their cars. Volkswagen used it to prevent independent researchers from discovering that they were cheating on emissions tests. Philips uses it to make sure you only buy Philips light bulbs to go in your Philips sockets. HP used it to plant a time bomb in its printers, which prevented printing with any cartridges that had been refilled or supplied by third parties. A Johnson & Johnson patent promises to use DRM to force people with artificial pancreases to buy proprietary insulin. John Deere wields its DRM to stop farmers from fixing their own tractors. Voting machine manufacturers use it to stop security researchers from publishing information about critical vulnerabilities.[54]

None of this has anything to do with copyright enforcement. Instead, the DMCA creates a new cause of action—felony contempt of business model—that's available to anyone who can use software to control what you do with the things that you own. And it has been exported globally. From Canada's Bill C-32 to Article 6 of the EU Copyright Directive, countries around the world have imposed far-reaching bans on breaking DRM. This gives corporations the power to make up their own private laws and have them enforced by public courts and the police. Amazon isn't the only monopsonist to take advantage of anticircumvention law to cement its dominance; Google and Facebook and Apple do the same thing. Addressing this is critical to breaking their power, and to preventing tomorrow's giants from using DRM to take more than their own fair share.

CHAPTER 3

HOW NEWS GOT BROKEN

In 1995, a self-described "nerd with limited social skills" started email-ing around to alert people to arts and tech events in San Francisco. At first they were addressed to just ten or twelve people, but more and more asked to be added to the list. People started asking if he could post the oc-casional job or apartment. It snowballed. Within two years the email list had morphed into a website with a million hits a month, connecting buy-ers to sellers for any number of services and goods. It was called Craigslist.

Craigslist was (and still is!) radically different from the hypercapital-ist, surveillance-filled websites we are mostly stuck with today. Ad-free and no frills, it has never been interested in maximizing revenues. Its founder, Craig Newmark, rejected advertising from the very beginning in favor of small fees on employers posting job ads in some cities. The company has focused on giving customers what they want, rather than sucking them dry for the value of their attention.

This approach has long baffled the tech bros who were surfing their way to billionaire status alongside it, including StubHub cofounder Eric Baker. He estimated that in 2005 alone Craigslist could have had reve-nues of over half a billion dollars had it been willing to fully monetize its user base (though this guess has since been criticized as being wildly overblown). "Craigslist is sitting on a potential gold mine of revenue, if only it would abandon its Communist Manifesto." But Craigslist's CEO Jim Buckmaster has consistently described the site as a public service. "We're not interested in selling our users short in order to try to become insanely wealthy."[1]

39

Although Craigslist never brought in all that much money, it did siphon off revenues that once flowed to newspapers and magazines. Users made their preference clear: given the option of paying much less (usually nothing at all) to reach a much bigger audience, they abandoned local newspaper classifieds in droves. One academic study estimated that Craigslist cost US local newspapers over $5 billion in revenue between 2000 and 2007.[2]

Then there were all the other online marketplaces that popped up. Many of the most lucrative classifieds, for high ticket items like cars and real estate, found their way onto specialist sites. And auction sites like eBay connected buyers and sellers faster and more efficiently than newspapers ever could. This was a huge blow for local newspapers that relied largely on classifieds to pay their bills.

Notably, though, this is part of a longer decline. Print ad revenues had been eaten up by the burgeoning TV industry since the 1950s. They were also affected by the same lax merger scrutiny we've repeatedly lamented. Heavy consolidation in retail meant there were fewer and fewer buyers for those full-page display ads that had previously advertised a range of local grocery, department, and sporting goods stores. Left vulnerable, the US news sector became an early pioneer of dirty financial engineering, debt-funded takeovers, and questionable business decisions. Early in the neoliberal era, newspapers were targeted for leveraged buyouts, where a Wall Street fund convinces a bank to lend it money to buy a business while using the business they're buying as collateral. It's like buying out your neighbor's house by taking a mortgage out against it—without your neighbor's permission.

Some businesses acquired through leveraged buyouts are struggling before the acquisition, but they all struggle after the buyout. After all, once the business has been acquired, it has a huge new debt load: the money that was borrowed against its assets to pay for it to be taken over. The new owners typically commemorate their purchase by paying themselves huge special dividends and emptying the business's coffers, and then set about finding "efficiencies" that the business's precarious, debt-heavy position demands.

Typically, this means some combination of selling and laying off assets and workers. Physical plants are sold off and either leased back or done away with altogether, in favor of outsourced suppliers, sometimes overseas where labor is cheap. Lifelong staff are fired—with unionized staff preferentially targeted for cuts—and either replaced by cheaper workers, or by colleagues who are now expected to do two (or three, or four) employees' work.

All this and more happened to the US news industry. Family-owned newspapers sold out to sharp operators from the finance sector that merged papers into vast, national chains. Those new owners promptly sold off their printing presses and plants and leased them back, yielding one-time gains at the expense of eternal exposure to rent and interest rate shocks, either of which would drive these essential costs through the roof.

These new, corporatized papers merged their newsrooms, closing foreign bureaus and firing national reporters (when ten papers merge into a single conglomerate there's no need for ten separate DC desks, or even ten reporters in the state capital—one will do). Eventually, many of the surviving reporters were also axed in favor of wire service coverage— why pay a stringer to cover international or national news when the AP and Reuters will do it cheaper? Even local reporters got the chop—how much value do they generate, anyway? To a private equity privateer, some zero-wage J-school intern can cover the hot dog–eating contest and the school-board meetings.

It wasn't just the news side of the business that faced these "efficiencies"—the sales force was also on the chopping block. If you're the only game in town for classified ads, why do you need to pay a salesperson who knows all the local merchants? Just get a 1-800 number and centralize classified sales in a right-to-work state where you don't have to worry about your workforce unionizing. Keep some salespeople at the central office and task them with selling national brand advertising to car companies, sneaker companies, and white-goods companies that want to reach the readers of all the papers in your chain.

All this happened before Craigslist began to offer a more attractive proposition to the classified advertisers of cities across America. US print circulations had been in decline from the early 1990s.[3] But when online classifieds arrived, all this "rationalization" meant that newspapers were less able to withstand the shock. Newspapers were creamed by the internet because they were already dying when the internet arrived. While Craigslist started to absorb easy classified ad dollars, the local salespeople who had spent their whole careers building relationships with, and anticipating the needs of, their community's businesses were working in other fields or nursing their paltry retirement checks, having been laid off by the masters of the universe who bought out their employers and declared them obsolete.

When newspapers went online, the fact that most outlets were running mostly the same articles became embarrassingly apparent, between national chains filing the same story for every paper and wire services serving all the chains and local papers alike. Perhaps newspapers could have adapted better if they had had a cushion to protect them from the shocks. But they didn't: their war-chests had been converted to special dividends for their corporate raider overlords and debt service to the investment banks that financed their leveraged buyouts. Actually, it was worse than that, because these papers now had to worry that if they had a shortfall, they might not be able to make payments on the presses and plants and buildings they'd once owned and now leased.

Newspapers responded by building up their online advertising, monetizing the huge growth in reach that came as people shifted their attention online. In the early 2000s, the web was open, with a seemingly infinite number of publishers and numerous search engines (anyone remember AltaVista?) and ad networks. Those conditions briefly helped online media to flourish, and in 2006, US newspapers generated record revenues: almost $50 billion, up from $38 billion just a decade before. But then Google achieved dominance over search advertising, and Facebook over social media. That was the beginning of the end.

COOKIE MONSTERS

Ultimately, both Google and Facebook are ad companies, deriving about 80 percent and 98 percent (respectively) of their revenues from advertising. Between them, they control 70 percent of the US ad market, and more than 65 percent in the UK.[4] They have sewn up the search and social ad markets in ways that let them extract ever more value—to the cost of the journalists, video makers, musicians, and other creative workers who provide the culture and information to which those ads get attached.

Google's strategy for locking in suppliers like news publishers has been to vertically integrate throughout the ad chain. It now serves up the ads, buys ad space from publishers and sells it to others, provides the analytics that sites use to persuade advertisers to place content on them, and operates the search engine ad-supported sites rely on for traffic. An investigation by the UK's Competition and Markets Authority found that Google controlled the whole online ad market, controlling at least 50 percent and up to 100 percent at different points of the chain.[5]

Google provides at least a basic version of each of these services to businesses for free, which initially seemed like a boon but was actually a trap. Josh Marshall of Talking Points Memo despairs of ever extracting his site. "Running TPM absent Google's various services is almost unthinkable. . . . Some of them are critical and I wouldn't know where to start for replacing them. In many cases, alternatives don't exist because no business can get a footing with a product Google lets people use for free."[6]

Google makes the online market even more hostile to new entrants by putting some of its monopoly profits toward maintaining its dominance. It has bought its way to search default on every platform: device manufacturers (including Apple, LG, Motorola, and Samsung), wireless carriers (like AT&T, T-Mobile, and Verizon), and browser developers (such as Mozilla and Opera) all take money to deliver their users into Google's maw. It pays billions each year to Apple alone. That enables Google to capture almost 90 percent of all general search engine queries and almost 95 percent on mobile devices. With Google providing the answers to almost every question we ask, it's no wonder publishers despair of breaking free.

Dina Srinivasan researches the opaque online ad industry, after ten years working within it. She points out that Google dominates ad markets via conduct that would be illegal in other trading markets: "Google's exchange shares superior trading information and speed with the Google-owned intermediaries, Google steers buy and sell orders to its exchange and websites (Search and YouTube), and Google abuses its access to inside information."[7] This iron-fisted control gives Google a stalker's view into publishers' businesses. But it's not the only one who gets to peek inside. The way Google has historically sold its ads gives that information away to huge numbers of others—and that's been hugely damaging to news publishers too.

You probably already know that today's internet is based on mass surveillance of you and everyone you know. Dossiers about your activity and preferences are constantly being compiled and updated, facilitated by cookies, the tiny data packets that identify and track you online. When you navigate to a web page, the ad server uses cookies to identify you, summons your dossier, correlates it with your identity across multiple databases, and offers brokers (sometimes dozens of them!) the opportunity to show you an ad. That's how you end up with those creepy ads that follow you around the web after you carry out a search on, say, erectile dysfunction: you get a tag called "person interested in boners" and that attracts bids from boner-pill vendors.

All of that is reasonably well known. But what's less well known, and just as important, is what happens to the losers of the real-time auctions when you visit a site. Say you visit the *Washington Post*. Dozens of brokers bid on the chance to advertise to you. All but one loses the auction. But every one of those losers gets to add a tag to its dossier about you: "*Washington Post* reader." Advertising on the *Washington Post* is expensive. "*Washington Post* reader" is a valuable category: a lot of blue-chip firms will draw up marketing plans that say, "Make sure we tell *Washington Post* readers about this product!"

Here's the thing: the companies want to advertise to *Washington Post* readers, but they don't always care about advertising in the *Washington Post*. And now there are dozens of auction "losers" who can sell the right to advertise to you, as a *Post* reader, when you visit cheaper sites.

When you click through one of those dreadful "Here's twenty-two reasons to put a rubber band on your hotel room's door handle" websites, every one of those twenty-two pages can be sold to advertisers who want to reach *Post* readers, at a fraction of what the *Post* charges.

In other words, the ad auction system enables advertisers to buy the publication's audience without contributing to the publication itself. Some brands, especially luxury brands, still value appearing in the prestige source—Chanel and Mercedes Benz want to be associated with the *New York Times*, not a tacky "twenty-two reasons" site. But not all advertisers care how they reach you. And so, to a large extent, this system disintermediated news publishers from the value of their creations.

That was a huge problem. News had long relied on an ad revenue model that itself relied on more profitable content to subsidize other important public interest work. As Clay Shirky says, in the print world "Walmart was willing to subsidize the Baghdad bureau. That wasn't because of any deep link between advertising and reporting, nor was it about any real desire on the part of Walmart to have their marketing budget go to international correspondents. It was just an accident. Advertisers had little choice other than to have their money used that way, since they didn't really have any other vehicle for display ads."[8] Newspapers didn't have to do much to capture ad revenue, since advertisers had little other choice.

The online world gave advertisers a range of new options, and brands (naturally!) took advantage of them. However, the consequence was that news publishers lost the premium that enabled them to invest in costly and vital content.

Although these changes cost news publishers extraordinary amounts, they generated rich rivers of gold for others. There's almost no transparency in online ad markets, so nobody really knows how much money goes where, but huge sums are being gobbled up by ad-tech platforms like Google's.

One known technique for maximizing profits is for Google to buy up ad space from publishers at a discounted rate and sell it on to advertisers for a huge and undisclosed premium. When the *Guardian* purchased some of its own ad inventory and followed the money, it discovered that up to 70 percent of revenues were siphoned off before ever reaching the publisher.[9] Middlemen were snatching most of the value, leaving news providers with as little as 30 cents of each dollar spent on ads attached to their content. Back in 2003, by contrast, almost the full dollar went to the publishers.[10]

Online advertising is a seriously lucrative business. A 2020 report of the UK's Competition and Markets Authority found that Google's cost of capital was about 9 percent, on which it was earning supracompetitive returns of over 40 percent. Facebook, which has a similar playbook but focused on social media rather than search, had even higher returns—a ludicrous 50 percent.[11] In a competitive market, publishers would sell their ads elsewhere. But the Google-Facebook duopoly gives them no such choice.

Facebook's strategy has also focused on integration, though more horizontal than vertical. As CEO Mark Zuckerberg explained in a 2008 email, "It is better to buy than compete." That's why it paid $1 billion in 2012 for Instagram, then a tiny company with thirteen employees. It snapped up WhatsApp for $19 billion just two years later. At the time these were jaw-dropping prices, but the acquisitions soon came to make sense. People who want to exit Facebook's data-hungry, privacy-invading walled gardens have nowhere to go—not if they still want to connect online to their family and friends. They're held hostage, their every action surveilled, their every moment of attention monetized.

These chokepoints keep many news organizations beholden to Facebook's algorithms too. While some have been able to successfully switch to subscription models, others still rely heavily on social media to generate traffic. But, in most countries at least, they don't get paid for their news being shared on Facebook, even though it profits handsomely from the ads sold around that content.

Facebook also directly competes with news media for advertising dollars. Advertisers have a finite amount to spend and have to decide how much goes to news media versus social media channels like Facebook. As Tim Hwang observes, this contributes to the challenges news producers face: "As advertisers give less money to media like newspapers, they also cripple the ability of newspapers to offer the content that subscribers demand. This makes it harder for legacy media companies to compete against their digital rivals."[12] Local newspapers are particularly vulnerable, since they're less able than the big nationals to achieve the kind of subscription revenue that could offset the ad revenue loss.

We're not saying the link between news and advertising is inevitable, or that it's the way we should fund news in the future (we get into these questions more in the second part of this book). But it is clear that, in a competitive market, the advertising supply chain would not work like this. There would be more transparency. Google and Facebook would have smaller margins. More of the money generated by those ads would go to the people who actually create the culture and knowledge to which it's attached.

These aren't the only companies redirecting money from publishers. As Matt Stoller says, "that's what's happening throughout the economy, especially in the media industry: middlemen everywhere are trying to find ways to redirect the flow of other people's revenue to themselves."[13] With so much money being siphoned off, carnage in news was inevitable. Beset by years of shakedowns, vertical and horizontal integration, and ring-fencing of the open web, US newspaper revenues plummeted from almost $50 billion in 2006 to just $14 billion in 2018.[14] Publishers and journalists are still scrambling to respond to this gaping hole in their revenue model. There's been cutback after cutback: no more subsidy for the Baghdad bureau eventually means no Baghdad bureau. And there has been a constant stream of layoffs, with US newsrooms losing fully half their staff in the eleven years from 2008.[15] More and more news, insofar as it's still covered at all, is generated by AI without human involvement. About a third of Bloomberg News's content is generated by a robot reporter. It's how the Associated Press reports on minor league baseball and how the *LA Times* gets out its initial stories on earthquakes.[16]

Many publishers have resorted to ever more intrusive advertising and ever more clickable content, making themselves ever less attractive to subscribers. Some of these initiatives blur the line between editorial and ads—like *Rolling Stone*'s offer to let "thought leaders" pay two thousand dollars to write for them and "shape the future of culture,"[17] or *Forbes*, which sells advertisers the right to blog on its site.[18]

This revenue hole is disastrous on any number of fronts. For democracy, because there are so few commercial resources remaining to fund investigative journalism and scrutinize government, enabling corruption and waste to flourish. For the arts, because there's little ability to cover any but the biggest books and productions (Scott Timberg, author of *Culture Crash*, points out that "there are NFL wives who get more mainstream media coverage than every living jazz artist put together"[19]). For social causes, like Black Lives Matter and #MeToo, which get less nuanced coverage than they need and deserve (this is exacerbated by fears around brand safety, which see advertisers increasingly sheer away from content deemed controversial—including by blocking their ads from being served on content that mentions terms like "Black Lives Matter," "George Floyd," and even "Black people"[20]). For the planet, with too few reporters to do justice to cataclysmic climate change, the biggest, slowest-moving story to ever break. And of course, for writers: not only by making it far harder for journalists to make a living, but by eviscerating a revenue source that once subsidized the birth of so many books.

What have we gained in exchange? Remarkably little. Leaving aside the obvious costs to democracy, culture, and the state of human knowledge, it's becoming clear that even advertisers don't fare particularly well from the extremely complicated, data-enriched, behavioral advertising model pushed by Google and Facebook. Because the online ad industry is incestuous and deliberately opaque it took some time to figure out what's really been going on, but it now seems clear that the whole thing has been a giant con.

Take Facebook's video numbers for example. In 2014 it began providing advertisers with data about how long users spent watching videos. What it didn't mention was that, in making that calculation, it ignored every view that lasted fewer than three seconds. This had the effect of inflating viewing times by at least 60–80 percent (according to Facebook, when it eventually copped to the con) and up to 900 percent (according to the advertisers who were burned). But the advertisers were far from the only victims. Facebook actively encouraged struggling news sites to pivot to video, laying off some of their text-oriented employees in favor of video producers. But contrary to the story painted by Facebook's numbers, few people were interested in watching them, and those expensive investments fell flat. The videographers and producers had to be laid off too, and millions of badly needed dollars were washed down the drain.[21] Even after this, though, Facebook didn't bother getting its numbers right. In 2017, it was promising advertisers it could reach twenty-five million more people in the US than actually existed.[22]

Another massive fraud was inadvertently uncovered by Kevin Frisch, an analytics executive for Uber who had been copping heat from his bosses because the company's ads were appearing on far-right website Breitbart. He'd blacklisted the site, but the ads kept coming, and the online ad system is so opaque he couldn't even figure out which network they were coming from. So he started shutting off ad networks, one by one, and discovered something extraordinary: it made absolutely no difference to the number of new customers signing up. "We turned off two thirds of our ad spend—$100m out of annual spend of $150m—and basically saw no change in our number of rider app installs. What we saw is a lot of installs we thought had come through paid channels suddenly came through organic."[23] Eventually, it turned out that about $120 million, or 80 percent of the annual spend, was attributable to fraud.

Here's how the scam had worked: scummy marketers fielded low-quality, high-volume apps (like battery monitors) that requested root access. These apps spied on every app you installed. If one happened to be Uber, they "fired a click" to the system to report you as having been "converted" by an ad. It was that simple. Uber had been losing at least

$100 million a year to fraud—and *nobody had even realized.* These days, Frisch advises that "you should start by assuming that half of what's on the display channels is fraud. Then ask yourself: Are you being smart enough to get rid of it?"[24]

The online ad market is beset by scams. First there are the automated scripts and click farms of bored-out-of-their-minds humans who click on ads to make it look like they're actually driving traffic to advertisers. One 2018 study suggested this made up about 28 percent of web traffic, and another estimated the cost to the advertising industry as $19 billion in the same year.[25] Then there's domain spoofing. Scammers set up new domains that look like legitimate, premium sites (say, thet1mes.co.uk), and auction off ads on them. When News UK—which publishes the *Times of London, The Sun,* and other British papers—carried out a fraud test in 2017, it discovered that 2.9 million bids were being made every hour on fake inventory and estimated the scammers were raking in £700,000 a month that should instead have gone to them.

The more you look, the more it seems that everything in the ad-tech stack is fraudulent: fake audiences firing fake clicks at fake videos on fake sites that suck real dollars out of advertisers' accounts. And the reason it's been so hard to pin this down? The ad system has built-in layers of misdirection because the people profiting most don't want you to recognize it for the shell game it is.

Perhaps the biggest fraud of all is the theory itself: the idea that with enough surveillance data and machine learning, ad tech can sell anyone anything. It sure sounds plausible that Google and Facebook, with all that information they've invasively sniffed out about you, can do a much better job of targeting you with ads than an advertiser who just targets readers of a particular publication. But that case is growing less and less convincing.

Department store magnate John Wanamaker once infamously remarked, "Half the money I spend on advertising is wasted; the trouble is, I don't know which half." The statement is a testament to the persuasiveness of the admen who pitched Wanamaker: imagine thinking that only half your ad dollars are wasted! An increasing number of big advertisers are starting to ask probing questions about whether online ads are as valuable as was promised. Numerous companies including eBay, Procter & Gamble, and Chase have now turned off hundreds of millions of dollars' worth of online advertising without losing any business.[26] Think about what this means. We're being surveilled, doxed, and digitally discriminated against all to put on a show that separates marks from their dollars.

We're now in the position where the business model of almost the entire internet is based on ads that are overvalued and underperforming. Tim Hwang calls it a bubble, much like the subprime mortgage bubble—and fears that its popping might create an even bigger crisis for news: "Like it or not, advertising is a critical, if tenuous, force for funding journalists and a vast universe of smaller media outlets and niche media."[27] If we continue letting so much of that money be sucked out by middlemen, the consequences—for democracy, writers, all of us—will be severe.

But for would-be trustbusters (like us), there is some potential good news. Yale's Fiona Scott Morton and David C. Dinielli have persuasively argued that the data advantage Big Tech uses to siphon ad dollars away from producers is remarkably brittle.[28]

Investors have shied away from funding competitors to Google and Facebook in part because they believe the narrative crafted by those companies about how their long-term surveillance of our online habits gives them an unbeatable advantage when it comes to ad targeting. Even if you could raise the capital to plant surveillance systems all around the web at a scale that competes with Big Tech, that would only give you a picture of what's happening now. Google and Facebook would maintain their monopoly on what has gone before.

But all that old data is only valuable if it actually helps better target ads. A recent investigation by the UK Competition and Markets Authority (analyzed by Morton and Dinielli) found that's not actually so. Overwhelmingly, it's extremely recent data that drives the most valuable targeting. For example, location data is hugely valuable while the user is in that location, but after that it becomes basically worthless. If I know you're walking past my coffee shop, I might spend a bunch of money to send you an ad to entice you to come in and get hooked on my delicious pastries. But once you've gotten on the subway and headed off across town? Who cares about you and your potential pastry-eating habits!

This is similarly true of retargeting ads: If I know you're shopping for a pair of sneakers, I might be willing to spend a lot of money showing you my sneaker ads. But two weeks later, you are dead to me. You've got your sneakers, or you've changed your mind. Either way, you're no longer of any value.

The upshot of this is that the mythology of Google and Facebook's deep, longitudinal surveillance databases may be more valuable than the data itself. Interventions in online ad markets—perhaps to stop Google and Facebook from collecting such intimate data or to facilitate competitors who operate in more ethical and transparent ways—could quickly erase a large part of Big Tech's data advantage and start widening its chokepoints out.

CHAPTER 4

WHY PRINCE CHANGED HIS NAME

I n the early 1990s, Prince began appearing in the public with the word *SLAVE* inked on his cheek. This caused his label much discomfiture, which was exactly the point. Warner had originally signed Prince in 1977, when he was just eighteen years old. After the artist achieved extraordinary commercial and critical success, however, their interests diverged. Prince was a prolific music maker and wanted to release that work to the public. But Warner was concerned that if albums were released too often there would be less excitement and fewer sales. *SLAVE* also protested the fact he didn't own his master recordings—the originals from which all copies are made. "If you don't own your masters," he said, "your master owns you."[1] Escalating the fight still further, in 1993 he changed his name to an unpronounceable symbol, refusing to release any new music under his original moniker: "The company owns the name Prince and all related music marketed under Prince. I became merely a pawn used to produce more money for Warner Brothers."

This bitter fight was playing out at a time that major record labels had a vice grip on the industry. They controlled radio airplay, print and television media, as well as distribution into stores. And they were abusing that power in breathtaking ways.

One trick was to allocate almost all costs to artists and almost all proceeds to themselves. This included charging artists enormous amounts for things like "breakage" and "packaging" (including even on digital files that couldn't break *or* be packaged!). Royalties were abysmally low, especially for artists who were just starting out. Country star Lyle Lovett once lamented that he "never made a dime" from almost five million records. Toni Braxton sold $170 million worth of records on her first contract, and received a royalty check for just $1,972. Courtney Love broke down the numbers in 2000, showing how on the sale of a million records, a band can easily end up working for minimum wage while the label profits by the millions.[2]

This is largely attributable to a peculiar, longstanding feature of recording contracts—recoupment. Before a penny from a song's sales actually makes it into their pocket, artists have to recoup not only any advance that was paid upfront but most of the label's other expenses of making the record. What gets put on artists' accounts is limited only by the imaginations of their contract's drafters. Specialist music accountant Craig Williams recounts reviewing one band's accounting statement to discover "they'd been charged for the champagne, food and taxis home from their own signing party!"[3]

Artists are warned not to sign contracts that give labels a "blank check—like unlimited deductions for travel, hotel stays, car rental, meals and entertainment," or deductions for the company's general costs of doing business.[4] But even if they avoid that trap, it's still usual for them to find themselves on the hook for all recording costs, including paying the producer, production costs, tour costs, marketing costs, and travel, plus all (or at least half) the cost of any videos. To make things worse, musicians are often required to use the label's internal suppliers or preferred partners for these services, and these suppliers engage in ghastly price gouging, knowing their "customers" have no choice but to pay whatever number appears on the invoice.

This is radically different from most other forms of cultural production. In a standard trade book industry deal for example, authors begin earning royalties as soon as they have paid back their advance. They don't have to first pay back the costs of editing, typesetting, printing, binding, cover design, and promotion. And while some of the midsize trade publishers have pioneered a new standard book deal in which authors split production and promotion costs with the publisher, these deals usually come with a fifty-fifty profit split between the author and the publisher—not the miserly rates that have been for so long paid to recording artists.

The structure of these deals reveals why it's so difficult for even "successful" acts to recoup. Consider a 1970s-era group, advanced forty thousand dollars (ten thousand each to keep them going for the two years or so it took to make the record) plus recording and tour costs of $110,000, on a contract with a 5 percent royalty. For every hundred dollars their music brings in, ninety-five goes direct to the label, and five goes toward chipping away at their debt. It's not until their music has generated *three million* that the original $150,000 debt will finally be erased, and the band will start to be paid for the first time since they received that initial advance (still, just five dollars for every hundred their music brings in).

Sound bad? That would have been a *good* deal—we omitted some details to keep it simple. In real life, additional costs would have been added to the band's debt, royalties would have been deducted for packaging, breakage, and promos, and foreign sales would have only been paid at half the rate of domestic. It's no wonder then that vanishingly few acts ever recoup. While there is no transparency around this, Richard Burgess, president of the American Association of Independent Music (A2IM), estimates that fewer than 5 percent of major label artists manage to do so.[5] Even if they do, their record labels will *still* own their master recordings—those from which all others are made. Legendary American guitarist Nile Rodgers says, "The music business is the only business where after you pay off the mortgage on the house, they still own the house. It does not make any sense. There is no other business on earth that does that. We pay back all the royalties, and they still own our property."[6]

By the early 2000s, even though the industry's coffers were overflowing with revenue from the CD bubble, the share that was going to suppliers—the performers and songwriters who actually created their product—was a miserly 7 percent.[7]

Some labels refused even to pay that paltry share, having their pressing plants secretly run a "third shift" to manufacture huge numbers of records that never officially existed on the books, and on which royalties were never paid. Not even the Beatles could get their due: in the early 2000s, an audit found their label had written off millions of records as scrap before secretly selling them and pocketing the proceeds. By this point, labels' "accounting errors" were so endemic that it had become standard practice for best-selling acts to audit their labels—and it turned out those errors ran, almost universally, in one direction. One accountant whose firm conducted thousands of royalty compliance audits and recovered more than $100 million recalled just one instance where it was the artist who owed money to the label instead of the other way around.[8]

Labels knew acts that broke through and became famous and powerful in their own right wouldn't sign up for the same treatment again, so they maximized their profits by making the initial deals as long as they possibly could. A typical album release cycle was two to three years, and seven album deals were not uncommon. LeAnn Rimes was notoriously signed to a twenty-one-album deal in the 1990s when she was just twelve years old. Further illustrating the abuses of the era, that same contract prohibited her from living anywhere but Texas or Tennessee.

Some artists became so desperate to escape unfair contracts they took the extreme step of filing for bankruptcy. American R&B trailblazers TLC did so after taking home just 2 percent of the $175 million generated by their music. Toni Braxton followed suit. Rather than changing the way they treated artists, the record industry responded by lobbying Congress to change the bankruptcy law to keep them locked in no matter what. Cary Sherman, former chairman and CEO of the Recording Industry Association of America, claimed all labels want is "some semblance of equality in the negotiating relationship."[9] But that's exactly what they didn't want. It was the labels' enormous power over artists that allowed them to transfer so much wealth from creators to their shareholders.

The internet changed all of that. It's not our intention to overly romanticize this period. The early 2000s were one of the most challenging times musicians have ever been through: file sharing smashed the record industry's business model, thousands of creative workers and support crew lost their jobs, and countless artists who had been making a living from selling their music could suddenly no longer do so.

With hindsight, however, it's clear that new digital technologies and the internet also did much to democratize music recording and distribution. Previously, the recorded music market had had that dangerous hourglass shape, with musicians, songwriters, and recording artists at one end and listeners at the other. A handful of enormously powerful labels sat in the middle, where they controlled listeners' access to artists, and artists' access to listeners. It was a classic chokepoint market.

But then new tools enabled professional quality recordings to be produced far more cheaply than ever before. The internet brought the ability to distribute them without cost, instantaneously, all over the world. It fragmented audiences down infinite online rabbit holes, causing TV, radio, and print to lose much of their taste-making power. Social media gave artists the ability to reach their fans directly for the first time, opening up any number of new ways to generate revenue, like direct sales of albums, tickets, and merch. It also opened up access to capital, enabling artists to finance ambitious albums and videos outside the label system. Fans have now contributed more than a quarter billion dollars toward music projects on Kickstarter alone. The major labels still controlled radio airplay and physical distribution into stores, but that didn't matter nearly so much once artists could break through without either.

Once artists had genuine alternatives to the major label system, the chokepoint began to balloon out. Today's labels are no longer the boogeymen of decades past—not because they saw the error of their ways, but because the shift in power dynamics brought about by the open internet forced them to change. Artists now have a much more equal relationship, partnering with labels to access capital, manage their rights and distribution, and access skilled marketing and promotional staff and analytics that tell them where to target their energies. Rather than focusing exclusively on a small stable of talent, the major labels have also entered the artist services market, which gives them a customer service focus like they never had before. Now there are such strong alternatives to the services they offer that they have to actually compete for new signings. And artists get treated better as a result.

Having said all that, shakedowns remain endemic to the music business. The lucrative streaming market is controlled by Spotify and four companies owned by Big Tech. If you're watching music videos, you're almost certainly doing it on YouTube. Live Nation Entertainment controls concert promotion and ticketing. In the US, SiriusXM rules satellite radio while iHeartRadio dominates terrestrial. Just three record labels—Universal Music Group (UMG), Sony Music Entertainment, and Warner Music Group—currently control almost 70 percent of the global market for recorded music, and they also own the three music publishers that control almost 60 percent of global song rights.

As we show in the next few chapters, these pieces all fit together. To understand how, we have to start with the way the unfair deals signed by so many artists in those abusive decades still have an enormously distorting effect on the music business today.

Given the number of musicians, the century-long history of recorded music, and the sheer amount and diversity of music that has been produced, the concentrated ownership of songs and recordings is staggering. Those labels didn't actually invest in producing all of it themselves: much was acquired via mergers and acquisitions, including a great deal bought up cheaply from distressed companies after file sharing sank the record industry's business model. The label Sanctuary, for example, had been trading at £130 (about $190 in US dollars) a share in 2001. But as the business model shifted, it was snapped up by UMG for £0.225 per share just six years later (about $0.45 in US dollars).

We saw how Amazon managed to suck away so much of the value of books. First it offered low prices to attract customers, then used the power of its market share to demand ever bigger discounts, and then, as the ebook and audiobook markets emerged, cemented in readers and publishers with its digital locks. Google and Facebook used very different strategies to capture the value of news advertising: vertically and horizontally integrating to become so pervasively enmeshed in the distribution ecosystems that they were able to extract a bigger and bigger share of the ad revenue generated by that content.

The Big Three record labels and music publishers have similar extractive power, but it comes from yet a different source: the industrial aggregation of copyrights. Record contracts routinely last for the entire copyright term. In the US, for recordings after 1978, that's the author's entire lifetime plus another seventy years, or, in the case of "works for hire," ninety-five years from the time they're published. There is a termination law that enables a tiny percentage of artists to claw back their rights after thirty-five years, but labels insist it doesn't apply to most albums, and even for singles the law is so complex and expensive to navigate that most artists end up stuck with their original deals forever. With few exceptions, then, contracts signed from the 1970s to the 2000s, when the major labels were at their peak power and abuses against artists were most rife, still govern use of that music today.

These copyrights and contracts are highly effective at converting temporary market advantages into more enduring law-backed ones. As a society, we have agreed to bestow a monopoly over every book, song, painting, sculpture, and movie in exchange for the broader social benefits we want it to achieve: to encourage the creation and widespread dissemination of knowledge and culture, and to reward the people who made it. But those aims are being perverted by over-powerful corporations.

Copyrights are exclusive rights to perform particular activities—like copying or transmitting—related to works such as films, books, or songs. Some of those works turn out to be valuable in the marketplace, but a copyright doesn't grant market power by default. When copyrights are aggregated on an industrial scale, however, they bestow the power to shape markets.

One of the few antitrust violations still enforced by regulators is "maintenance of monopoly," or taking actions in the market to ensure that no one can compete with you. This is why Mark Zuckerberg is in so much trouble for admitting that Facebook acquired Instagram so that he could continue to dominate the digital lives of the millions of Facebook users who were bailing on FB and joining Insta.

But there's no rule against maintaining your copyright monopoly. An antitrust regulator won't punish UMG for "defending their copyrights," even if that makes their market monopoly more pervasive and powerful. Indeed, when a big company "defends its intellectual property," governments step in to *help*. That's the case even when those rights have been coerced in vast quantities from creators via nonnegotiable "agreements" in exchange for reaching the audiences those companies hold hostage.

Their acquisitions of most of the world's rights have given the biggest record labels and music publishers the power to shape music markets, to take more than their fair share of the value, and to control the future of music. Consider how royalties are paid. Since music is now so much cheaper to produce and distribute, and because, as we explained above, the internet has created so much more competition, royalty rates are higher now than they've ever been. Twenty-five percent is becoming standard. Some labels will pay 50 percent, especially if they don't pay an advance.

The majors have to be competitive with these rates when they sign new artists. But those already under contract aren't so lucky. Many of them are governed by decades-old contracts, negotiated when artists had much less power, and when the costs of making and shipping records was much higher than it is today. In the 1950s to 1970s, royalty rates as low as 4 percent were not uncommon. The Beatles' first EMI deal came with no advance and royalties of just a penny per record (from which they had to pay their manager, then split the rest four ways).[10] Radiohead's deal, signed in 1991, gave them 12 percent.[11]

A few artists achieve the stratospheric success that gives them the power to renegotiate exploitative old contracts. But most don't. As a result, huge numbers of heritage artists, including leaders in jazz, R&B, disco, soul, and hip-hop, remain bound to their terrible original deals, even though their labels now pay far less for manufacture and shipping.

When record companies professed support for the Black Lives Matter movement in mid-2020, professor and author Josh Kun called out the hypocrisy: if they really wanted to support Black lives, he said, they could "start with amending contracts, distributing royalties, diversifying boardrooms, and retroactively paying back all the black artists, and their families, they have built their empires on."[12] One way in which they could do that is by universally raising all royalties on digital exploitations. Martin Mills, CEO of the influential indie Beggars Group, began calling for a minimum rate of 15 percent in 2016. Although this is far less than current norms, it would still be much more than most heritage artists get now. Another response would be to forgive recoupment debts once a certain period has passed (Beggars does this after fifteen years). Under substantial pressure, Sony finally announced in 2021 it would do something similar. At the time this book went to press, however, UMG and Warner still hadn't followed suit.[13]

The unconscionably low rates paid out on catalog don't just hurt heritage artists; they also make it much more difficult for independent labels to compete—and thus disrupt the majors' hegemony.

When music was embodied in physical discs and sold in stores with limited shelf space, most sales were of front list (the new stuff). In the digital era, however, catalog (older music) has become increasingly important. UMG is the biggest of the major labels. In 2019, for example, 57 percent of its global digital revenues came from music released at least three years earlier (what the industry calls "deep catalog"). It turns out that, given the choice of almost all music that has ever been commercially released, listeners are seeking out a very different selection to what had been offered to them before. People really do like the old stuff better than the new stuff. (This makes it all the more tragic that UMG, which long left its archives of heritage recordings moldering in a warehouse because it couldn't figure out how best to store them, lost hundreds of artists' masters—sometimes the sole remaining copies—in a 2008 fire.)

Since catalog has basically no overhead, the more of it a label controls, the more income it will have to subsidize everything else. You can see how their huge repertoires tilt the business in the majors' favor. They already had the best economies of scale, the most lavish promotion and marketing budgets, the connections necessary to get radio airplay, and the networks to distribute physical records to stores. On top of that, they get a windfall payday from catalog's unanticipated new profitability in the digital era. And the cherry on top is that unfair and outdated contracts mean all their newly valuable old repertoire has far higher profit margins than anything new produced today. That helps explain their brightening financial situation. A 2020 UK parliamentary inquiry into the economics of music streaming found that "major label turnover [had] increased by 21 percent, but operating profit grew by an unprecedented 64 percent." In other words, the report concluded, "not only are the majors earning more money than in the last twenty years, they are also making more profit from these incomes."[14]

That's translating into huge windfalls for corporate execs, with evidence suggesting "the top five Warner executives received remuneration packages equal to the earnings of 2019's top 27 tracks as well as a share package worth $590 million." It's the majors' oligopsony status, the report finds, that is enabling them to "disproportionately benefit" from music streaming relative to the creators they purport to represent: "This has resulted in record high levels of income and profit growth and historic levels of profitability for the major labels whilst performers' incomes average less than the median wage."[15] Jake Beaumont-Nesbitt, policy advisor to the International Music Managers Forum, says these copyright reservoirs disadvantage newer labels who have less back catalog to supply them with passive income. "Building an audience for a new artist in the distraction economy takes a rolling campaign of content and communication over many months," he told us. "It's all high risk in an immensely competitive and unpredictable market; losses are normal. Established labels with evergreen catalogues can offset that R&D risk against established income, new self-releasing artists or labels cannot."[16]

Control over catalog doesn't just enable the majors to vacuum up the value of the music of the past—it also allows them to charge rent to today's new artists.

People make music with the instruments and tools of their time. Since the computer revolution of the 1980s, one of the most significant tools has been sampling, which takes existing recorded sounds and collages them into new compositions.[17] When hip-hop was first emerging, sampling was a free-for-all. Most musicians didn't even consider whether sampling was a copyright violation (no more than Dizzy Gillespie working sixteen bars of John Schonberger's "Whispering" into his solo in "Groovin' High" was), and if they did, they either assumed it was fair use, or "de minimis" (too trifling for the law to consider).

In that brief golden age, groups like Public Enemy, the Beastie Boys, and De La Soul experimented with using hundreds of samples to create dense walls of sound that began transforming the sound of contemporary music. But as the new art form grew in popularity and began to make money, the labels who owned the copyrights in the sampled recordings began demanding a cut. Over time, they successfully asserted the right to control sampling of their catalogs, relying on narrow readings of copyright exceptions that suggest even very short snippets usually need to be licensed.[18]

Two licenses are needed: one from the record label who controls the copyright in the recording, and the other from the music publisher who controls the copyright in the underlying song. Artists can rarely get around it by sampling sounds that are out of copyright; rights last so long, and the history of recorded music is so short, that nearly everything remains restricted. If the rights aren't cleared, labels won't risk releasing the tracks for fear of costly litigation and statutory damages of up to $150,000 per infringement.

License costs depend on the sample's duration, recognizability, and fame but can run to five or six figures. Entertainment lawyer Dina LaPolt sums it up bluntly: "There's two kinds of samples: the really fucking expensive type, and the really, *really* fucking expensive type."[19] Artists signed to indies often have to pay these costs out of their own pockets, because their labels can't afford to front them the cash.[20] Sometimes rights holders ask for a share of the new copyright instead of (or in addition to) the upfront fee. That can get tricky when there is more than one sample: "You might get all . . . copyright holders demanding to own 100 percent of your new sampled composition. Three times 100 percent is 300 percent, but you only have 100 percent to give."[21] Journalist Harry Allen estimates that sample-heavy hip-hop like Public Enemy's "It Takes a Nation of Millions to Hold Us Back" would have had to be sold for $159 "just to pay all the royalties from publishers making claims for 100 percent on your compositions."[22] This is a real problem for artists. If they don't recoup on their record contracts, the only royalties they'll ever see will come from the song rights; if they're obliged to transfer the song rights too, they can be left with no income at all.

These economic realities have forced complex, sample-heavy music out of the commercial market. Even one or two samples can be prohibitive to clear. Former label executive Mark Kates told McLeod and DiCola, "You generally start at paying $5,000 to even have a conversation. They won't even really consider it for less than that."[23] That was a decade ago, and the costs are higher still now, as music publishers and labels have continued to ratchet up their rates. "It has literally knocked the smaller artists out of the game altogether. Only the ones who are very, very well off can afford to sample anymore."[24]

Even those who do have the money might not be able to secure a license, because relationships and influence are also critical: you need the right people to usher the request through. Artists signed to majors are much more likely to get the clearance they need than those signed to indies or working outside the label system. Clearance expert Bill Stafford describes licensing for artists on independent labels as "very, very difficult. Without someone there to help them along, it's the bottom of the pile."[25] Big Daddy Kane found this out when he couldn't release a track sampling the Staple Singers because Prince (who owned those rights) just wasn't interested. The song languished until Big Daddy signed with Warner. Prince was also on their roster, and the clearance came through.[26] Even Chance the Rapper, who has remained independent despite his huge commercial and critical success, struggles to clear rights, and his frustration with navigating the system leaks into his music: "No Problem" begins with the lyric "If one more label try to stop me. . . ."

The complexities with clearing samples might help explain why no other unlabeled rappers have yet been able to replicate his success.

These high costs are doing little to help artists. At first, the new clearance culture *did* create a windfall for some of those R&B and soul artists who had been forced into unfair deals decades before. Their records were sampled, the samples were cleared, and they received some cash. Increasingly, though, artists who signed up with labels found that their contracts expropriated them of future sample revenues by mandating that any revenue would be offset against those all-but-undischargeable debts for the costs of recording their records. The new sampling revenue went straight to the label.

Thus the majors have the sampling market sewn up at both ends. If you're an artist, chances are a massive label owns the recording you want to clear and a massive publisher owns the rights to the song. It's going to be monumentally difficult to make music the way you want and that speaks to the culture of the moment unless you sign with one of them. The money you pay will go to the label, and if someone down the line decides to sample your music in turn, that money will go to them too. The rules are designed to drive up the cost of making music, creating barriers to entry that make it harder for independents to compete while adding little to artists' bottom lines.

This system maintains major label dominance. Every time an artist signs up to a major in order to make their music-making possible, it gets to add *their* copyrights to the label's strategic repertoire for another century.

Giving more copyright (in this case, the right to control sampling) to musicians in the concentrated world of recorded music is, again, like giving your bullied kid more lunch money. The bullies just take the extra money too. If we didn't let labels extract artists' entire copyrights, they wouldn't be able to get such a powerful advantage. But we haven't learned this lesson: we keep giving musicians more to take.

In 2015, a US court awarded Marvin Gaye's heirs $5 million because Robin Thicke, Pharrell Williams, and T.I.'s song "Blurred Lines" was too close to Gaye's "vibe." The court didn't find that the song copied *anything* from Gaye, but rather, that it was recognizable as *the kind of song that Gaye might have composed*. There were some bad facts in that case: Robin Thicke's admissions that he was high on Vicodin when writing the song, and publicity interviews where he said he set out to make something with Gaye's "groove" likely influenced the jury's finding. Nonetheless, the judgment created a cottage industry in similar suits, targeting the likes of Katy Perry and Ed Sheeran. Over two hundred leading artists, including John Oates, Jennifer Hudson, Jean Baptiste, and members of Tool and Linkin Park filed an amicus brief supporting an appeal against the Blurred Lines decision, telling the court that it threatened the songwriting industry: "All music shares inspiration from prior musical works, especially within a particular musical genre. By eliminating any meaningful standard for drawing the line between permissible *inspiration* and unlawful *copying*, the judgment is certain to stifle creativity and impede the creative process."[27]

Musician, critic, and industry expert Ted Gioia says this environment is making it even harder for new musicians to break through: "The fear of copyright lawsuits has made many in the industry deathly afraid of listening to unsolicited demo recordings. If you hear a demo today, you might get sued for stealing its melody—or maybe just its rhythmic groove—five years from now. Try mailing a demo to a label or producer, and watch it return unopened."[28]

Even the Recording Industry Association of America (RIAA), which lobbies for the major labels and has historically argued for the most expansive version of copyright imaginable, has started filing briefs in these cases arguing that there's too much copyright around these days, because their members are parties to these lawsuits over "vibes" and it's endangering their business.

But while the RIAA's members are suffering in the short term, it's easy to see how they'll adapt: new record contracts will simply make signing away your "vibe" rights a nonnegotiable condition of the deal. This would transfer ownership of *entire music genres* to the Big Three labels, who may fight among themselves over their overlapping claims to them, but, more likely, will cross-license to one another as they do with samples today. That would add even further to their primacy, not least because this kind of litigation is so expensive to both bring and defend that it's inaccessible to any but the deepest-pocketed labels. If anyone recording music in a recognizable genre required permission from one of the Big Three to do so, it would become virtually impossible to record *any* music without their permission, and they would inevitably wield that power to wring ever greater concessions from artists. We know this because that's what they've done every other time they've had the ability to do so. When Prince inked *SLAVE* on his cheek, he was pointing out an uncomfortable reality: that the way we've designed copyright law funnels power away from artists and subjugates them to masters.

CHAPTER 5

WHY STREAMING DOESN'T PAY

A nybody who follows music knows that income from streaming is a
joke unless you're one of the most successful artists. The rates paid
are usually governed by secretive private contracts—first between platforms and labels, then between labels and artists—so it's difficult to get a
clear picture of exactly what's generated per stream. However, there are
some windows into this opaque world. Independent cellist and composer
Zoë Keating has been posting her streaming earnings data since 2012.
In September 2019, for example, her music was streamed on Spotify
over 200,000 times, for a payout of $753—about 36 hundredths of a
cent ($0.0036) per play.[1] That lets us make some ballpark deductions
about what labeled artists might be getting. Even on a relatively generous royalty rate like 25 percent, it might be just 9 hundredths of a
cent ($0.0009). And for those artists locked into decades-old contracts
with, say, 6 percent royalties, it might take a hundred thousand plays to
generate enough to buy a twenty-dollar pizza. That's before tax. And,
if they haven't recouped their recording costs, none of these artists will
see a dime.

Obviously then, making a success of streaming requires huge scale.
That's too bad for music that doesn't lend itself to being listened to infinitely on repeat, a point repeatedly made by experimental musician
and composer Holly Herndon. When commenting on a composition by
Krzysztof Penderecki, she said, *"Threnody to the Victims of Hiroshima* is a
really intense orchestral piece that has changed me musically, and I'm

really happy it exists, but I'm definitely not putting that on during a dinner party. You listen to it once and you gain access to the idea and you're changed forever."[2] A few hundredths of a cent for a stream of nine-minute track isn't going to go far—especially distributed across an entire orchestra!

Herndon's collaborator Mat Dryhurst also despairs of ever making money from streaming: "For album-making artists like us, where it's really important you listen to songs 1 through 12, and we make one like every three years, the whole per stream payout thing doesn't make any sense."[3] Most artists are in the same boat. Spotify won't say how many are on its platform, but it's in the tens of millions. A mere 43,000 of those are responsible for 90 percent of streams.[4]

Streaming can probably never be a feasible way for lower volume artists and composers to make a living, but it doesn't have to work *this* badly for them. The reason it does is because it was designed that way. As journalist and music commentator Liz Pelly told us, streaming "was shaped *by* the majors *for* the majors." While streaming companies cop a lot of flak for these terrible outcomes (and we dig into their responsibility in the chapter that follows), it was the major labels who set the system up in the first place. Because they control so much catalog, anyone who wants to start a streaming service must go through them. That gives the Big Three the power to "operate without the usual rules that apply in highly competitive markets," according to Gadi Oron of the International Confederation of Authors and Composers Societies, which represents almost 250 creator societies around the globe.[5]

Not surprisingly, they created another winner-takes-all system that disproportionately benefits the very top artists and the very top labels. As David Turner explains, "oligopolistic strong-arming by major labels occurred with the emergence of each new streaming service, ensuring the royalty setup would be pro-label, not musicians."[6] That's why their profits are ballooning even as their artists see their share plummet—recall from earlier that their income has recently increased by 21 percent, but profits by *64 percent*.[7] It's not surprising that the CEO of the British Phonographic Industry (a trade association for record labels) told the UK parliamentary inquiry into the economics of music streaming that the "focus should be on growing the streaming pie rather than trying to argue over where that streaming pie should go."[8] Like Vegas stage magicians, they want us looking in the wrong direction to hide the sleight of hand that's tipping so much of the value of music into their corporate coffers.

One structural feature that particularly advantages the majors is in the way royalties are divided up. All the major platforms operate a pro-rata system where the royalty money from all subscribers is pooled, then paid out by share of plays. If, say, Drake gets 5 percent of them, his label gets 5 percent of the money—even from subscribers who have never listened to one of his tracks.

Keating says this isn't how fans think it works: "They think that if they are playing all Zoë Keating, that the portion of their subscription that is going to the artist is all going to me. But it's not."[9] This pool system means those who listen less (perhaps because they're fans of more challenging music, like Keating's avant-garde classical, or Herndon and Dryhurst's experimental electronic) end up funneling less money to their favorite artists than those who listen to unchallenging background music day in and out. French streaming platform Deezer says the pro-rata system hurts local and niche acts by giving popular artists and genres more than their fair share.[10]

One response is to switch to a "user-centric" model. Instead of going into a single pool, the recording royalties component of each subscription (about 52 percent of the whole) would be distributed between the artists the user actually listened to. If a subscriber only listened to Keating that month, that full amount ($5.19 on a $9.99 subscription) would go to her. In effect, those who listen less would reward their preferred artists with higher royalties. Those who use music to background their days would deliver relatively less to each artist.

There has been only limited modeling of how user-centric payments would shift money, and the winners and losers are by no means clear-cut.[11] Artist rights organizations like the UK Musicians' Union are supportive but clear-eyed about user-centric systems: they don't see them as a panacea, but think they could create more transparency and at least improve outcomes at the margins. Turner has criticized the model for being an individualistic solution, straight out of the neoliberal playbook: "This consumerist solution removes the responsibility to fairly compensate artists from record labels/streaming services and reassigns it to individual fans." But he still says he'd welcome its adoption. "The shift would represent such a major pivot in how music streaming works and would allow for a much healthier conversation around the entire business model."[12]

Deezer has been trying to trial such a system for literally years, but resistance from the majors has prevented it from doing so. That suggests the biggest players are well aware they're sucking away more than their fair share of value.

RIGGED: HORIZONTALLY AND VERTICALLY

Songwriters are another group that have suffered from the majors' role in designing the structure of streaming. It's like a bad joke: "What's the one thing that's worse than the streaming royalties paid to recording artists?" Answer: what you earn from writing those songs.

The music industry is not just horizontally integrated, with three major labels controlling the vast majority of the market, it's vertically integrated too. The Big Three record labels—UMG, Sony, and Warner—also own the Big Three music publishers. And that creates a gargantuan conflict of interest.

Above, we mentioned that the share of streaming revenue that goes to recording artists is about 52 percent of Spotify's total revenue. That's bad enough—but the share that goes to songwriters ranges from just *10 to 15 percent*. That's how someone like Fiona Bevan can end up earning a paltry £100 in royalties for co-writing a track on Kylie Minogue's *Disco*, even though it topped the charts.

In the US, the composer share for interactive streaming like on Spotify is set by a statutory license, rather than dictated by the music publishers. For years, it was set at just 10.5 percent of revenues, courtesy of a weird formula we talk about more later. While Big Music gave lip service toward protesting that rate, on closer examination, this actually worked out exceptionally well for the major labels who also own the world's biggest music publishers.

In the previous chapter, we explained that peculiar feature of music industry contracts: recoupment, or the practice of requiring artists to repay any upfront advance plus most of the label's other expenses of making the record. Vertical integration within the music industry combines with this practice in a way that hurts composers. Since recordings are more costly to make than compositions, companies that own both record labels and music publishers have a perverse incentive to push as much revenue to the label side as possible.[13] If songwriters earn more, they'll earn out their own advances and start actually getting paychecks. But if the lion's share goes to recording artists, who are much less likely to earn out, that money stays in-house, and the corporation's profits are fattened instead. The conflict of interest is obvious, and its consequences tangible.

Paltry songwriting revenues are making the industry ever less sustainable and forcing composers to give up their craft: the number of full-time songwriters in Nashville has fallen by 80 percent in just fifteen years.[14] For shareholders, however, it works out great. Leading music industry lawyer Amanda Harcourt has called for the relative shares of composers and recording artists to be rebalanced but isn't optimistic about the chances of it happening: "With so much horizontal integration it is unlikely to occur."[15] This is yet another way in which the dominance of Big Music enables them to shape markets to funnel money away from the very creators they are supposed to benefit.

THE UNATTRIBUTABLE MONEY HUSTLE

In 2015 a contract between Spotify and Sony was leaked—and the music world was agog. In the US, interactive streaming services like Spotify and Apple Music license music directly from record labels and other distributors on whatever terms the parties agree. The terms of those deals are kept tightly under wraps. Big Business is well aware that the less you know about what's going on, the less likely you'll be able to fight it.

Industry insiders had for years suspected that the majors had negotiated deals that were prioritizing their own interests over those of their artists—and certainly over the interests of their independent rivals. Until the leak, however, that was just hearsay. The leaked contract proved it.

Most notably, the deal entitled Sony to as much as $42.5 million in advances and up to $9-million-worth of free ad space (which it could use or sell) with another $15-million-worth at a discounted rate.

Labels commonly require advance payments or minimum revenue guarantees as a condition of licensing their catalogs. Assume an advance of $5 million for three months. Spotify pays the label that $5 million upfront. If its users stream enough songs to reach $5 million in royalties payable to that label in that quarter, Spotify effectively recoups its advance. If they stream more, Spotify pays additional royalties to get square. The contract controversy was primarily about what would happen if users streamed *less*. Would the excess be shared with artists or simply pocketed by the label?

Record deals had long distinguished between revenue attributable to specific uses of songs (which must be shared between the creator and labels), and unattributable or general revenue (which the label got to keep).[16] That gave labels a perverse incentive to maximize "breakage," a term that originally referred to a deduction for the costs of broken physical records, on which artists would not receive royalties, but which later came to refer to all payments that aren't linked to specific use of repertoire. Arranging deals to maximize breakage cuts out the artists the labels are meant to represent. Because the contracts that affect them are usually kept secret, however, there's no transparency around whether deals have been deliberately structured to eliminate the artist's share—or how much money breakage ultimately costs them.

The leaked contract shone some light into this darkness. The only reason Sony was able to negotiate such large advances and those free and discounted ads was because it controlled such a vast number of artists' rights. But the contract showed that it used them to structure arrangements that would favor itself instead. This racket isn't new. In the 1950s and '60s, the majors would enter into deals with record clubs based on massive advances and minuscule royalty rates. Everyone knew those fat advances would never earn out, but the labels knew the non-recouped bit wouldn't be attributable to any particular artist, and they'd have no obligation to give their artists even the stingy share they were owed.[17]

But that was just a two-bit scam. In the streaming era, structuring deals to maximize breakage and thus minimize the share that has to be passed on to artists became a much bigger part of the business. Sound-Exchange's former executive director John Simson has described major labels as "hell-bent on receiving unattributable money."[18] Since only the most powerful artists have the power to contractually demand a share of breakage,[19] doing so effectively increases the label's margin by the amount that should rightfully have gone to artists.

To illustrate how distorting such advances can be, Merlin, which licenses digital music rights on behalf of independent labels, once reported over $1 million in breakage from unrecouped advances via just two global streaming deals. In one, the unrecouped portion was more than half of what had been earned in royalties; in the other, almost *five times* as much. On the latter deal, had Merlin been a traditional record label, it could have kept $500 for every $100 it shared with artists. Artists on a 25 percent royalty rate would have ended up with just $25 out of every $600, instead of the $150 they would have been entitled to if the payment had been structured as royalties instead.[20]

As it happens, Merlin passes all such revenues on to the independent labels it represents. Although they rarely have any contractual obligation to pass it on to their artists, many leading indies publicly pledged early on to give their artists a good faith pro-rata share of unattributable revenue from digital services.[21]

The majors had long refused to address the breakage question, but their hands were forced when the leaked contract showed the extent of the unattributable value being transferred from artists. All three issued statements assuring artists they shared breakage from advances (if not the other benefits the contract disclosed). Industry insiders accepted Warner's assurances,[22] but for Sony and Universal, however, there was (and still is!) much skepticism. Just what were they paying *on*, and how long had they been paying it *for*?

Not long, apparently: independent expert analysis of a 2014 royalty statement of a successful UMG–signed band turned up plenty of errors and inconsistencies, but "no evidence of the payment of breakage."[23] Charles Caldas, then CEO of Merlin, believes it was only the leak of the contract that got them "to (in a very, *very* carefully worded way!) say they would pay breakage on streaming advances" at all.[24] And they gave no answers about how they'd share the value of all that free and discounted ad space. Because royalty statements are so deliberately opaque, and because labels have few transparency obligations to their artists, even today, it's often not clear when, and on what terms, breakage is actually shared.

Advances and ad money aren't the only way labels siphon value away from artists. An even bigger profit center is the practice of taking free or heavily discounted equity in emerging technology platforms as a condition of licensing their catalogs. Take the streaming platform Sound-Cloud, which struggled to persuade the majors to license their music. Warner was the first to agree to do so. In addition to the fees it negotiated for use of its catalog, the music giant secured a 5 percent ownership stake, rumored to have been acquired at a 50 percent discount compared to that paid by other investors.[25] Such equity arrangements are deals "that all sides seem to prefer go unnoticed," but they are a key part of the new media landscape, and give the majors another huge economic advantage over independents.

It doesn't stop with SoundCloud: the Big Three have taken stakes in a whole range of new music endeavors, including Shazam, Deezer, and even YouTube (when it was bought by Google, the majors reportedly negotiated for an equity stake valued at up to $50 million, or about 3 percent[26]). Contrast this with Kobalt, a music publishing company that has won market share (including key artists such as Childish Gambino) with its "radically transparent" ethos, and which refuses equity stakes in streaming companies in favor of higher per-stream payouts.[27]

Of all these deals, it's the ones with Spotify that have proved most lucrative. Inked in 2008, the year the company launched, these deals gave 6 percent of the company to Sony, 5 to Universal, 4 to Warner, and 2 to EMI—which eventually ended up with Universal after the two giants merged. A final 1 percent went to Merlin, the global digital rights agency representing independent labels that then made up about 12 percent of the global market.[28] The price? Less than $10,000 for the lot.[29] Compared to the amounts paid by other early investors, that was virtually free. The payoff was handsome: when Spotify went public in 2018, Sony's share alone was valued at about $1.5 billion.[30] That's a return on investment of 45,000,000 percent.

Once again, the conflict of interest is obvious. The majors wanted Spotify to go public with the highest possible valuation so as to maximize the value of their stock, but also had an interest in negotiating the highest possible royalties for their musicians, which would drive that value down. "How can they negotiate with themselves, theoretically?" one industry insider asked. "What's a fair royalty, what's a fair advance, when they *are* both sides?"[31]

This question was on everyone's minds as Spotify's IPO drew near. The majors' long-term contracts had expired, and they were licensing their recordings to Spotify on a month-to-month basis. New long-term deals were an essential prerequisite for Spotify's IPO: the company would be worth far more if it could assure potential investors that the platform wasn't about to lose access to the most popular repertoire. At this time too, Spotify was still losing hundreds of millions of dollars a year, and "needed to reduce royalty payments to show investors the potential for profit."[32] Universal, Sony, and Warner were in a strong bargaining position because Spotify desperately needed their content, but nonetheless each decided to accept royalty cuts of about 3 percentage points.[33] That is, they exercised their power in a way that reduced the market rate for recorded music, but which raised Spotify's value to investors.

It's unclear how much this cut actually affected their bottom line—they may well have insisted on additional kickbacks in the form of over-large advances and free ads and other perks to offset the cost on top of the fillip it gave their equity investments. But it *is* clear that this move harmed their independent competition. As the leaked Spotify contract showed, the majors have "most favored nation" clauses in their contracts with the streaming platforms, guaranteeing nobody else will get a higher rate. That meant when the independent labels came back to the negotiating table, the ceiling was lower than it had been before. In other words, the majors used the power of their vast rights catalogs to directly hurt independent artists and producers.

As if that weren't enough, it was long unclear whether the majors would share any part of the resulting windfall with their artists. Merlin had promised early on to pass on the full value of its equity stake to its members, and many of those independent labels had in turn committed to passing it on to artists. But the Big Three dragged their feet. Even under huge pressure from artists and managers, Sony glaringly failed to address this issue in its response to the leaked Spotify contract. It was not until 2016, seven years after it secured its equity stake, that Warner finally announced it would share the proceeds. That prompted Sony to follow suit just hours later. UMG kept silent for a full two years more before it finally also promised to share the cash with its artists.

The billion-dollar question then became *how* the money would be divided up. Since the windfall from the share sale was unattributable to any specific use, the majors had complete discretion about whether and how to pass it on, except in outlier cases involving acts who were powerful enough to have written an entitlement into their contracts.

One option would have been to treat it like general licensing revenue. Recording contracts typically set out two main royalty rates: a lower one for sales that reflect the additional costs and risk involved in actually manufacturing and selling a record, and a higher one where labels simply license their works to another party to exploit (say, in a TV commercial) and don't have to do anything except make the deal and take the money. Licensing royalties are typically 50 percent of revenues—far higher than the 5–25 percent artists usually get for sales, depending on when their contracts were signed. Outrageously, digital music sales get called "licenses" for consumers, which is how consumers can be bound to terms including prohibitions on resale, but are called "sales" to musicians, which ensures they get paid at the lower rate. Artist advocates called for the equity windfall to be treated the same as licensing deals, which would have seen half the money go to artists. The three majors all came up with different ways of splitting the cash, each one less advantageous to artists than that.

Warner, which sold its full shareholding in Spotify shortly after the IPO for over half a billion dollars, allocated a flat 25 percent of the proceeds for sharing between artists and distributed labels. That's likely to have been a bit more than the sales royalty rate of most artists, but just half the regular licensing rate. Controversially, however, Warner applied the equity proceeds to artists' royalty accounts. Remember those huge, all-but-unrecoupable debts most acts are saddled with thanks to the system that makes them pay virtually all the costs of making and marketing their records? This decision meant that the sale proceeds were offset against those debts. Because there was no transparency around this process we don't know exactly who got how much, but it's likely that most Warner-signed artists simply had their debts reduced slightly without ever seeing a single real dollar in their bank accounts.

Sony sold half its stake in Spotify for $750 million. It used artists' sales royalty rates to calculate their pro-rata share, likely ranging from about 5–25 percent depending on the age of the contract. That's lower than Warner, and far below the usual licensing rate. Importantly, though, the earnings did not count against unrecouped earnings, which meant artists did actually receive some cash.

UMG took yet another approach. Recall it took two full years longer than the other majors to confirm it would share the proceeds when it sold its stake, and when it finally did it was via a terse one-line statement: "Consistent with UMG's approach to artist compensation, artists would share in the proceeds of a [Spotify] equity sale."[34] Industry watchers were left to speculate about the percentage that would go to artists, whether or not it would be recoupable, and how distributed labels would be treated.

At the time of writing, UMG still hasn't sold any of its shares, which had appreciated in value to an astonishing $2 billion by the end of 2020. But artists do finally have some clarity about how it will be paid—thanks, unexpectedly, to Taylor Swift. In 2018 she became a free agent after thirteen years signed to Big Machine Records. As one of the most bankable stars on the planet she had an enormous amount of negotiating power. On signing a new deal with UMG, she used it to maintain ownership of her master recordings, a feat almost without precedent for a major label deal. On top of that, she insisted that UMG agree to share Spotify sale proceeds with all its artists on a non-recoupable basis. It's still unclear at what rate they plan to pay—the meager sales royalty rate adopted by Sony, Warner's 25 percent, or the 50 percent licensing rate that most fairly reflects their risk and reward. But when the shares are sold, UMG artists will receive at least *some* money in their pockets.

A 2019 Deutsche Bank report estimates that streaming is the most profitable form of music distribution, generating an 18 percent margin, compared to 13 percent on downloads and just 11 percent on physical. But as we've seen, those profits aren't being evenly enjoyed. Daniel Glass, president and founder of Glassnote Records, says, "There's very little middle- and lower-class in recording. That world has dried up." This history helps show why.

Music copyrights are supposed to enable artists and songwriters to create new works, reward them for doing so, and encourage investors to get them to market. But with the industrial aggregation of copyrights concentrating them in so few hands, those aims are being subverted. Between them, the Big Three sign only about 650 acts each year—a tiny fraction of working artists.[35] Nonetheless, their vast copyright reservoirs give them outsized power to determine how music pays for everyone else. The massive advances and other kickbacks they routinely demand as a cost of doing business increase barriers to entry, making it harder for competition to flourish. And, since contracts last the entire term of copyright, which can be a century or more, they keep artists locked in even when their labels are acting against their interests. The result is an industry controlled by a tiny handful of anticompetitive empires, shored up by legal privileges they can call upon states to enforce.

We have known about the risks posed by highly concentrated owner-ship and inordinately long contracts for years. Public Knowledge and the Consumer Federation of America explicitly warned against permitting the merger of EMI and UMG in 2012: "Incumbent major record labels have the incentive to stifle new digital distribution platforms because those platforms begin to level the playing field among major labels, inde-pendent labels, and unsigned artists."[36] But that deal was approved, and since then we have been watching that stifling play out.

Remarkably, despite all this, the market share of independent labels is actually growing. In 2012 the majors controlled 76 percent of the global recorded music market; by 2018 that had fallen to 66 percent.[37] A2IM's president, Richard Burgess, suggests this is because the algorith-mic models used by some streaming platforms "tend to help surface less mainstream recordings for people who have more niche tastes." Data suggests these listeners are also the most likely to pay for their music—Merlin's analysis of half a trillion streams found its independent mem-bers' repertoire "performs over 25 percent better in market share terms on paid tiers vs free tiers."[38] The trend has been apparent for years but was easy to ignore when the indies were growing from a low base. That's no longer the case. It took Merlin nine years to distribute its first bil-lion dollars to member labels, but just eighteen months to distribute the second.[39] In 2019, the majors grew their streaming revenue by 22 per-cent, while independents increased by 39 percent. And, when you break down market share by copyright ownership (which takes out music the majors distribute but don't own), indies now claim a full 40 percent of the market.[40] Just imagine how much more of a threat they could be to the majors' hegemony—and how they might broaden out the industry's chokepoints—if the playing field were closer to level.

CHAPTER 6

WHY SPOTIFY WANTS YOU TO RELY ON PLAYLISTS

Paul Johnson's life was like any other struggling musician's—working multiple jobs, picking up gigs, hustling. Then his warm acoustic folk-pop tune "Firework" made it on to one of Spotify's Fresh Finds playlists, designed to surface brand new artists. Spotify and other streaming platforms invest heavily in playlists, ranging from the algorithmically generated Discover Weekly (which predicts new music subscribers might like) to the editorial RapCaviar (the most desired real estate in hip-hop). Playlist placements are highly coveted, both for how they rack up the streams—more than seven billion in five years in the case of RapCaviar—and the way they expose music to new listeners. The latter paid off for Johnson. His first playlisting shot him from a few thousand streams a day to twenty thousand, and later, as his music landed more and more spots, to hundreds of thousands. Thanks to this exposure he's now making around $200,000 a year, mostly in royalties from streaming.

That's brilliant for Paul. But, like almost all successes in music, it's a Horatio Alger story. Spotify wants you to believe the rags to riches transformation is due to hard work and talent when it actually requires a huge amount of luck. Ignoring that luck element elides how difficult it is for musicians to support themselves via streaming revenues—and how many hard working, talented people will be unable ever to do so.

We've already talked about the infinitesimal fractions of cents paid per stream, which mean that making a living from it requires extraordinary scale. Nevertheless, streaming has become the main game in recorded music, with revenues of $13.4 billion in 2020—62 percent of the global market.[1]

As we've seen, immediately before the streaming era began, we went through one of the rare moments in the history of recorded music when power flowed in the direction of artists. Although it was an economically disastrous time for many of them, the democratization brought by digital technologies and the internet also finally forced record labels to reform abuses they'd carried off for decades. Sony Music's CEO Rob Stringer even expressed regret for the past maltreatment, acknowledging that "a lot of people did stuff they shouldn't have done: screwed over an artist or trod on someone's head to get somewhere."[2]

Now, however, the recorded music market is again taking on that hourglass shape, this time with the streaming platforms at the center. In the last couple of chapters, we explained how the music industry has been organized to let labels and publishers scoop up much of the value of music. Here, we show how the streaming platforms, as they become more powerful, are positioning themselves to do the same.

The most dominant, Spotify, tells investors it plans to leverage its listeners into a massive digital ad play that would make it a market leader behind only Google and Facebook.[3] It pushes playlists with names like Mood Booster, Happy Hits, Life Sucks, and Coping with Loss to extract what the company claims is subscribers' real-time mood and activity data, then flogs it to sell ads.[4] But this is almost certainly a counterfeit claim: like the rest of Big Tech, Spotify is better at selling advertisers the idea it has a mind-control ray to make people buy stuff than at actually persuading people to buy stuff. The real money will come from Spotify inserting itself as a gatekeeper between musicians and listeners. And those very same playlists that gave Paul Johnson and other artists their breakout success will be central to its ability to do so.

Streaming is sold as a way for listeners to access almost any music on command. Increasingly, however, obeying nudges from streaming platforms, subscribers listen to playlists prepared by algorithms or human curators instead of making their own selections. As the International

Federation of Musicians points out, playlists are increasingly pervasive: "There is one playlist for each moment of the day: wake-up, breakfast, work-out, relaxation, meditation, running, partying etc. One single click of a button and music is on for the next 30 minutes or the entire evening or night."[5]

Indeed, playlists have become so important that being left off can flop even megastar releases (as Katy Perry discovered after Spotify blackballed her for giving rival Apple Music a temporary exclusive, reminiscent of Amazon cutting off publishers who wouldn't give it big enough discounts). Music journalist and commentator David Turner sees them as repeating the same old tune: "The tone of playlisting shifted very quickly in the last couple of years, from excitement to disillusionment, once we recognized that the same issues of gatekeeping that existed in forms like radio are just simply being repeated."[6]

Playlist culture imports old power imbalances. When writer and music commentator Liz Pelly analyzed the gender of artists featured on Spotify's most popular playlists, she found just one woman-led song featured on RapCaviar's evolving fifty-track playlist over four weeks, with other leading lists doing little better.[7] The biggest editorial playlists on every platform also prioritize American voices: a recent study found that almost half of all acts featured by Spotify were from the US. It was even higher for Amazon Music, at 67 percent. And, as in the past, the system often helps acts repped by the biggest labels get the most exposure. Their staff have direct access to pitch songs to editorial teams and are helped by the fact that platforms need to stay on the majors' good sides to secure favorable terms next time their license comes up for negotiation. Having said that, however, the majors don't have it all their own way. There are more artists sharing the top 10 percent of streams between them than there have been before, meaning Top 40 pop hits are getting fewer streams, while everything else gets more.[8]

Streaming is also changing the very *sound* of music. Spotify wants subscribers to listen as much as possible, and one way of ensuring that is to feed them "streambait"—the kind of background music that can be left on all day without fatigue. To that end, Spotify pushes undemanding options—Chill Hits, Chill Vibes, Chill Rap, De-Stress Chill, Chilled Soul, Peaceful Piano. Musicians looking for the monster volume it takes to make a living from streaming are steered toward creating unchallenging, forgettable tunes. Per-stream payments even seem to be influencing song length, which has dropped substantially over the streaming era. Drake's 2018 album *Scorpion* features twenty-five songs, averaging just over three and a half minutes apiece.

By nudging listeners toward playlists, Spotify is also training us to outsource our decisions about what to listen to. The more listeners automatically head to Spotify's ¡Viva Latino! or Baila Reggaeton or Rock Classics, the more streaming comes to mimic radio. The difference is that with radio there were thousands of DJs deciding what to play, including many that were passionate about breaking new local talent. With streaming, just one faceless global giant programs each channel.

This trend threatens to disintermediate artists and labels, just as Amazon sought to disintermediate publishers by encouraging writers to publish direct. Liz Pelly has been warning of this danger for years: "A music culture dependent on playlists is dependent on Spotify, whereas a music culture dependent on albums is dependent on record labels."[9] Passive listeners are less likely to form connections with the musicians who make it or seek out their gigs. Instead, they just keep loading up the playlists that promise more of the same and accept whichever interchangeable artists are loaded next.

When streaming platforms exert so much control over what gets listened to, they gain more and more ability to shift value from the artist and labels, songwriters and publishers. Spotify is already flexing that muscle. Its ambient playlists have for years been dominated by pseudonymous songwriters and performers with no online presence but millions upon millions of streamed song-plays, and leading ambient acts like Brian Eno and Bibio have been dropped in their favor.[10] One investigation found over 90 percent of tracks featured on Spotify's Ambient Chill list came from these mystery viral artists, all originating from Swedish production house Epidemic Sound. The top fifty of these artists have racked up almost three billion streams between them.[11] To put that number in context, Spotify's RapCaviar, the most influential playlist in streaming, only recently passed seven billion.

The suspicion is that Spotify has negotiated lower than normal royalties with Epidemic Sound, then prioritized its music to fatten margins. A former Spotify insider confirmed as much to *Variety*, describing the practice as "one of a number of internal initiatives to lower the royalties they're paying to the major labels."[12] This can save substantial cash: *Rolling Stone* estimates Spotify would have had to pay out about $5 million in royalties just to the top ten of these manufactured artists had it been paying industry-standard rates.

Spotify has also begun extracting co-op, a polite euphemism for payola, from creative producers—part of the "two-sided marketplace" that lets it not only sell artists to listeners but also listeners to artists. This has become a textbook tech play: recall how Amazon shakes down publishers for advertising costs and how Facebook encouraged companies to use it to connect to customers before suddenly demanding that they pay for access.

In late 2020, Spotify launched an "experimental" feature that would boost artists' plays—but only if they agreed to lower "promotional" rates.[13] Most are already being paid so little that they might be willing to make this trade-off, in the hope that increased exposure might lead to new album, merch, and ticket sales—or even better, the kind of breakthrough that launched Paul Johnson to fame. That would be a slippery slope to the bottom, with artists and labels feeling they have no option than to accept ever lower rates to access the audiences that Spotify now controls so tightly.

Another initiative, Marquee, invites artists and labels to buy pop-up ads to prompt listeners to check out their music. At fifty-five cents per click, most labels say they don't see much direct return on investment from their ads, but some say the payments seem to bump their chances of landing those longed-for playlist spots. George Howard, a professor at the Berklee College of Music, explains that these kinds of practices "continue what payola always has done—the major labels, which have the most money and the most frequent releases, get the most play, consolidating the amount of art that is put out there." A2IM president, Richard Burgess, says Spotify had promised it would never do this, and that it's yet another way of putting downward pressure on label margins: "Some labels feel like the program promotes their music to people they would reach anyway, and the expense, effectively, just reduces the royalty they make." Being able to treat the suppliers of your core input as a profit center is a neat trick and shows just how much value might be shifted from creators to shareholders if streaming's dominance continues.

On top of this, Spotify and other platforms are simply moving margin from creators and artists to themselves as they gain the power to do so. In

2016, music platforms kept 31.6 percent of revenue. By 2018, their share had grown to 32.7 percent—even though their systems were by then more mature, which would suggest less rather than more overhead and thus justify a smaller rather than larger share.[14]

Investors are betting that, with strategies like these, Spotify can cement its hold on the recorded music market. Although it has lost money every year since launch, its stock price still doubled within two years of its 2018 initial public offering. As with Amazon, investors believe it will capture sufficient market power to be able to dictate terms and divert more of streaming's rivers of gold from artists and labels. And those rivers are only getting deeper: Goldman Sachs has predicted the streaming market will exceed $37 billion by 2030.[15] Venture capital firm Andreessen Horowitz agrees Spotify could pull this off: "Historically, music labels have commanded certain economics from streaming services, but if Spotify's existing large user base continues to gain share, the negotiation could flip, allowing Spotify to achieve meaningfully differentiated economics relative to the competition."[16]

Spotify controls just over a third of the market. The rest is dominated by Big Tech: Apple (with 19 percent), Amazon (15 percent), Tencent (in joint venture with Spotify, 11 percent), and Google (6 percent).[17] These other players are pushing the same playlist culture, and for the same reasons. Between them, they believe they can return the music market to its old hourglass shape, this time with them at the center.

If we leave things as they are, it will be hard to prevent them. Plenty of driven, artist-focused people are keen to set up alternative platforms that work better for artists but are kept out by sky-high barriers to entry. If you want to start a streaming service, you'd better have deep pockets. Music licensing is fiendishly complex. Sound recordings and the underlying compositions are owned by different people and have to be licensed separately using different rules. As well as individually negotiating sound recording licenses with all major distributors, you'll need to jump through all the hoops associated with clearing the mechanical rights for the underlying songs, in every country you wish to operate. Leading music industry lawyer Amanda Harcourt, outlining what's involved in clearing just the composition rights to set up a streaming service in Europe, describes it as "dreary" and "unduly complex," with high transaction costs making it especially difficult for small and medium-sized companies.[18]

In the early 2000s, unlicensed peer-to-peer software providers and streaming platforms abounded. Record sales plummeted and a panicked recording industry adopted a policy of scorched earth litigation, driving them out of the market. The link between these technologies and the fall in revenues led them to characterize music fans as unprincipled thieves obsessed with getting everything for free. But as we see from the rapid growth of licensed streaming, once that finally became an option, what was really winning fans over was the offer of instant access to all the world's popular music. Had the recording industry taken the opportunity to work with lawmakers to streamline licensing for these new distribution methods at the time, its transition could have been far less painful, and we would now have licensing rules more fit for purpose than today's archaic mazes.

Spotify CEO Daniel Ek describes these licensing complexities as one of the biggest limits on the platform's growth.[19] That's undoubtedly true, but these mazes still work to its advantage. Sure, they force Spotify to grow more slowly, but they also stop rivals from ever starting up. That makes them crucial to Spotify's own anticompetitive flywheel: paying these high transaction costs saves it from having to actually compete. On top of that, as we saw in a previous chapter, the major record labels routinely shake down new players as a condition of granting them the licenses they need to get started, adding further to the cost of entering the market. That explains why Spotify's only rivals of any significance are deep-pocketed tech giants—they're the only ones with the resources to do so.

With Spotify and the tech players already so dominant in the market, it's hard to imagine how these licensing mazes and high start-up costs leave room for anyone else to become established. That makes it likely that streaming platforms' power will continue to grow relative to that of artists or labels. It's their explicit aim to achieve this: Tencent Music Entertainment and Spotify recently exchanged equity "to give both companies better leverage in negotiations with the major music groups."[20] While Spotify undoubtedly played a crucial role in towing the music industry out of the crater left behind by the collapse of the CD bubble and the rise of Napster, that doesn't mean the system it pioneered will ultimately be healthier or more sustainable for music.

The record industry's potential responses to this growing threat are limited. They're too reliant on streaming revenues to withdraw their catalogs from Spotify completely, and they don't want to risk their catalogs being de-emphasized in place of cheaper alternatives, as is already happening in the ambient space. They could insist on more favorable terms, but the biggest players, Sony Music and UMG, still have big equity stakes in the company, and doing so could threaten those investments. That might explain why, after an initially hostile reaction to Spotify's two-sided marketplace, UMG inked a new multiyear deal embracing it. Already, "major songs feature on popular Spotify playlists at a disproportionately higher rate than independent songs."[21] Perhaps it sees that, given the recent inroads of independents, its relatively fatter margins, and its hefty stake in the company, an arrangement where labels are forced to buy access to listeners could work to UMG's advantage.

Crucially, too, cutting out Spotify would help its Big Tech rivals become relatively stronger. That's also dangerous. Labels know—from direct experience with Apple and YouTube, and from *everyone*'s experience with Amazon—that these companies will play hardball as soon as they achieve dominance themselves. That makes it vital to keep Spotify in the game, and further limits their possible responses.

THE PODCAST PLAY

Spotify isn't only interested in sewing up music—it's going after podcasting too. In just two years it has spent close to a billion dollars buying up leading podcasts, production houses, and tools, with the obvious aim of vertically integrating an industry that has been flourishing with hundreds of players. This podcast gambit lets us see something that has happened historically play out in real time.

As we began writing this book, podcasts were one of the few remaining vestiges of the open internet. The industry had the same three layers as online news once did: production, distribution, and ads, all controlled by different players. Since then, however, we've seen a handful of would-be oligopolists trying to take control of the different layers the same tactic Google used to position itself to suck so much of the value out of news. Spotify is one of them, and Amazon and SiriusXM are making big plays as well. If they succeed, it will mean less scope for podcasting to act as a public square. That risk was bullhorn-announced when Amazon first added podcasts to its music platform, together with a condition banning podcasts from containing any anti-Amazon content.[22] Realizing the overstep, the giant quickly walked it back. But it's a stark reminder of the power we give up when we allow powerful companies to take over the infrastructure we might need to organize against them.

Podcasting started in the early 2000s by piggybacking on RSS, a widely used syndication protocol that facilitates a decentralized information ecosystem. Anyone can publish an RSS feed, and podcasts have traditionally simply been published as RSS feeds that include a link to an MP3 housed on the public internet. When you subscribe to a podcast, you're just telling your feed-reader to check in with the servers that host that RSS feed every now and again to see if it's been updated, and, if it has, to download the MP3 the new entry links to.

The intrinsically decentralized nature of RSS and thus podcasts has enabled podcasting to thrive as a cottage industry, composed of millions of people who create, share, and listen. Some had budgets, studios, and advertisers. Some were just a single person with a voice memo app— think of early YouTube personalities, except that instead of all those weird and diverse voices and formats being crammed into YouTube's proprietary silo, they were spread out all over the internet, on millions of servers hosted by large and small providers with a wide diversity of business models and priorities.

Spotify's podcasting play is all about turning this open ecosystem into another walled garden. In just two years it spent almost a billion dollars buying production companies and podcast creation tools. Another $100 million went on securing exclusive content like Joe Rogan's podcast, which quickly became their most popular—leaving them highly exposed as Rogan increasingly spewed vaccine misinformation and racist ideas[23]—and it has been rolling up talent like the Obamas and Bruce Springsteen too. RSS has no place in Spotify's vision because the whole point is to close the open system. You will need a Spotify account to hear any of its content, and Spotify will be spying on you when you do.

Take a moment to think about the kind of podcasts you listen to. By surveilling your listening habits, Spotify will be able to figure out your politics, sexuality, and insecurities, and then sell advertisers direct access to your ears. Just as with newspapers, the extra value of wealthy listeners will be siphoned off by the platform, instead of going to creators themselves. And premium subscribers, who haven't previously been subjected to ads, will become a whole new product.

As Spotify vertically integrates an industry that once flourished with thousands of individual players, we're seeing what happened with news play out again in real time. Spotify's aim is to create another chokepoint market, with audiences at one end and creators at the other. It will squat in the middle, charging audiences tolls for reaching creators, and creators tolls for reaching audiences. The bigger the audience and content pool it controls, the more it will be able to shake down creators.

Even in its first steps into this market we can see how Spotify is working to make audiences dependent on playlists rather than specific podcasts or producers. It offers curated programming on topics ranging from news to football to food to true crime, flowing freely from one show to the next.

This development should strike fear into the heart of every creator who relies on podcast income. As Pelly explains, "Playlists are designed to create and condition dedicated fans of Spotify products, not artists or podcasters." That culture "strips agency and power from the people who make the work that sustains the platform: if users are coming to the platform for a playlist instead of a specific artist or podcaster, whether or not Spotify is able to retain those artists or podcasters on its platform matters very little to their bottom line." Individual creators and producers lose their power: "If they screw over the independent food podcasters and they all decide to leave the platform, what difference does that make to the listener who is just used to hitting play on the 'Chill Dinner Time Talk' podcast playlist and won't know the difference anyway? Spotify will find another podcaster to add to a playlist, or even better, get some new stuff going in Spotify Studios."[24]

This makes podcasting critic Nick Quah fear for the next generation of podcasters. "My biggest concern is that if you don't have a preexisting relationship with a platform, . . . if you don't have a platform yourself, if you're an up-and-coming nobody from a demographic that's historically [underserved] by traditional media companies, do you still have a shot? And to what proportion do you have a shot relative to other demographics?"

The pivot to podcasts—and, particularly, Spotify's in-house production of them—might also contribute to making things even worse for musicians than they are already. One of Spotify's challenges is that so much of its revenue goes toward paying music royalties. Since that's usually a fixed proportion of revenue (those mystery viral artists aside!), it doesn't improve with scale. When Spotify creates its own podcasts, however, it can serve them up to as many listeners as it pleases, all for one fixed price. Naturally, it's going to nudge its listeners toward the lower cost product, as we've already seen it promise to do with those promotional rates. Musicians who were making a pittance from 200,000 streams a month are *really* going to struggle if their plays get halved because listeners have been steered toward podcasts instead.

If Spotify does succeed in vertically integrating podcasting and walling it off from the open internet (and the size of its investment sure suggests it is determined to), it will be able to divert an increasing share of the value they generate away from creators. Its share price has spiked around its podcast announcements, suggesting investors believe it can do so.

When this exact same thing happened with news, few people realized what was at stake until the battle was lost. This time we know exactly what's going on. The live question is whether we'll let it happen anyway.

CHAPTER 7

WHAT THE US SHARES WITH RWANDA, IRAN, AND NORTH KOREA

R adio is one of the most important players in the music ecosystem, bringing in an annual haul of over $40 billion worldwide. Of that, US terrestrial radio brings in some $13 billion.[1] But for recording artists, it might as well be nothing. That's because the US is one of the only countries in the world that doesn't pay royalties to the owners of the recordings they play, putting them in an exclusive club with members like Rwanda, Iran, and North Korea.[2]

Big Radio's longtime argument has been that airplay equals free promotion, which sells records despite evidence that those who listen to more music radio actually buy *less* music.[3] Now that pretty much nobody buys records, they have updated their rhetoric to argue airplay also shifts concert tickets and merch.

Broadcast lobbyists say that if they had to pay record labels and musicians it would "financially cripple local radio stations, harming the millions of listeners who rely on local radio for news, emergency information, weather updates and entertainment."[4] Somehow, though, US internet and satellite radio stations, who do have to pay, manage to make it work!

Some station owners have begun entering into private deals with bigger labels that see them voluntarily pay for radio use in exchange for reduced fees for online uses—a practice that has been criticized for having the potential to drive down the statutory rates payable for the latter, disproportionately harming smaller labels who lack the power to negotiate radio payments to offset it.[5] It's no substitute for a legal obligation like the ones in force almost everywhere else in the world.

When broadcast lobbyists claim local radio would be threatened by an obligation to pay artists and labels, they also ignore the reality that it has *already* been gutted—by the same lack of competition that has become endemic throughout the culture industries. The 1996 Telecommunications Act deregulated the US radio industry, including by removing the cap on the number of stations a single company could own nationwide. Reed Hundt, who was the FCC chair at the time, promised "diversity in programming and diversity in the viewpoints expressed on this powerful medium that so shapes our culture."[6] Predictably, though, the shift brought the opposite. The number of radio station owners went into freefall after deregulation, with Clear Channel (now rebranded as the cuddlier-sounding "iHeartMedia") ballooning from 40 stations to 1,200 in just five years.

As ownership became more concentrated, money and power did too. In 1993, the top four companies earned 12 percent of all marketing revenue. By 2004, they were raking in 50 percent, sucking a huge amount of money away from locally owned stations.[7] These big networks also brought homogenization. It's "common now for a single automated center to feed content to a slew of stations across the country," and local DJs have disappeared.[8]

A2IM's Richard Burgess mourns this loss, telling us it means indies have fewer options to break artists via local stations, thus making it even harder for them to compete with the majors: "One way that managers and small labels used to break artists was by going to their local radio station. They might play it at 4 a.m. If they got a few phone-in responses, they would move it to a better time slot. And you could grow and break a record this way. Now, in many cases, there's nobody there."[9] That centralized control also makes it possible for these powerful buyers to cancel artists they don't like, as Clear Channel did when the Dixie Chicks criticized George W. Bush.[10]

It's not that Big Radio can't afford to pay. At about $13 billion a year, US terrestrial radio revenues eclipse those of the domestic record industry, and they're predicted to remain strong.[11] Every single month, iHeartMedia reaches 90 percent of Americans. In 2018 it boasted a 27 percent margin, higher than any other advertising-supported audio media.[12] It nonetheless entered bankruptcy protection that very same year—not because its fundamentals were weak, but because the company was staggering under the unbearable debt it had been saddled with as part of a leveraged buyout in late 2006.

Leveraged buyouts—where people take out loans against companies they don't yet own—are a key feature of the private equity playbook. Typically, about 70 percent of the purchase price comes from debt.[13] Just a tiny fraction of the purchase price is put up by the general partners in the fund itself, with the remaining equity coming from outside investors. Typically, the leveraged company will try to buy competitors in an attempt to monopolize the industry, then use that power to squeeze suppliers, while simultaneously using their massive debt overhangs to squeeze workers and creditors as well. The idea is for the partners to exit after three to five years with a fat capital profit, having pocketed hefty advisory and management fees along the way.

These deals are structured to give the fund an outsized return in the event the investment goes well and insulate them from the downside if it fails. Experts Eileen Appelbaum and Rosemary Batt describe this as a classic case of "moral hazard," because "the general partner who makes the decision to load the portfolio company with debt that it is obligated to repay bears very little of the potential costs associated with those risks."[14] Because private equity firms are so much better at capturing value than creating it, carnage often follows. These effects are by no means limited to the creative industries: in the US, ten of the fourteen largest retail bankruptcies since 2012 have come under the aegis of private equity firms, directly costing almost 600,000 jobs, plus 728,000 more at suppliers and related firms.[15] The devastation can extend to former workers who have their pensions wiped out. Who wins? Not the economy, which is stripped of previously productive businesses, nor employees, who no longer have work. Creditors certainly lose out—iHeartMedia's bankruptcy restructure saw its debt reduced to $16.1 million from $5.75 billion, almost the exact amount that had been loaded onto it via the leveraged buyout. Even most of the people who actually invest don't really win: since 2006, private equity has returned about the same as the market overall—the same as you'd get from a Vanguard index fund—despite requiring investors to tie up their money indefinitely and take on a lot more risk and pay much higher fees.[16]

Taxpayers are big losers from this too, since they're increasingly left holding the bag when these investments go south. In 2020 the US Federal Reserve promised to buy corporate bonds, including the riskiest "investment-grade" debt, for the first time in history. This was intended to save productive businesses in the COVID-struck economy, but private equity took the opportunity to load up their companies with even more debt, and then use "dividend recapitalizations" to pour the proceeds directly into their owners' pockets. An astonishing 24 percent of the money raised in the US loan market during the first half of September 2020 was used to pay dividends to private equity owners—six times the usual average.[17] The only real beneficiaries of this parasitical form of private equity are the billionaires at the top of the tree. The fact that these practices go so unregulated, despite the carnage that ensues, is just another way in which the deck is stacked in favor of enriching the already wealthy at everyone else's expense.

Big Radio's power is different from that of Amazon (which relies heavily on sky-high switching costs), record labels (since it doesn't industrially aggregate copyrights), and streaming platforms (there's no licensing, so there are no licensing mazes!). Instead, it relies on regulatory capture. That's where regulators come to be dominated by the interests they are supposed to police, rather than the public interest they're there to protect. Watchdogs become pets. When thinking about removing the legal supports that enable corporations to capture an unfair share of value, we shouldn't forget this one.

The term *regulatory capture* has a funny history: it came into common parlance through the Chicago School economists, those architects of unregulated, monopoly capitalism. The Chicago School advocated for letting companies buy their way to total market dominance—and observed that once a market was monopolized, the companies in it would shower their surplus cash on the regulators who were supposed to be overseeing their activities. The regulators would become agents of the companies, creating rules intended to punish upstarts that challenged the dominant companies, cementing the incumbent firms' advantage. The Chicago School called this "regulatory capture" and correctly identified it as a serious problem with monopolized markets.

However, the Chicago School had a unique remedy for the problem of monopolists being able to pervert their regulators: eliminate regulation altogether! No regulation, no regulators, no regulatory capture, no problem (somehow, preventing monopolies from forming in the first place didn't seem to cross their minds).

The US radio industry exemplifies regulatory capture. After using their regulatory monopolies over airwaves to accrue huge audiences and revenues, they converted them to influence—mobilizing their monopoly profits to buy policies that would further strengthen their hold. That's why they've been able to defeat the literally dozens of bills seeking to extend the US public performance right to radio airplay, even as newer, weaker entrants into internet and satellite radio have been forced to pay.[18]

That influence also helped them secure the 1996 deregulation without any of the checks or balances that could have made sure it would actually deliver the competitive stimulus that was promised. The upshot? Virtually untrammeled consolidation, with no obligation to pay for one of their primary inputs, giving them a leg up over competitors and supracompetitive profits.

Radio's refusal to pay for recordings doesn't just hurt US artists—artists from other nations earn nothing from the use of their work in the world's largest market either. And it has other downstream effects too. When US recordings are played in the United Kingdom or Australia, royalties are collected but not paid through to artists because performance rights rely on reciprocity. As the Future of Music Coalition explains, "This leaves tens of millions of dollars of royalties on the table annually rather than in the pockets of American artists."[19]

Sometimes that revenue is distributed amongst foreign artists, which at least goes some way toward redressing the fact of their work being ripped off in the US. Other times, however, it gets paid out to the local arm of a multinational label, like Sony. John Simson, who formerly headed up SoundExchange, says that in such cases "it's just not clear whether the UK label has any obligation to pay it through to the US label and performer. . . . Typically, it's not paid through."[20] Instead, it goes into a black box, fattening the label's margin at their artists' expense.

Regulatory capture isn't limited to radio. Every big business knows that having sympathetic lawmakers is a good investment. Maybe it'll help them avoid regulation altogether, as radio has so effectively managed. Or maybe it'll result in regulation that potential competitors can't afford to comply with, shaking them out of the market. Apple regularly sits on a hoard of about $200 billion in cash. At last check, Google had $132 billion and Amazon almost $70 billion. That's a lot of influence they can buy—which makes it all the more urgent to rein them in.

When corporations have outsized influence over policy, it subverts democracy—exactly what those pre-Borkian antitrust regulators were trying to prevent by framing standards that targeted "bigness" rather than mere consumer welfare. Clear Channel (now iHeart) didn't just invest the money it saved from not paying artists into lobbying—chunks went toward seeding hate and division. In his book *Monopolized!* David Dayen describes how Clear Channel and fellow giant Cumulus Media created the right-wing radio culture that, thanks to their dominance, gave commuters and other listeners no choice but "an unfiltered stream of aggressive conservative invective." That countrywide indoctrination promoted Clear Channel's overarching interest in lower taxes and even less regulation, which was of course shared by its private equity masters.[21]

There's an obvious, if slightly attenuated, link between the kind of supercompetitive profits that come from not paying workers and suppliers fairly, subversion of the democratic process and the storming of the US Capitol. The American project has always involved defending elite minorities from the majorities who produce their fortunes. Sometimes that involves overt coercion, such as the enslavement of Africans. Sometimes the coercion is more systemic, as when workers are denied the legal right to organize and strike (with the threat of spectacular violence if they do so anyway).

Defending this system in a country that styles itself "the land of the free" is a heavy narrative and ideological lift, and America has always relied on storytellers, blowhards, and demagogues to keep it divided. As President Lyndon B. Johnson once said, "If you can convince the lowest white man he's better than the best colored man, he won't notice you're picking his pocket. Hell, give him somebody to look down on, and he'll empty his pockets for you." Those in service to the oligarchy keep workers pitted against each other, too, partly through narratives aimed at attributing financial hardship to individual rather than systemic causes, hence the suggestion that "socialism never took root in America because the poor see themselves not as an exploited proletariat, but as temporarily embarrassed millionaires."[22] Right-wing talk radio has a symbiotic relationship with ultra-wealthy elites. They may not listen to it, but they fund it, nurture it, and promote it, and it delivers a fabulous return on investment in the form of a whole flock of turkeys who'll reliably vote for Thanksgiving. If sowing hate is going to maximize profits, we can expect more of it to come.

CHAPTER 8

HOW LIVE NATION
CHICKENIZED LIVE MUSIC

Three poultry processors control almost every chicken sold in America. They achieved their power by buying up everything to do with chicken production; then insisting farmers buy their chicken houses, chicks, medicine, and feed; and finally by using contracts to dictate exactly how they'd be raised. Farmers find themselves in a nightmarish panopticon where these companies know and can control everything about their business while getting almost no information in exchange. Their contracts don't stipulate a fixed price in advance for their meat, but also don't allow them to bargain, and they prohibit farmers from comparing notes with neighbors to understand whether they've been fairly paid. While they were at it, the processors divided up the country in a way that means they rarely actually compete. (The evidence suggests that in fact they "secretly coordinate" to "stay off each other's turf."[1])

Christopher Leonard dubbed the system of radical centralized control that follows from this kind of vertical integration "chickenization," and it's spreading rapidly through agricultural markets. Pork processors adopted the model almost wholesale. Monsanto was following the same playbook when it bought up the suppliers of seeds, fertilizer, and pesticides, and then offered farmers big incentives to use their suite of products. Now they're locked in by contracts that would make it financially ruinous to use any other supplier's seeds.

96

Chokepoint capitalists want to chickenize everything they can, so they can control—and capture the lion's share of value from—other people's labor. Now the live music industry is being chickenized too. Previously, running live events required artist managers, talent bookers, event promoters, venues, and ticketers, each operating largely independently from the rest. Now, though, a leviathan called Live Nation Entertainment has vertically integrated every element. It manages artists and books and promotes talent to play in venues it owns, runs, and tickets. It's horizontally integrated too, to the point where it's the world's largest live entertainment company, the largest producer of live music concerts, one of the world's biggest artist management companies (representing more than five hundred of the world's biggest artists), and the world's biggest live entertainment ticketer.[2] All this gives it enormous control over live music.

When thinking about the conditions that enable corporations to create chokepoint markets, vertical and horizontal integration is one of the signal culprits: there's nothing quite like ensuring there are no other players in the market to keep both sellers and buyers firmly welded to you! Integration has long been seen as the province of antitrust, and its regulators are the ones tasked with deciding whether such tie-ups ought to be permitted.

As we explained at the get-go, this book is not focused on antitrust law per se, so you might be wondering why we've identified vertical and horizontal integration as a focus. The answer is that we want to convince you that the resulting chokepoints are problematic even if antitrust regulators disagree, and that there are a whole bunch of remedies *outside of antitrust* that can and should help widen them out. That's what the whole second half of this book is about.

We've seen how impossible the current economics of streaming are for all but the most popular acts. Artists have been told not to worry, though, because they can always make a living from gigs!

When COVID-19 canceled everything we saw that event income actually *cannot* be relied on. And even before that, such airy assurances elided the brutal grind of touring life—the physical toll of performing, regular adrenaline crashes, poor food and sleep, long-term separations from family and community. Still, pre-pandemic, it was not uncommon for musicians to make 95 percent of their income from live events. Those gigs also sustained countless other workers, including roadies, food and drink suppliers, security, and marketing. A healthy live scene is critical to keeping music afloat.

For over a decade, however, Live Nation has been sapping the industry's lifeblood. In 2010, it merged with Ticketmaster in a deal that could have been blocked under the existing antitrust law, but which the Justice Department waved through. The result was a particularly elegant flywheel of anticompetitive exploitation.

The Ticketmaster tie-up gives Live Nation a voyeur's view of its competitors' businesses. By controlling competitors' ticketing, it gets detailed real-time insights into their financial positions, programming innovations, successes, and failures, which it can then imitate or avoid. It can access detailed information about demand for acts, where that demand is centered, how it's evolving over time, and whether fans are willing to pay inflated prices to scalpers in the secondary market. That then allows it to make better decisions about who to book and how much to pay them (in the venue market), and also enables it to swoop in and take over acts that have been developed by independent managers when they're just about to break through (in the management space). All that improves its margins, so it is able to offer the best prices to the most profitable artists, securing the most lucrative gigs for itself and further cementing its dominance.

Live Nation's ticket business also creates a serious conflict of interest. Artist managers tend to be vehemently against ticket scalping (the practice of reselling tickets above face value) because it upsets fans while diverting value away from artists. But ticketers love this "secondary market," because it nets them a second and even more lucrative fee on the same product they have already sold once.[3] Since 2012, shortly after its Ticketmaster tie-up, Live Nation's annual reports have identified growing this market as one of its core strategic planks.[4]

When the two companies merged, the Justice Department had required Live Nation to pinkie swear it would not retaliate against venue owners for contracting with other ticketing companies, and not condition or threaten to condition events on venues using their ticketing services.

Live Nation began breaking those promises almost as soon as the merger was approved. In 2019, the Justice Department finally began to investigate. By then, Live Nation's reputation for "threatening behavior and retaliation" was so strong, and its power so pervasive, that it was difficult to find anyone who was willing to speak out. Eventually, however, six venues, with their identities kept secret for fear of reprisals, all described a similar pattern. One was warned that if it went with a competitor for ticketing, Ticketmaster's response "would be 'nuclear,'" and that, "though he would deny it if [the venue executive] repeated it, Live Nation would never do a show in our building, that they would find other places for their content."[5] Another, after signing with a competitor, found calls from Live Nation to discuss show bookings dropped from weekly to nonexistent. They resumed immediately once the venue came "back in the family."

Venues quickly understood "that refusing to contract with Ticketmaster w[ould] result in the venue receiving fewer Live Nation concerts or none at all."[6] This effectively forced them into Ticketmaster contracts, drastically reducing the ability of other ticketers to compete. That might help explain why ticket fees have massively outpaced growth in event prices. According to a 2018 study by the US Government Accountability Office, fees now account for an extraordinary 27 percent of ticket price, a burden borne by consumers. (In the UK, where venues and promoters usually contract with several ticketers rather than have exclusive deals, fees range from 10–15 percent.)[7] It's no wonder that, while ticketing makes up just 13 percent of Live Nation's revenue, it generates more than a third of its profit.

Live Nation's defense? As summed up by *Billboard*, that "it's not a threat if you're just laying out a person's options."[8] That's exactly what your friendly neighborhood mob goon might say when shaking you down for protection money.

When interviewing people for this book, we always gave them the option not to be named. Almost nobody took us up on it—except those we spoke to about Live Nation. In most cases, those people were anxious even about speaking off the record. As one live music insider told us, "They manage some of the biggest artists in the world. They book and own some of the biggest rooms in the world. If you want to work with any of those artists, then you have to play ball. If you're a booking agent, if you're a venue promoter, if you're another artist, then you have to make sure that you're on their good side."[9]

Despite the Justice Department's clear findings that Live Nation had repeatedly breached the terms of the consent decree attached to the merger, Live Nation got off with a slap on the wrist: the decree was extended for five years, although it was amended to make it easier for the government to enforce in the future, assuming any venues would still have the nerve to stand up for themselves, and the company was obliged to pay the government's $3 million costs. Live Nation paid up, while insisting it "strongly disagree[d]" with the Justice Department's findings. To put that monetary penalty in context, Live Nation generated $11.55 billion in revenue in 2019, including $1.54 billion from ticketing. Antitrust lawyer Jennifer M. Oliver says this shows that behavioral remedies like consent decrees "are too easily ignored or abused by post-merger behemoths, and the benefits of violation often outweigh the punishment."[10] Or, as economists Uri Gneezy and Aldo Rustichini famously put it, "A fine is a price."[11]

The merger between Live Nation and Ticketmaster is made worse by the ticket division's deceitful practices. If you've ever tried to buy tickets to a popular event, you'll know that people are usually restricted to buying six or eight seats at a time and are subjected annoying tests to prove they aren't bots scooping tickets up for resale. That makes it *feel* like Ticketmaster is doing all it can to stamp out scalping, and its public statements match. In private, however, it's a different story.

In 2018, undercover reporters from Canada's CBC News and *Toronto Star* caught Ticketmaster representatives boasting of customers harvesting tickets via hundreds of accounts.[12] Ticketmaster's TradeDesk software automatically syncs the accounts of such users to reseller sites, including its own, making it easier for scalpers to flog their plunder. Ticketmaster's "Professional Reseller Handbook" also dangled the promise of fee discounts if "scalpers hit milestones such as $500,000 or $1 million in annual sales"[13]—something that's never going to happen at six or eight tickets per show. Ticketmaster benefits because it gets paid each time the tickets are sold, and higher prices in the reseller market mean more money: $25.75 on a $209.50 ticket the first time it's sold, and $76 more if it's resold for $400.[14] Ticketmaster responded by insisting it didn't provide tickets to scalpers ahead of regular users (something the exposé hadn't actually alleged).[15]

Just three months after the amended consent decree was entered into judgment, Live Nation was hit with a new class action lawsuit seeking to recover damages for the supracompetitive fees consumers were obliged to pay thanks to Ticketmaster's monopoly. It claims, among other things, that Ticketmaster's new supposed anti-scalping measures are actually designed to lock in customers so they have to resell their extra tickets on Ticketmaster's own site, thus ensuring Ticketmaster will reap the fees and giving the company a huge advantage over secondary market rivals like StubHub. Live Nation and Ticketmaster denied the court had jurisdiction to deal with the claim, since its users are forced to waive their class action rights and agree to mandatory arbitration as a condition of accessing the site. Such clauses are regularly used to strip power from suppliers and workers; here's an example of them put to the same use against consumers.

To sum up: artists are told that to make money from music they have to tour. If they tour, they have to do it via venues that use Ticketmaster (since it controls over 70 percent of the market), and if they use Ticketmaster it will gouge their fans and give Live Nation a competitive leg up over independent rivals. It's a system no one but Live Nation's shareholders could love.

The COVID-19 pandemic mothballed live music venues around the world. With many independent venues already operating with razor-thin margins, that put them under extraordinary new financial stress. One person working in that scene told us she was receiving emails announcing venue closures almost every day: "These rooms have been, in some cases, owned by the same family for generations, and don't have ancillary income sources or access to funding like a multinational or publicly traded company would. Without being able to operate their businesses and without government support to get them through the pandemic, what other options do the owners of these locally owned rooms have?"[16]

Live Nation is being squeezed by the pandemic too, but it has access to capital markets that all but ensure it will still be around when live music is back on track—this time with still fewer competitors, and an even more dominant market position. Investors are convinced of that. Investment magazine *Barron's* gushes over Live Nation's "impenetrable moat that has a monopoly-like structure" and Ticketmaster's "upper hand in negotiating with venues" thanks to the company's control over talent. It suggests the firm "will continue to strategically purchase firms that aren't able to sustain this latest cycle"—a polite way of saying they will gobble up distressed businesses at fire sale prices.[17] Live Nation raised $1.2 billion in new capital in May 2020, and its share price has more than doubled since the early pandemic nadir. That was helped along by Saudi Arabia's sovereign wealth fund, which became the third-largest shareholder after buying up a 5.7 percent stake.[18]

Through this book, we've been focusing on chokepoints, but this needs to be understood as an effect, rather than a cause. The cause of chokepoint capitalism is *oligarchy*, the concentration of wealth and power into too few hands. No one epitomizes oligarchy like the Saudi royals, the oil trillionaires who openly kidnap and dismember journalists who criticize them. The House of Saud has embarked upon a project to shift its business interests out of oil and has been firehosing money into other sectors in bids to monopolize them. The Saudi royals are the major financiers of Softbank, the investors behind Uber, WeWork, and other notorious money-losing tech companies. Softbank's strategy—that is, the Saudi strategy—is to lose money for as long as it takes to establish a monopoly, and if no monopoly is forthcoming, to unload those investments through IPOs, which are bought up by naive investors who assume that if, say, Uber was able to keep going for more than a decade, there must be some way it will eventually be profitable. So far it hasn't been, but Softbank sure cleaned up on its IPO. It is *never* a good sign when a key player in your industry takes a major investment from the House of Saud.

While the Saudis epitomize oligarchy, the United States is not far behind. An analysis of 1,779 policy outcomes found "economic elites and organized groups representing business interests have substantial independent impacts on U.S. government policy," and that "mass-based interest groups and average citizens have little or no independent influence."[19] In 2015, former US president Jimmy Carter described the US as having become "an oligarchy with unlimited political bribery" after the Supreme Court decision in *Citizens United* effectively removed limits on political donations.[20] That was confirmed by the 2016 election, on which Wall Street invested a record two billion dollars. That buys a lot of influence.

Live Nation's power comes from vertical integration on a huge scale, combined with insufficient merger scrutiny and failures to enforce consumer protection laws. The story of how it came to achieve its dominance shows the problem isn't so much in the text of antitrust law, but in the failure to enforce it. There was ample scope for regulators to shut this deal down, or even to approve it with stricter conditions. They didn't, because antitrust law has been in a forty-year Reagan-induced coma, the agencies starved of budget and demoralized, the judiciary brainwashed by lavish "continuing education" seminars—the Manne Seminars—at a Florida resort, which 40 percent of the US federal judiciary attended to learn about why antitrust law shouldn't be enforced. US antitrust law is actually pretty great (and new bills in the pipeline as we write this would strengthen it further), but the US political consensus has been that antitrust is mostly a dead letter, a quirk of history that can be ignored the same way we ignore laws that require you to hire a boy to run ahead of your auto-car with a lantern and a bell to warn horse-riders that you're coming.

Antitrust's enforcement failures have led to a huge reduction in competition and impoverishment of independent venues right at the time when music industry workers, hit by the decline in record sales, most needed these revenues. As another live music insider told us (again on condition of anonymity), "Monopolistic practices do not encourage creativity, they do not encourage local ownership, they do not encourage entrepreneurship. They generally are not pro-worker. So you have to wonder, who benefits from it?"[21] The answer is clear from society's growing inequality: The top 0.1 percent benefit. The rest of us don't.

CHAPTER 9

WHY SEVEN THOUSAND HOLLYWOOD WRITERS FIRED THEIR AGENTS

April 2019 was a bad month to be a talent agent in Hollywood. Phone calls, emails, and texts flowed in, tones ranging from accusatory to apologetic. Within days it was done. Seven thousand Hollywood writers had fired their agents.

The talent agent's role is to set up meetings at which clients pitch their work, then negotiate terms and seal the deal. Traditionally, agents take a 10 percent commission on the price of the job, which aligned their interests with those of their clients: the more the client earned, the bigger the agent's paycheck.

As in every other culture industry we've looked at, talent agencies have consolidated into a few big firms. The giants are William Morris Endeavor (WME) and Creative Artists Agency (CAA), both now part-owned by private equity. Together with the much smaller United Talent Agency (UTA) and ICM Partners, they make up the Big Four agencies. (As this book goes to press, CAA is trying to swallow up ICM, threatening to concentrate the industry still further.) Between them, these agencies represent nearly all the most bookable writers, actors, and directors in the US film and TV industries. That gives them a great deal of power. And, just like every corporation that gets strong enough to do so, they use it to further their own interests.

In this instance, that involved a con called "packaging." The consolidated agencies had huge portions of Hollywood talent on their rosters and, over decades, had come to increasingly sell their clients' services to studios as "packages," bundling together the key actors, writers, and director for each project. These clients—the talent—were told this was good news, because their agents would no longer charge them that 10 percent commission. Instead, the agencies charged packaging fees to the studio: usually a hefty upfront fee, a further lump sum when the show achieved net profits, and then a percentage of gross profits for the lifetime of the show.

This practice uncoupled agent compensation from what their clients got paid. Rather than settling for a measly 10 percent, agencies discovered that they were able to negotiate to get *more* than their clients. For example, CAA's packaging fee on *Cold Case* was $75,000 per episode—more than writer and creator Meredith Stiehm received during its first two seasons. Overall, she estimates that the agency made ninety-four cents on every dollar she earned from the show.[1] That's a far cry from the customary 10 percent fee that is still charged by smaller agencies.

The conflict of interest is obvious. Movie and TV studios *also* have a great deal of power. If they're giving away fees of this magnitude, it's because they're getting something in return. The Writers Guild of America (WGA) has alleged that agencies now "routinely refuse to negotiate greater salaries for staff writers," instead taking the first offer to protect their own fees. Chip Johannessen, who has written for shows like *24*, *Moonlight*, and *Beverley Hills, 90210*, says ICM pressured him to give up benefits that he was contractually entitled to because there otherwise wasn't enough money to get his show made; later on, he found that it also "extracted a substantial packaging fee with a more favorable profit definition, . . . deliberately enriching itself at [his] expense." *Grey's Anatomy* showrunner Krista Vernoff says her entertainment lawyer friends "have endless stories about agents asking them to 'take the lead' in aggressive writer negotiations because the agents are afraid to anger their agency bosses."[2]

Agencies try to prevent their talent from working on productions with colleagues represented by other firms, because that would mean they'd have to split the packaging fee. They pressure creatives to take on projects that aren't in their best interests but would give the agency the most saleable package. This structure also incentivizes agencies to sell programs to the studios who are willing to pay the fattest fee, rather than those willing to pay the most overall or offering the best development or creative fit.

As of 2019, about 90 percent of TV shows were packaged, mostly by the Big Four, which had by then swallowed up most of their competitors. These agencies benefit massively from network effects—the more writers and actors and directors they represent, the more valuable their packages become. This feeds into their anticompetitive flywheel: talent that isn't signed to one of those agencies gets locked out of most deals, which forces them to come on board, which makes those packages still more valuable and prevalent, which makes it ever harder for other creative workers to opt out of this system.

Once agencies represented all the most valuable creatives, they were able to extract ever more value. "Though packaging fees initially came about because agencies provided more than one piece of the project," David Goodman told us, "over time the Big Four agencies gained so much power that the agency would get a packaging fee just for representing one creative in the project. In television that was almost always the writer/creator. So packaging fees were a 'shakedown'—you want my client, you have to pay me."[3]

In recent years the biggest agencies took even more advantage of their control of the talent by starting up or acquiring their own production companies—most notably WME with its Endeavor Content division, which finances and produces original content. CAA and UTA followed suit, albeit on a smaller scale. In shows that they produce, these agencies were negotiating with themselves, which the WGA describes as an "indefensible" conflict of interest: "Acting as an employer and representing a client in salary negotiations are fundamentally at odds: an employer's incentive is to maximize its profits and keep labor costs low, while the agency is duty-bound to get the best deal it can for its client."[4]

Not only have agents become hopelessly conflicted, but there's also fewer of them around to handle more work. One former agent points out that, "when Endeavor merged with William Morris to make WME, they took on around 250 more clients for TV and kept only three WMA agents, letting go over 100 reps and support staff."[5] Still more staff have been lost to "efficiency" improvements demanded by WME and CAA's private equity partners. This means agents have less time to proactively work their contacts to figure out what deals might be on the horizon and get in first for their clients.

In response to these problems, many writers have found themselves forced to hire lawyers and managers to look after the interests their agents had been supposed to care for. For the privilege of doing so, they have to pay another 10 percent. Ironically, many of those managers are former agents who have been let go to cut costs. Longtime agent Gavin Polone says, "In effect, the agency has off-loaded the cost of extra career guidance for an individual client by getting that client to pay for that service directly with an additional 10 percent fee."[6] He analogizes this to a restaurant firing its dishwashers and insisting customers rent clean plates elsewhere—all while charging the same prices and increasing its profits. But of course that wouldn't work in the restaurant business, because there's too much competition: "Customers would just go elsewhere for meals where the plates are provided for free."

Hollywood writers can't do that. So many agencies have been rolled up into those four dominant firms that there's no other restaurant to go to. It's another chokepoint market.

The result is that, even after hiring new managers and lawyers, writers kept losing ground. Between the 2013–14 season and 2017–18 seasons alone, the WGA calculates salaries fell 16 percent, even as the number of scripted shows surged.[7]

In part, these falls are attributable to changes in the way television is being produced. In the past, a writer would commonly work on a twenty-two-episode network show and get paid their episode fee twenty-two times a year.

Now, however, with the increase of streaming and prestige cable offerings, there are a lot of shows that shoot just ten episodes. Kimberly Ndombe, a rising writer with credits on shows like *Good Trouble* and *Chicago Fire*, says one show is not enough: "You have to be able to jump around. There are more shows to staff on, but I think it's harder to make a living."[8]

But jumping around isn't always possible. The talent agencies, so busy negotiating up their own rates, dropped the ball on negotiating exclusivity (how long a writer would devote themselves to a single show) and span (the amount of time they can be required to work on a single script before they have to get more pay), with the effect that writers on these shorter shows were being held longer and longer. That blocks them from picking up other work, which has become a serious drag on salaries.

We spoke to David Slack, who has written for shows like *Law & Order* and *Person of Interest*, and who sits on the WGA board. He told us that even senior writers on a "pretty significant" per episode fee were getting amortized down to the scale rate—the very minimum mandated by the Guild, which had previously been paid only to the most junior writers.

Those shorter runs hit in other ways too. All writers get weekly fees for working in writers' rooms, but higher-level writers get that supplemented by script fees given to the credited author of any given episode. The WGA minimum for that is about $27,000 for a half-hour broadcast show. Typically, the showrunner—the person with primary creative and managerial control—gets credit for the first and last episodes of a season, and other senior writers each expect credit (and the associated script fee) on at least one. As reporter and critic Kyle Paoletta explains, "When a show order only calls for six or eight episodes and its writing staff includes a showrunner and a handful of veterans, the chances of a low-level staffer getting a script fee drop precipitously."[9] That has knock-on effects by slowing down career progression, because assistant writers usually can't land a staff writing job until they've had episode credits.

But the rate falls can't all be explained by shorter-run shows and the shift to streaming. *Grey's Anatomy* is a network show and its seasons are among the longest in the business—typically twenty-five episodes. But showrunner Krista Vernoff says that when she began writing for *Grey's Anatomy* fifteen years previously, she made more money per episode than the same level writers on the show are making now—even though *Grey's* apparently pays better than most.[10] As WGA's David Slack told us, "It's harder and harder and harder for creative people to get compensated for the actual monetary value of what we contribute."[11] The reality is that, despite this being the golden age of television, fewer and fewer of the spoils are going to the creators who make it happen—just as in all the other culture industries we've looked at.

Convinced these declines came about because the agencies' interests had become disconnected, or even opposed to, those of the writers they were supposed to represent, in 2019 the Guild sued the Big Four for breach of fiduciary duty. But the lawsuit wasn't the writers' only—or even primary—plan for relief. Their ace in the hole was collective action.

With overwhelming support from its members, the WGA adopted a new code of conduct abolishing packaging fees and prohibiting agencies from holding more than a 20 percent stake in any production house. In line with union rules, it then directed members to terminate relationships with any agents who didn't sign on. That's why those seven thousand members fired their agents. Within days, the Big Four agencies' business had ground to a halt. We pick up the story of what happened next in our chapter on collective action.

DEFENDING THE BACK END

TV writers aren't just struggling to defend their incomes in the rigged agency game; they're also battling to maintain their rights to share in the profits of their work. Traditionally, key writers have had entitlements to residuals or "the back end," which means a share of profits from all kinds of uses, including domestic broadcasting, international licensing, and streaming.

When a show becomes a hit, the back end can far outweigh how much the talent earns during the first years of its run. Writers, actors, and directors have long relied on these payments to cushion them during the gaps between jobs, and they've been particularly handy for writers scrambling to transition to shorter writing seasons and lower rates.

Traditionally, when there are dealings between affiliated parties (say NBCUniversal owns a show that it wants to stream on its own platform), they've been required to reach terms based on a fair market rate. That's why NBC had to shell out $500 million over five years for streaming rights to *The Office*, a show it already owned, beating out Netflix's bid of $90 million a year, and why WarnerMedia had to pay almost the same to reclaim *Friends*. It's a safeguard for all the other people who are entitled to share in the profits.

Not all owners play by the rules. Fox drew headlines in 2019 when it was ordered to pay more than $50 million for defrauding the creators of the *Bones* crime procedural by giving its own affiliates preferential terms on international licensing and streaming deals. Unusually, Fox's own employees, executives, and witnesses provided some of the most damning evidence against it, admitting that Fox's top executives had not only flagrantly disregarded the corporation's obligations to the show's creators, but also given false testimony to try and cover up their wrong-doing.[12] There's an obvious financial incentive to pull this kind of trick: everything that gets stolen from creators goes straight to the corporation's bottom line.

As the media landscape becomes more and more vertically integrated, the most powerful players want to change the way this system works. All the biggest studios have now launched their own streaming platforms: Disney owns Disney Plus and ESPN Plus (and also Hulu, since Disney's merger with Twenty-First Century Fox), NBC has Peacock, CBS has Paramount Plus, and WarnerMedia has HBO Max. They don't want to keep having to pay creators market rates for putting their shows on their own platforms. They want to keep the upside for themselves.

That's why corporations are making moves to change this model. Disney, for example, has started to offer producers contracts that entitle them to payments out of a predefined profit pool, with their share based on a show's success and longevity. However, they would not be directly linked to licensing revenues, and so don't require the company to offer fair market value.[13] That removes one of the last truly competitive elements from the market.

This takes a leaf out of a playbook that was written by Netflix and Amazon for their own video streaming platforms. When those services buy a show, they try to take global rights, and don't license it to any other platforms. That means the old residual system doesn't make sense. Instead, Netflix covers production costs plus a negotiated "profit payment" starting with the very first episode, while Amazon pays a bonus starting from a show's third season based on the value the company determines it has. Effectively, these arrangements buy out the back end.

We're not suggesting the residual system should keep working exactly the way it did before. Indeed, in many ways that perpetuates the winner-takes-all nature of creative labor markets, which sees a handful of the most successful stars take home the lion's share of revenue. That's because the current formula disproportionately rewards blockbusters— shows like *Friends* and *Modern Family*, whose enormous success probably gave their creators enough power to renegotiate their deals anyway. That's not good either. As Scott Timberg argued in *Culture Crash*, a world where a tiny group takes a vast majority of the spoils while everyone else fights one another for crumbs is "the world in which today's creative class finds it ever harder to ply its craft, pay the rent, collect its meager revenues."[14]

Some industry insiders have argued that, while Disney's new deal template might limit the upside for mega hits like *The Big Bang Theory*, those "middling/mildly successful series that go on for a couple of seasons to respectable/modest ratings and would not normally be able to generate a meaningful back end under the traditional mechanism" could actually do better under the new arrangement.[14] That would be a welcome outcome—but there are better ways to achieve it than by giving untrammeled new power to the studios that already dominate so many film and TV creators.

CHAPTER 10

WHY *FORTNITE* SUED APPLE

W hen it released the first iPhone in 2007, Apple made *things*: software, yes, but mostly hardware—shiny, cutting-edge products that aimed to change the way people interacted with the world. The following year, Apple introduced its App Store as a kind of afterthought. Steve Jobs made it clear this wasn't meant to be a revenue-center—"We don't intend to make any money off the App Store"—but rather a feature that would help it sell more devices by attracting more developers and more apps. Users would not be able to install software from any other source, which Apple said was to keep them safe from malicious programs. Developers would get 70 percent of revenue; the rest would go to Apple to cover "upkeep."

iPhones became tremendously popular. Unlike the devices that came before them, iPhones could be used to easily enjoy news, books, movies, TV shows, and games. Content distributors leapt at the chance of reaching this new and affluent mobile audience. Their content made iPhones and then iPads ever more desirable, and device sales soared.

It wasn't long before Apple realized that controlling the sole source of their software opened revenue possibilities it hadn't originally dreamed of, and in 2011 it abruptly changed the rules in its favor. It had always taken its 30 percent cut on purchases made within apps, but companies had been allowed to direct their users to buy content in a web browser, rather than the App itself, handling payments themselves and bypassing Apple's fee.[1] Under the new rules, apps were no longer able to link to purchase options outside the Apple ecosystem, and Apple ensured a 30 percent cut on sales of ebooks, movies, games, news subscriptions—all content whatsoever. It was a huge change: the difference between paying Apple 30 percent of the initial purchase price for the app (which was often zero), versus having to surrender 30 percent of the lifetime revenue generated by that app (which could be thousands of dollars). While users could still access content they'd bought or subscribed to elsewhere, services were banned from even mentioning that within their apps.[2]

The anticompetitive flywheel is obvious: Apple started with an innovative, attractive product, which locked in the first users. Then it gave software developers and content distributors an easy way of reaching that audience, encouraging them to invest in new software offering an ever wider range of content. That attracted more users, all tied to the App Store as their only source of software. Once enough users were locked in, the suppliers were too. That's what gave Apple the power to unilaterally change the deal developers and creators had signed up to. They also gave themselves unlimited power to decide which apps made it into the store, with the developer guidelines not even pretending to offer any kind of procedural fairness: "We will reject apps for any content or behavior that we believe is over the line. What line, you ask? Well, as a Supreme Court Justice once said, 'I'll know it when I see it.' And we think that you will also know it when you cross it."[3] Researchers Nieborg and Poell describe this rule as "emblematic of the platform's strict content control, heavy curatorial bias, and above all, low level of accountability."[4]

Today, apps generate enormous revenue. As we write, all but one of the top two hundred highest-grossing iPhone apps are free to install, with developers making their money from subscriptions and in-app purchases. Apple takes a cut from each.[5] It refuses to break out how much revenue comes from apps, but the leading app analytics firm estimated it at over $70 billion in 2020—over a quarter of its yearly revenue.[6]

Apple's ban on external payments marked a turning point. It had started off making money from devices. Now it was making money as ferryman: the only one that could cross the river between buyers and sellers.

LIFE IN THE WALLED GARDEN

Apple's toll hits content creators hard. Forty of the top fifty highest-grossing apps are either creative products themselves (games), or platforms that distribute those of others: audiobooks, streaming video, and music. Apple's 30 percent vigorish dramatically impacts the amounts available to the people who actually create that content.

Apple doesn't have to make any of the films, TV shows, games, books, or music that get streamed or downloaded over its mobile operating system. It doesn't have to promote them, obtain the licenses for them, or provide the app on which they are played. It just has to process payments and shuffle a few files around the internet. For that, it gets to cream off 30 percent of revenue. That's 30 percent that isn't available for makers further down the chain.

The economics are impossible for streaming music too. As we saw, streaming companies pay out close to 70 percent of subscription fees to copyright holders; if they give Apple the remaining 30 percent, there would be nothing left to keep the lights on. Spotify's initial response to the toll was to charge a higher price to Apple users, but this just helped boost Apple's position by making its own product, Apple Music, relatively cheaper on iOS. (Apple helps itself by self-preferencing too: its own apps are the top App Store results when people search for content like music, books, and audio titles.)[7]

By 2016, the 30 percent rate on ongoing subscriptions became too embarrassing for even Apple to sustain, and the company reduced it to 15 percent after the first year.[8] By way of comparison, credit card processing usually costs between 2 and 3 percent, so that's still a huge amount for a basic service that could easily and cheaply be offered in other ways.

Some of the biggest companies with the highest market shares are strong enough to resist this tax. Amazon flatly refused to pay from the get-go. This means that, while you can read Kindle books on your Apple devices, you cannot use the Kindle app on iOS to buy new titles. Spotify similarly blocked new in-app signups from 2016, once it had enough market penetration to be able to withstand the inevitable loss of users. Instead, new customers had to sign up on its website, which then avoided Apple's toll. That undoubtedly deterred some people who wanted to pay for music from doing so, with obvious downstream effects for the people who make it. In 2018, Netflix had been the highest-grossing program in the App Store, with $853 million in revenue, of which hundreds of millions went straight to Apple.[9] Netflix had to tolerate this shakedown while growing its market share, but as soon as it had enough customers, it too eliminated in-app signups.

Smaller companies have less power, sticking them with an unenviable choice: pay the tax (resulting in unviable margins that make it impossible to compete with the Amazons and Spotifys and Netflixes selling the same kind of content) or remove the ability for customers to subscribe or buy within their apps, knowing it will be far harder for them to reach critical mass (and thus, again, making it impossible to compete with the major players).

Thus, Apple's chokepoint feeds other chokepoints. Sometimes this happens in ways that are shockingly direct: in 2020, for example, Apple cut a deal allowing Amazon and a few other premium subscription video providers to use their own payment methods for their video streaming apps. The reason? Apple is trying to make the Apple TV app the default way people watch shows and movies—that is, to create yet *another* monopoly for itself. It cut this deal to persuade those video providers to integrate their content.[10] This is disastrous for competition, both in the short term (the non-favored video distributors will have to pay out up to 30 percent more revenue than the favored ones for essentially the same product) and the longer (because the more eyeballs Apple can divert to its own TV app, the harder it will be for anyone else to survive). While content sellers like Amazon, Netflix, and Spotify can bypass the tax by signing subscribers up elsewhere on the web (at least once they've managed to sew up most of the market!) it's much more difficult for those who rely on in-app purchases—a key revenue source for game developers.

Games are increasingly important cultural products. Generating about $160 billion in 2020, the global computer game industry is bigger than film and music combined. About half of that is on mobile, where games generate three-quarters of all app revenue.[11]

A sizeable portion of that comes from *Fortnite Battle Royale*, which pits a hundred players against one another in a *Hunger Games*–esque fight to the death. The game quickly became ludicrously popular, notching up 350 million users across various platforms, including iOS and Android.

While the game is free to play, its creators make money when players buy extras, like "battle passes" (which give access to exclusive features), slick costumes (Rebecca's little sisters want new ones all the time), and cooler gear (players like to destroy one another in style!). This all adds up: in 2019 alone, *Fortnite* generated revenues of $1.8 billion.

Fortnite's developers, Epic Games, were understandably unenthused about the prospect of handing over a 30 percent rake just for processing payments. (Since this kind of in-game purchase doesn't count as a "subscription" the discounted rate Apple introduced in 2016 did not apply.) Google charges the same usurious rate, but unlike Apple, it permits the "sideloading" of apps on Android—that is, for users to install software from outside the Play Store, Google's equivalent of Apple's App Store. Determined to hold on to more of its revenue, Epic announced it would bypass the Play Store to avoid paying its 30 percent vig, instead asking its Android users to load the software from an external site.

However, Epic soon realized the apparent freedom to sideload apps to Android phones was illusory. Its Android customers were subjected to "scary, repetitive security pop-ups," technical blocks, and suggestions that third-party software like *Fortnite* was dangerous malware. All this scared potential users away, cutting into revenues. After eighteen months of trying to make it work, Epic reluctantly gave in and made the game available on Google's Play Store after all.[12]

This highlights a reality that is easy to miss when we rely exclusively on centrally sanctioned apps and functionalities: that mega-corporations deliberately restrict the capabilities of our devices in order to maintain their iron control.

Cory got a lesson in this when he crowdfunded an audiobook for his novel *Attack Surface*. Since he refuses to let DRM be attached to his audiobooks, and since Amazon's Audible refuses to carry them without it, his audiobook rights are basically worthless to publishers. He wanted to show there was a market outside Audible—and his fans emphatically showed up to do so, buying $267,613 worth of books. That sounds like a resounding success, right? Well, kind of.

Once the files were delivered, it became clear that a *lot* of users were struggling to play them on their phones. They had to download them, unzip, install a compatible audiobook reader if they didn't already have one, point them to the files, and then hope for the best. Rebecca considers herself tech savvy, but the first two audiobook apps she tried didn't work at all, and the third one couldn't proceed past the first quarter of the book for no reason she could figure out before giving up.

Moving around and playing open file formats is some of the most basic functionality we expect from computers, but it doesn't take much to figure out why it's nearly impossible to do so on mobile devices. If we could do this outside the apps they control, Apple and Google would be less able to lock us in, and less able to shake down the people who make the content we play, listen to, read, and watch. After all, the iPhone's predecessor, the iPod, had no trouble with this kind of operation—the ability to easily download and play music without using an app has been removed from the devices that came after it. Those who provide us with these devices consider the lack of functionality to be a feature, not a bug.

Though Epic grudgingly put *Fortnite* in the Play Store, it grew increasingly resentful at the usurious tolls the mobile giants were exacting. It formally asked Apple to let it provide direct payment options and to create its own competing App Store, with the idea of reducing consumer prices and raising the share that would go to developers.[13] When it refused, Epic began to plot.

In August 2020, it activated a hidden feature in its iOS and Android versions, allowing users to pay directly. Cleverly, Epic used that flawed "consumer harm" standard in its favor, offering customers who opted to pay through its website cheaper prices than those who kept using the app. Its flagrant violation of the app store rules got *Fortnite* booted out of the Apple and Google stores within hours, and Epic launched an antitrust lawsuit against Apple the very same day.

Apple, keenly aware how much was at stake, played dirty. It didn't just throw *Fortnite* out of the App Store but threatened to terminate the developer accounts of Epic's related companies. This retaliatory strike was squarely aimed at the Unreal Engine, a graphics engine owned by Epic that is widely used by independent developers to create their own video games, as well as filmmakers (Lucasfilm used it to make *The Mandalorian*).[14]

Since cutting off access would put Epic's entire business at risk, Apple's threat drastically raised the stakes. It may have been enough to force Epic to back down, had a federal court not issued a permanent injunction prohibiting Apple from following through.[15]

This is obviously no David vs. Goliath battle, but rather a trillion-dollar company pitted against a multi-billion-dollar company. That's why Epic had the resources to initiate the antitrust lawsuit and to defend itself from

Apple's retaliation. But that's what's needed to take on such a behemoth. Apple holds so much power and has given itself such discretion about how to exercise it that smaller developers are terrified of getting on its bad side—much as we saw with Live Nation.[16]

The bad press from the *Fortnite* fight caused Apple to introduce an additional fee reduction, halving the rate charged to the 98 percent of developers earning less than $1 million per year down to (a still usurious!) 15 percent. That was a face-saving response to bad publicity but made little difference in practice, since the beneficiary developers bring in just 5 percent of revenue between them.[17] And it's all but useless for those who sell material like books, movies, TV shows, or news: the prices of such content all but ensure they won't fall within the discount threshold.

"FREE" AS IN "FREE MARKET"

If you learned your economics from Heinlein novels or the University of Chicago, you probably think that "free market" describes an economic system that is free from government interference—where all consensual transactions between two or more parties are allowed.

But if you went to the source, Adam Smith's *Wealth of Nations*, you'll have found a very different definition of a free market: Smith's concern wasn't freedom from governments, it was freedom from *rentiers*.

A rentier is someone who derives their income from "economic rents": revenues derived from merely owning something. With a factory, you have workers who contribute labor, you have investors who build and maintain the physical plant, and you have the landlord, who siphons off some of the revenues derived from this activity because of his title to the dirt underneath the factory.

Every dollar the landlord extracts is a dollar that can't go to the workers as wages, or be rolled into the factory's upkeep and improvement, or enrich the people who build and maintain the plant.

One of the most powerful ways to extract economic rents is to have a monopoly. A ferryman who charges high prices isn't necessarily extracting rents because someone else can build a bridge or run a rival ferry service. But if the ferryman uses his profits to successfully lobby for a ban on bridges and competing ferry services, *then* he's extracting rents, because the price his passengers pay is high merely because there's no alternative.

Monopolies are self-reinforcing. Canny monopolists hold back some of these rents for special projects, like bribing politicians to secure favorable treatment, buying out competitors, or securing those competitors' doom with predatory pricing and other dirty tricks. Thus, the ferryman might use his monopoly rents to poach all the rival's key employees. Or he might lower ticket prices to below the cost of operating, subsidizing the fare out of his monopoly rent war chest until the competitor goes bust and sells out at pennies on the dollar, and then put the price back up.

The ferryman might also spend some of his excess profits on lobbying lawmakers to pass rules mandating a minimum number of boats be operating at any one time—making it hard for any new operator to start up. Where a person or corporation seeks to increase their profits through more favorable regulation, it's called *rent-seeking*.

We saw how regulatory capture can harm creative producers in the context of radio: changes to ownership laws allowed Clear Channel to buy its way to a dominant position, use that position to crush rivals, and use some of the resulting profits to maintain its outrageous advantage in not having to pay recording artists or labels for their music.

A market is "free" if what's for sale and how much it costs are set by the capabilities of producers and the desires of buyers. Every rent collected in the market whittles away that freedom, as choices about what to sell and what to buy disappear into the pockets of rentiers who own things instead of making things.

Apple, with its App Store, is a rentier. After investigating it and its fellow tech giants for more than a year, US House Democrats released a 450-page report finding that it created barriers to competition, charged developers supracompetitive prices, and discriminated against rivals, all while preferencing its own offerings.[18] Developers couldn't break free because they were locked in by its anticompetitive flywheel: "network effects, high barriers to entry, and high switching costs in the mobile operating system market."

Those entry barriers include the same DRM laws that enabled Amazon to steal away control of the ebook and audiobook markets.

Epic has a building full of engineers. It could have paid some of them to make its own app store for iOS and sell its games through it, keeping all the money. Just as it proposed to Apple, it could even have invited other app creators into its store and offered them a better deal, while still making a bit extra themselves.

Installing a third-party app store on iOS devices has some technical challenges, of course. Apple has gone to great lengths to prevent this, using a combination of software and hardware to enable its devices to uphold the interests of its shareholders against the interests of its customers. That said, engineers are fallible. And when it comes to security, defending is always harder than attacking: defenders have to make zero mistakes, while attackers only need to find one.

We know that eleven generations of iPhones are vulnerable to an exploit called Checkm8, which attacks a defect in the devices' Secure Enclave—a chip designed to resist any patching or modification, rendering these permanently vulnerable to Checkm8 attacks.[19]

Epic could field a third-party app store that used Checkm8 to install itself on compatible iPhones and access millions of the customers it lost by being turfed out of the official App Store—for a mere fraction of what its decade-long antitrust lawsuit will cost it. Indeed, lawsuits will only cost Epic money, while an Epic Store for iOS could actually turn a profit.

Epic wants to make that store, but its lawyers have doubtlessly explained that giving people a tool to install a rival app store would violate Section 1201 of the DMCA and risk a five-year prison sentence and a $500,000 fine per act of circumvention, and this would be even more costly than suing a monopolist worth $1 trillion that has access to some of the most aggressive litigators in the world.

Figuring out how to get your program played on a phone without paying a toll to the phone maker isn't a copyright violation, but it *is* a business-model violation. Congress could easily have written section 1201 of the DMCA to say, "Bypassing DRM to violate copyright is illegal," but it didn't. It created a new crime—"felony contempt of business model"—which actually *supports* anticompetitive conduct. By giving Apple's App Store moat the force of law, the DMCA stops it from being competed away, allowing monopolists to keep collecting money that should be going to makers, not rentiers.

Interoperability is essential to competition. Your sneaker maker doesn't get a veto over whose socks you wear. We have done away with coal bosses who pay in noninteroperable scrip that can only be spent at the company store. Microsoft couldn't stop Apple from making the iWork Suite, which reads and writes every one of Microsoft Office's baroque file formats.

And yet Apple and its defenders insist Epic is the one overstepping here. They say Apple customers *like* the fact that Apple gets a cut of every app sale, just as they are said to prefer that independent repair of Apple devices be banned so that Apple alone can fix their phones (and decide when those phones can't be repaired and so must be replaced). They say Apple's veto lets it protect its users by blocking malicious apps, and that it would never abuse this power for its own gain.

This argument is *laughable*. If Apple believes that its customers prefer cutting the company that charged them $1,000 for a phone 30 percent of every app they run on that phone, it could just give them the choice: "Buy *Fortnite* through the App Store or through Epic's app; it's up to you! Think different!"

The idea that Apple customers prefer to buy from Apple is belied by Apple's extreme measures to prevent them from buying elsewhere. We didn't believe East German bureaucrats who insisted that the Berlin Wall's purpose wasn't to keep the people locked in, but rather to stop outsiders from breaking into the workers' paradise of the German Democratic Republic. We shouldn't believe Apple when it insists that preventing interoperability is just a way of enforcing its customers' preferences. Apple can easily prove that its customers don't want to escape its walled garden: just let Epic install a gate and see if anyone goes through.

THESE HARMS ARE NOT JUST COMMERCIAL

Giving corporations like Apple and Google the right to control such important gates doesn't just have consequences for the creators and producers who are being shaken down, or the users who are forced to pay more. It cuts at our most essential freedoms.

Chekhov exhorted writers not to put a gun onstage unless a character was going to fire it. But this advice has a corollary for audiences: "If there's a pistol on the mantelpiece in Act I, it'll go off by Act III."

Apple should have paid attention. Although it was not the first company to use DRM to prevent users from installing software on devices without its approval (game console manufacturers did this for decades before), it *was* the first company to popularize the model for general-purpose devices.

Ten years ago, Cory predicted that once Apple gave itself the power to decide which software you were allowed to use, governments would start ordering it to prevent you from using software they didn't like.[20] It didn't take long for that prophecy to be fulfilled.

In 2017, Apple kicked all working VPNs out of the Chinese App Store, so the Chinese state—which was then in the midst of rounding up one million Uyghurs and putting them in concentration camps—could spy on its population more effectively.[21] In 2020, Apple purged the Chinese App Store of RSS readers, which had been helping Apple customers in China evade state censorship and surveillance.[22] The consequences of these losses can be lethal.

If you're reading this, but you're not a Chinese dissident, that shouldn't give you much succor. Right now, we live within a system of what Bruce Schneier calls "feudal security."[23] In most countries, inadequate state-granted user protections (against spying, surveillance, malware, and fraud) force us to seek protection from feudal seigneurs (e.g., tech companies) and hope that their business interests happen to align with our human rights.

Google might use its power to protect your privacy by blocking some of the worst online surveillance, like when it started blocking third-party cookies in Chrome. But the protection is incidental—it doesn't want to protect your privacy; it wants to make sure it's the only one who gets to violate it. If you're worried about Google itself or one of its trusted parties abusing your data, that ban won't help.

Likewise, Apple makes a big (and deserved) deal out of its privacy orientation, but that privacy is in service to a marketing message: "Apple is the pro-privacy alternative." Apple cares about selling devices, and privacy is a means to that end. If its business model changed to make it more profitable to surveil you, it would do that instead.

The feudal lords of the internet secure us against the lawless bandits that roam outside of their castle walls. But they don't love us. They don't want us to be safe. They want to make money. If they can get richer by sacrificing our safety, they'll do so in a heartbeat.

In this feudal security system, a small elite of mercantilist warlords get all the property rights (the right to decide how the infrastructure is used) and the rest of us get tenants' rights (the right to make limited use of the warlords' property).

The warlords promise to defend us from bandits and build high walls to keep the bandits out. But if someone suborns the warlord to act against us, suddenly those walls lock us *in*, leaving us helpless.

Indeed, the walls aren't just a protection; they're a temptation. Anyone who coerces or bribes a warlord into letting them inside the compound enjoys a smorgasbord of defenseless prey—the walled garden becomes an all-you-can-eat buffet for the benefit of these predators.

The power Apple gave itself *invites* states to make demands just like those of the Chinese government. By deciding to manufacture and sell devices in China, while insisting on full control over the apps that could be used, Apple all but guaranteed it would be deputized to aid in mass roundups for concentration camps.

If its users could sideload apps that subverted harmful government orders, those orders would be less effective—offering less temptation for governments to make them in the first place. If they did anyway, users would have an out. That's important for citizens the world over, not just in China. Because if there's one thing we've learned in the last half dozen years, it's that there's no saying what kind of government we might end up with next.

CHAPTER 11

YOUTUBE: BAKING CHOKEPOINTS IN

YouTube is *the* online video platform. More than two billion users spend the equivalent of 114,000 years each day watching sports highlights, music and craft instructables, music videos, banal home recordings, conspiracy theorists, vintage Algerian TV, cats riding robot vacuum cleaners, and everything else the human mind can conceive. Users upload five hundred hours of content each minute. When kids are asked to rank the most desirable professions, "YouTuber" regularly tops the list.[1] For many creators, there is no alternative: their work has to be on the platform, or it might as well not exist.

When YouTube started, there were few clues it would become such a juggernaut. The company was founded in early 2005 by three PayPal employees—Jawed Karim, Steve Chen, and Chad Hurley. They set up office above a pizza shop between Palo Alto and San Francisco, and the first video was a nineteen-second clip of Karim inanely describing elephant trunks (at the time of writing, it has been viewed over 180 million times). As YouTube experts Jean Burgess and Joshua Green explain, the founders were "agnostic" about the kind of content on the platform, focusing on the social networking side instead: "In practice YouTube really didn't mind what kind of content their users were uploading, as long as the scale of the platform's user population and their activity levels continued to grow."[2]

As it happened, though, it was the *content* that proved key to success. People loved being able to easily upload, watch, and share videos online, and the site mushroomed. Many of the clips were posted without the copyright owner's permission. By March 2006, YouTube began limiting videos to ten minutes with the intent of eliminating infringing movies and TV shows,[3] and even before that, uploads had been kept short by a 100MB file size limit.[4] However, unauthorized snippets of highly commercial copyrighted works remained widely available. In December 2005, a two-and-a-half minute *Saturday Night Live* sketch titled "Lazy Sunday" was famously uploaded. Viewed 1.2 million times in ten days, the clip increased YouTube's traffic by 83 percent, reignited interest in the fading sketch show, launched Andy Samberg's career, and catapulted YouTube into mainstream public consciousness.

Meanwhile, just a few miles away, Google was struggling to build its own online video offering. It had begun much earlier, in late 2003, but progress on the rather drearily named Google Video was slow. The service sought to offer a catalog of legally licensed professional content, but struggled to get off the ground, in large part because rights holders were so reluctant to license their content for online use. But rights negotiations weren't the only impediment: the service floundered on a technical level too. It wasn't until mid-2005 that Google Video even offered a way to play back its videos, and even then, clumsily, it required users to install separate software to do so.[5] Google was eating YouTube's dust.

That's not to say things were progressing entirely smoothly above the pizza shop. From the moment users began uploading videos, the founders were sweating under legal pressure from irate content companies demanding they do more to prevent copyright infringement. As journalist Steven Levy explains, however, they pressed on: "Even though YouTubers knew that people who were uploading videos didn't really have the right to do so, they believed that YouTube would be all right as long as there weren't complaints from copyright holders about specific videos, in which case they could respond."[6] This approach was backed by the US's "safe harbor" law, which protects platforms from liability for hosting infringing content that is uploaded by users, so long as they move "expeditiously" to remove it once it comes to their attention. Enacted by the United States in 1998, these laws were subsequently exported worldwide, including to the EU in 2000.[7]

Safe harbor laws are intended to balance two important considerations: protecting the interests of copyright holders and protecting online expression by reassuring those who operate services that host speech that they aren't required to vet and block every potential infringement, a situation that would limit the online public sphere to materials that had been vetted by lawyers and subjected to private indemnification agreements. After all, YouTube hosts all kinds of different material—classes (on everything from math and physics to languages, crafts, yoga, and swimming), beauty tips, political commentary, comedy, nursery rhymes, toy unboxing, advice on building cabinets and changing spark plugs and everything else you can imagine. It's an unfathomably valuable trove of knowledge, entertainment, and culture that would not be possible if hosts were liable for everything their users uploaded. That's why the safe harbors limit liability for copyright infringement to circumstances where the host fails to quickly take down infringing content once they have been notified of its existence. YouTube followed these rules, taking down infringing videos after receiving notices of infringement, but with the site growing exponentially and more infringing content being uploaded all the time, media companies grew exasperated with the apparently endless game of "whack-a-mole." The threat of expensive litigation loomed large.

Skyrocketing costs were also challenging the start-up. It was expensive to host and distribute all those videos, and YouTube was bringing in virtually no revenue. The site's exponential growth threatened to become more curse than blessing as it rapidly outpaced the team's efforts to monetize the site, and the founders soon realized they had to offload it to someone with deeper pockets.

At this time, Google Video had been taking a very different approach to infringement. While it eventually added a feature allowing users to upload videos, its model depended on persuading the big entertainment companies to license content, and it was anxious not to alienate them. Accordingly, Google policed infringement much more carefully than its rival, and *far* beyond its obligations under the safe harbor law. But the strategy was not rewarded: most movie studios and record labels still refused to allow Google to sell their video content. By the time it finally launched, "The most prominent movie studio Google convinced to show full-length movies on the service was an independent, Green-Cine," Levy recounts, and "the highlights of its meager inventory were films by the Polish director Andrzej Wajda and the documentary *Mau Mau Sex Sex*."[8]

And thus Google realized its video business was a dud just as You-Tube's founders were looking to offload their problematically successful child. As Google's then-counsel David Drummond tells it, "We looked up one day and saw YouTube building an edgy fun brand, in a way that Google Video wasn't. We imagined that if you put that on the Google platform, and, you know, with Google distribution, Google machines, and everything, you'd take it, you'd really, really accelerate."[9] The search giant pounced, paying $1.65 billion for the fledgling site—a full billion more than Google thought YouTube was actually worth. As Levy tells it, though, there were signs even early on that the move would pay off: as the deal was closing, Rupert Murdoch's Twentieth Century Fox "declared that whatever Google was paying, Fox would pay more."[10]

Google took possession in October 2006, just eighteen months after YouTube's birth. One of the new owner's first actions was to address the site's infringement problem. The company's lawyers believed the sheer amount of infringement on YouTube gave rise to enormous potential liability. The time limit on videos kept a lid on the number of infringing movies and TV shows but did little against unauthorized music. Although it was protected by the safe harbor rules, Google couldn't be sure the takedown framework wouldn't be interpreted narrowly (or abolished altogether!) if it was seen as permitting a free-for-all. So it immediately began figuring out how it could more proactively catch infringing material before it was made public on the platform.[11] By June 2007, it was trialing a new system that utilized audio and video "fingerprinting" technologies to automatically detect infringing videos as soon as they were uploaded.[12]

By then, however, media companies had lost patience. That March, Viacom had filed a lawsuit against YouTube for direct and indirect copyright infringement, seeking a billion dollars in damages. (It was later amended to make it clear it was only concerned with infringements from before Google's copyright filtering system was rolled out.) Eventually, the case was merged with other suits brought by rights holders including the English Premier League, which sought billions more.

Pretrial discovery unearthed embarrassing revelations for both sides. It turned out Viacom had tried hard to buy YouTube when it went on the market, either alone or in joint venture with Google. And it also appeared that it had secretly uploaded its content to YouTube even as it was complaining about infringement, deliberately "roughing up" videos to make them look stolen and even sending employees to upload content anonymously from public computers.[13] Meanwhile, damaging emails from YouTube's co-founders showed they were aware of rampant infringement on the site from very early on, and even that one of them, Jawed Karim, had uploaded some of it himself, while Google founder Sergey Brin was on record saying Google weakened its copyright compliance standards after acquiring YouTube so it "would profit from illegal downloads."[14]

Ultimately, however, the lawsuit failed. Critically, the plaintiffs had failed to convince the court that YouTube wasn't eligible for safe harbor protection. To be liable for infringement, the judge ruled, it wasn't enough for YouTube to be generally aware: it needed to know of "specific and identifiable infringements of particular individual items" and to have failed to act expeditiously to remove them. That wasn't made out on the facts. In fact, YouTube responded very rapidly to DMCA takedown notices. A month before filing suit, Viacom had spent months accumulating 100,000 video links, issuing them to YouTube via one mass take-down notice. Apparently impressed, the judge noted that, by the next business day, virtually all had been removed.[15]

Since YouTube had complied with its obligations under the DMCA, the safe harbor applied, and summary judgment was awarded in YouTube's favor. There were a couple of subsequent skirmishes on appeal, but overall Google came out on top. The parties eventually settled the litigation in 2014. While the deal terms were confidential, Reuters reported that no money changed hands.[16] For Viacom and the other plaintiffs, it was an enormously expensive loss. It's not known how much they spent on the suit, but Google reported spending $100 million in just the first three years.[17]

While all this was going on, YouTube had continued to grow rapidly, with Google's deep pockets saving it from having to worry too much about the sustainability of its business model. As cofounder Chad Hurley explains, this helped its meteoric rise: "We could have spent more time on how we're going to monetize the system, but we continued to focus on more growth, more users, better experience."[18] As recently as 2016 the company was still running at a deficit, with CEO Susan Wojcicki saying it was "still in investment mode" and had "no timetable" for becoming profitable.[19]

Google's ownership helped YouTube in other ways too. By 2009 some estimates suggested YouTube was spending $350 million a year serving videos to users. But Levy reports Google "privately tell[ing] journalists that those guesses were based on what *others* had to pay to move such massive numbers of bits. With its superefficient cloud infrastructure and its private fiber-optic network, Google's costs were less, much less." The notoriously secret company wasn't admitting just how much less, but Ramp-Rate, "another company conversant with infrastructure costs," estimated just $83 million—a quarter of what others would have to pay.[20] This gave YouTube another huge advantage over rivals.

Despite the courts' confirming that YouTube was not liable under the DMCA (and the law itself explicitly stating that protection wasn't conditioned on "a service provider monitoring its service or affirmatively seeking facts indicating infringing activity") YouTube continued investing in its automated infringement detection system. After over a decade and a hundred million dollars, the result is a vast compliance system called Content ID. It works like this: YouTube invites content owners to upload copies of their copyrighted works, adds them to a database, then checks every user-submitted video against those entries before permitting them to go live on the site. (They keep on checking, too, whenever their database is updated or algorithm tweaked. YouTubers regularly report receiving Content ID matches for content they published a decade before.)

Where apparent infringement is detected, the rights holder is given three options: to block the video, track its analytics, or "monetize." If it chooses monetization, the rights holder gets to share in the ad revenues generated by the video.[21] YouTube claims Content ID is 99.5 percent successful at resolving music content claims, and 98 percent successful for claims involving other forms of content, like movies, TV, and games.[22]

YouTube's preemptive filtering not only goes far beyond what current US law requires (that platforms "expeditiously" remove content once they know it is infringing) but creates an important new revenue stream for creators and producers.

Previously, if someone used the Village People's "YMCA" as a background track to a home video of their toddlers paddling in an inflatable pool, it would have been subject to a takedown notice and removed. With Content ID, however, it can generate revenue for rights holders instead. Google reported that, as of 2017, rights holders chose to monetize more than 90 percent of Content ID matches, rising to over 95 percent for music uses.[23]

In 2019, the first year Google broke out YouTube's revenues in its reporting, it brought in ad revenues of over $15 billion, and paid out about $8.5 billion to rights holders, including about $3 billion to music rights holders.[24] According to previously published stats, about half of what YouTube pays out to the music industry comes from the professional music videos they upload themselves, and the other half from user-uploaded content.[25] If that ratio still holds, YouTube paid out about $1.5 billion in 2019 to music industry rights holders for uses that, without Content ID, simply could not have been converted to cash. To put that in context, the entire global recorded music market that same year was estimated to be worth $20.2 billion, putting the contribution of YouTube-hosted user-generated content at about 7.5 percent of the market (with original licensed content contributing that much again).

Despite this, Content ID has few friends. The zeal with which it is programmed to detect infringements sometimes leads to false positives. Not every use of copyrighted material is prohibited by copyright law, and it's impossible for an algorithm to figure out whether a snippet of a news report, sports broadcast, or song is allowed. It may be that the amount taken is too insignificant to infringe, or that it's in the public domain—as is the case where copyright has expired. The president of Public.Resource.Org, Carl Malamud, told us they received over three hundred Content ID matches on some six thousand government videos they posted to YouTube and proved all but two were false positives. At least in part due to Malamud's efforts, YouTube added "It's public domain" to the list of reasons for contesting a Content ID match.

The use of copyrighted material does not infringe where it's permitted by law, for example where it's a fair use (in the United States) or fair dealing (in most of the Commonwealth). Determining whether a use is permitted requires careful balancing of factors like the amount taken, purpose (Is it a parody? Criticizing government policy? Reporting news? Transforming it into a new creative work?) and the extent to which the taking interferes with the market for the original work.[26] But Content ID isn't capable of determining that and errs on the side of blocking videos that, to a human judge, clearly aren't infringing. One musician received *five* automated claims against his ten-hour video of continuous white noise—that is, uncopyrightable generic electronic hissing.[27] Another user had a video blocked just because birds were singing in the background.[28]

This makes it difficult for creators of certain kinds of creative speech to benefit financially from their work. For example, when music and film experts critique media on YouTube, the snippets they use can be a permitted "fair use," but still get caught by Content ID and have the monetization opportunity offered to rights holders of the content they're criticizing instead. Classical musicians struggle in this system especially. They have a legal right to play music that's in the public domain, but when they upload recordings of themselves playing the likes of Mozart, Mendelssohn, and Liszt, Content ID gets triggered because the major record labels (primarily Sony) have uploaded their own recordings to the database. The system cannot distinguish between the new performance of the composition (permitted!) and a copy of say, a Sony Music–owned recording of it (which would be infringing). Thus, at least some of the content monetized by major rights holders under Content ID does so unjustly. The Electronic Frontier Foundation decries this as a kind of reverse Robin Hood: "Money is taken away from independent artists who happen to use parts of copyrighted material, and deposited into the pockets of major media companies, despite the fact that they would never be able to claim that money in court."[29]

While there is a system for challenging false positives, it's so unwieldy that even professors expert in copyright law struggle to navigate it! In 2020, NYU uploaded a video featuring musicologists debating the "Blurred Lines" lawsuit, with the point being to show watchers how expert evidence is constructed in copyright infringement cases. That necessitated playing portions of the songs, and the video was flagged by Content ID. While this was a textbook fair use, these sophisticated copyright experts had real trouble getting the flag lifted: "While the experts in intellectual property law at NYU Law were certain that the video did not infringe, they ended up lost in the byzantine process of disputing and appealing Content ID matches. They could not figure out whether or not challenging Content ID to the end and losing would result in the channel being deleted." Eventually the matches disappeared—with no explanation!—after faculty used personal connections to reach out to YouTube.[30] As an engineer would put it, "Solving your problem by personally contacting high-level YouTube executives is not a scalable solution." It's certainly not an option open to the vast majority of creators forced to rely on this system.

If a creator resists a rights holder's monetization claim (say, because they're sure their use is permitted under law) it can be converted to an official DMCA notice and then a copyright "strike" under YouTube's policy. Three strikes in ninety days will result in the creator's account being terminated and all videos deleted—which makes this dangerous territory for those (like classical musicians and music and film critics) who regularly get unfairly flagged. While false positives are merely annoying for the big record companies and movie studios who have dedicated account managers within YouTube to sort out such mishaps, they're a serious threat to those who can't access such white-glove service. For many creators, that would mean losing their livelihood, since YouTube's dominance means there's virtually nowhere else for them to work. That makes challenging false positives such a scary prospect that even those NYU law professors weren't confident enough to chance it.

Even the major rights holders who benefit most aren't unalloyed fans. Content ID is extremely successful at identifying infringing videos, enabling rights holders to block them from appearing on the site. But that also means missing out on the visibility and revenue that comes from monetization—and, since YouTube controls almost all the eyeballs within the video streaming universe, it's not like there's anywhere else offering a better deal. That forces their hand, making them agree to license their content, even though the rates YouTube offers are much lower than they believe they would get in a competitive market. In other words, copyright owners find themselves reluctantly agreeing to poor terms because it's better to have their music out there and make *some* money than not. Sound familiar? Sure, because it's the exact same reason artists signed up to those terrible deals with labels back when they, too, had no other choice!

YouTube's dominance also gives it outsized power to shape culture. Once a video finishes playing, YouTube's algorithm serves up the ones that come next. That makes algorithmic invisibility the biggest risk for creators, big and small: if YouTube doesn't autoplay your content to interested watchers, it's very difficult to build and sustain a subscriber base of any scale.

The inner workings of YouTube's recommendation algorithm are guarded closely, which has led to the emergence of a huge industry of self-proclaimed experts insisting they alone know the secret to getting attention for your content.[31] But they don't. Nobody does, outside of YouTube. For content creators, that algorithm decides whether they sink or thrive. "There are so many people who quit their full-time job because they were doing well enough to support themselves," British comedian and musician Emma Blackery told the *Guardian*. "Then the algorithm changes and suddenly they can't support themselves anymore."[32]

Social media platform expert Sophie Bishop says this "highlights the precarity of building a career contingent to platforms." YouTube's business model is based on advertising, which Bishop posits results in its algorithm prioritizing content that attracts more lucrative demographics: "Optimization teaches content creators how to fit within the contours of visibility on YouTube, which is in turn informed by advertisers' desires and their organizational strategies."[33] YouTube's algorithm shapes creativity: "The topics discussed in videos, genres engaged with, video lengths, titles utilized, video thumbnail design, and organization of speech."[34] Being a slave to the algorithm exacts a real toll, according to digital ethnographer Zoë Glatt: "Creators are encouraged to pursue a quantity-over-quality approach if they want to achieve success on YouTube. This, combined with a lack of clarity about what content exactly YouTube will promote and what might be demonetised, leads to an extremely precarious and stressful working life for creators."[35]

Those who aren't happy with the system have nowhere else to go. Until about 2015, many video bloggers were successfully making a living on Blip TV, "a more community-focused alternative to YouTube." Although it was founded the same year as YouTube, and at one point boasted almost a million video publishers, it "was quickly eclipsed by YouTube, which had a lot more resources at its disposal after it got acquired by Google." It was bought out by Maker Studios in 2013 with the aim of competing with YouTube. But Maker was then itself acquired by Disney, which promptly shut the platform down, encouraging Blip creators to monetize YouTube channels instead.[36] Imeem was similarly shut down in 2009 after being acquired by News Corporation's MySpace, as was Vessel when it was bought by Verizon. In each of these instances, enormous companies closed off alternative options for creators.

Countless other video platforms simply failed, unable to compete with YouTube's resources and reach, until we got to this point of YouTube being effectively the only game in town.

Major rights holders lay the blame for YouTube's current dominance squarely on the DMCA's safe harbors. If it had had to license copyrighted works from the outset, they argue, rights holders would have been able to negotiate higher licensing fees. This ignores the reality that even Google Video, with the entire might of the search giant behind it, was unable to secure the content licenses necessary to make an appealing service. Alternatively, they claim that the safe harbors helped YouTube gain the viewers it needed to become the behemoth it is today. This is more convincing, though every other hosting platform, including Vimeo (founded a few months before YouTube) and all the short-lived platforms that have come and gone before and since have benefited from those protections too. What's weird about this argument is that it ignores the fact that YouTube's automatic infringement monitoring goes far beyond its obligations under the DMCA and has been in place since early in the site's existence. YouTube's anticompetitive flywheel can't be explained by the DMCA's safe harbors.

YouTube's dominance began with network effects. The value of its network became higher as more people joined: the more videos that were posted, the more attractive the site became to viewers, and then the more videos were posted, and so on. This got continually reinforced by Google's self-preferencing—it uses its supremacy in search to funnel users to YouTube over alternate platforms.[37] Additionally, it didn't have to be as conciliatory with rights holders as it would have been if its monolithic owner had not had a cool $100 million to put behind defending infringement suits. On top of that, critically, it benefited from those magical economies of scale that came from being part of Google, which drove its costs far below what a smaller owner would have had to pay. It also enjoyed freedom to grow without worrying about the bottom line—something that wouldn't be possible if it weren't being subsidized from elsewhere. These are factors that the consumer welfare standard loves—efficiency! Low (in this case, zero) prices for consumers! But that's exactly what led to the core of creator and rights holder complaints against YouTube: its ability to shake down rights holders and creators.

In 2021, YouTube almost doubled its 2019 revenues, to $28.8 billion.[38] It pays out an estimated 55 percent to creators, and, while we don't know how much it costs to run, it seems clear that it's becoming *enormously* lucrative. Commercial market research firm YouGov reports that, in 2020, YouTube (free or paid) was the most popular music service in the US, France, and India, and second (after Spotify) in the UK.[39] However, YouTube pays substantially less in royalties than competing streaming platforms like Spotify and Amazon and Apple's music offerings. The major labels call the difference between what YouTube extracts from music and the amount that goes to artists and investors "the value gap," and describe it as "the biggest threat to the future sustainability of the music industry."[40] Just as they siphon away extraordinary wealth from artists and independent producers, YouTube does the same to them.

There are other similarities between the labels' fights with YouTube and artists' struggles with labels. Just as artists object to the lack of transparency around their sales and royalties, record companies accuse YouTube of obfuscating how much music is actually streamed via YouTube, how much it pays out, and how rates are decided.[41] YouTube doesn't publicly report on these matters, but it seems like all kinds of different deals are made: in 2018, for example, one influencer marketing firm reported working with clients receiving as little as $0.35 and as much as $5 per thousand views.[42] Google claims its rates on music are higher than Spotify's ad-supported tier,[43] but without transparency, there's no way of verifying that claim—and no way for creators and rights holders to use payments made to others as leverage for increasing their own.

In other words, YouTube acts just like the other powerful buyers we've looked at: using its power to avoid transparency and drive down the amounts payable to suppliers and workers. The "value gap" isn't caused by safe harbor laws. It's caused by an excessively powerful buyer shaking down the record industry *because its dominance allows it to do so.*

BAKING CHOKEPOINTS IN

By 2021, YouTube's dominance was unquestioned. With almost two billion global users, it had by far the biggest audience and reach of any online video site, and was the second most visited global website, behind only Google itself.[44] Creators upload their videos to YouTube because that's where the viewers are, and that, in turn, keeps those viewers coming. Today the platform hosts literally billions of videos, making it a natural first port of call for anyone looking for music videos, tutorials on making hollandaise, or the latest football highlights. This is a deep data moat: it would be hard for a competitor to build up a library to match it.

Having said that, however, YouTube is not immune to competition. It does not have creators locked in anywhere near as tightly as Amazon and Apple, for instance. That's evident in the popularity of TikTok, downloaded over three billion times in its first few years online.

If YouTube goes too far in ripping off the individuals and businesses who supply its content, they can take it elsewhere. YouTube's platform gives the most popular streamers the ability to communicate with tens of millions of subscribers—including passionately loyal fans willing to evangelize on their behalf. If the most popular YouTubers decided to make a coordinated switch to some new rival platform, one that promised more creator-friendly terms (and maybe not to radicalize your kids) it would have an enormous head start. And, given the megaprofits YouTube seems to be generating for corporate HQ, wannabe rivals are no doubt already plotting to do so.

Google knows competition from new platforms is a real risk to its bottom line. If it wants to avoid YouTube becoming another MySpace, it needs stronger fortifications—ones that lock customers in and competitors out. *That's* what Warren Buffett is looking for as he seeks out "economic castles protected by unbreachable moats."[45]

With help from the European Union, Google might have found its best moat yet. Facebook CEO Mark Zuckerberg once observed, "It is better to buy than to compete."[46] Big businesses know it's better to comply with expensive regulation than to compete too. While they naturally prefer power without responsibility, power *with* responsibility can be almost as good.

The Bell Telephone Company was once entitled to go to your house, inspect the device you had plugged into your phone line, and, if it came from a competitor and you refused to remove it, to cut off your service.[47] That allowed it to transform its state-bestowed right to regulate the telephone utility into a state-backed right to control its competition. It didn't matter if the rival company's product was better: Bell's law-backed moat could not be competed away.

Amazon and Apple follow the same playbook when they use anticircumvention laws to weaken copyright owners' abilities to create competition over ebooks and audiobooks. Those digital locks are moats that can't be competed away either.

This all harkens back to the paradox we alluded to earlier: that although markets are supposed to be risky and companies are supposed to be disciplined by their fear of a change in the order, the reality is that they instead devote their resources toward limiting that risk. That's why, as soon as a corporation manages to create a chokepoint, it will try to make it permanent. Rather than trying to retain their dominance by making the best products, they do this by locking in suppliers and workers, killing off or merging with rivals, and making their markets maximally inhospitable to new entrants.

Expensive regulation is an exceptionally helpful tool for doing this. Compliance costs might shave a few hundred million dollars off a big company's quarterly earnings, but in exchange, it'll get to watch as its less well-resourced rivals are killed off by the weight of regulation. And, critically, giants get a new barrier that makes it that much less attractive for anyone else to enter their market. In a world where short-term shareholder value is king, this is a much more attractive option than actually making great products in ways that respect workers and suppliers. This is one reason we ought to be careful about how we rein in excessive corporate power. If the tools we use make operating so expensive that only the biggest firms can afford to be in the game, we'll end up baking chokepoints in.

There was a strong element of that when the European Union passed the General Data Protection Regulation (GDPR) in 2016. This well-intentioned legislation sought to address the online privacy invasions that became endemic as the internet transitioned to being a surveillance-fueled ad machine. Unfortunately, some of its rules were so expensive to comply with that only the largest companies were able to do so. This eliminated most of the EU's homegrown ad-tech companies, delivering their market share to Facebook and Google. That gave them extra revenues they can use to pay for the compliance that was supposed to bring them to heel and makes it that much more difficult for new companies with privacy-respecting business models to try to compete. The GDPR offers many benefits to citizens, but these unintended consequences harm more than they help. The fatal mistake was in regulating invasive tracking, rather than banning it altogether. The result is that tracking continues, but at such a high operating cost that only the biggest companies can participate.

Article 17 of the EU's 2019 Copyright Directive will do even more to entrench incumbent platforms, like YouTube, that control cultural market chokepoints. It requires EU nations to pass laws that abolish the safe harbors and impose liability on almost all commercial platforms that host user-generated content (the law has a few, narrow carve-outs for newer and smaller organizations). But online services can get exempted from liability if they can demonstrate they have "made best efforts" to prevent the availability, and future upload, of infringing works. In other words, the biggest incumbents—those with licensing deals and the capacity to filter uploaded content for infringement (like YouTube!)—have the least to fear from this new regulation.

These new obligations require platforms to monitor their users—an activity that is unambiguously prohibited by the GDPR. And, at the same time, they impose severe penalties if they err on the side of caution when removing speech. Satisfying these competing requirements will require an unimaginably expensive army of moderators or farcically expensive filtering technology, which will have the effect of bankrupting all but the largest tech platforms. This is not just a case of additional regulations imposing a greater burden on less resourced entities. It's worse: this law effectively entrenches the most powerful incumbent platforms over all others.

The major record labels pushed for this law regardless, gambling that YouTube's new obligations under Article 17 would give them the leverage they needed to negotiate higher fees. But the EU law merely treats the problem's symptoms (the labels' being squeezed), not its cause (that YouTube's excessive power enables it to squeeze them).

There's no doubt the new regulation will be bad for users, especially creative users. Article 17 was eventually amended to require exceptions for things like quotation, parody, criticism, and review, but as we've seen, even the most expensive automated filtering systems can't tell the difference between infringing uses and lawful parodies, critiques, and transformative new works. And some European countries have been criticized for failing to properly implement these safeguards into their domestic laws at all.[48]

But these developments will be most harmful to those seeking to create alternative streaming platforms that could compete against YouTube. Google's $100-million-plus investment in Content ID provides it with an additional capital moat that will need to be matched by any company that seeks to challenge its dominance. Thus, on top of its network effects and self-preferencing and data advantage, the new regulation adds enormously to the costs of entering the market. That will force smaller players from the market and block new ones from entering, leaving creators with even fewer, even more powerful, buyers for their work. Rather than braking YouTube's anticompetitive flywheel, this intervention promises to speed it up.

Google knows this, which is why it backflipped from its original opposition to the EU proposal. In an opinion published in the *Financial Times*, YouTube CEO Susan Wojcicki sang the praises of Content ID as "the best solution" for managing global rights and called for the EU to develop similar technology-based solutions.[49]

The cultural industries should have figured out by now that, if it's good for Google, it's probably not good for them. Google's play is obvious: to be the only one that can afford to participate in the market for user-uploaded video content. That very real prospect was recognized by the UK Parliament's 2021 *Economics of Streaming* report, which expressed concern that "YouTube, as an existing, dominant entity continue to operate as currently but new entrants that might compete for YouTube's market share may disproportionately face additional barriers to entry."[50]

There are excellent reasons to mobilize against Big Tech. It is turning the internet into a surveillance machine, weakening democracies, radicalizing our families and friends and turning communities against one another—all to generate a few extra bucks for shareholders who already have more than enough. But the backlash against Big Tech is focusing too much on its Techness, and not enough on its Bigness. Misapprehending the source of the danger risks actually making it worse. If you think Google is bad now, just imagine what it will become if we keep creating rules that make it all but impossible for alternatives to emerge.

PART 2

BRAKING ANTICOMPETITIVE FLYWHEELS

CHAPTER 12

IDEAS LYING AROUND

C reative workers are told their problems will be fixed if they just get more copyright, or stronger digital locks, or if the internet is filtered. But as we showed in the first half of this book, the real reason they earn so little from the culture they make is that the most profitable supply chains have been colonized by powerful corporations who use their control over chokepoints to co-opt most of its value.

We showed how businesses fortify themselves against competition by aggregating copyrights on an industrial scale and by taking advantage of network effects, licensing mazes, regulatory capture, horizontal and vertical integration, and self-preferencing. All this keeps competitors out and lets middlemen muscle their way in between audiences and culture producers to capture a greater and greater share of the money that flows from one to the other.

While anticompetitive flywheels vary by industry, each chokepoint capitalist seeks to do the same thing: lock in users, lock in suppliers, make markets hostile to new entrants, and, ultimately, use the lack of choice to force workers and suppliers to accept unsustainably low prices. That's exactly what we depicted with our anti-competitive flywheel at the be- ginning of this book.

Locking in users often begins with network effects—that phenom- enon through which the value a user gets from a service increases with every additional user. But dominant businesses then try to convert those temporary advantages to more enduring moats. Spotify ties artists and labels to its platform by training listeners to outsource decisions about what they should listen to. Amazon does it by chaining books with digital locks that are illegal to remove, and by persuading you to buy a year's worth of shipping up front. Record companies lock listeners in by requiring their artists to sign century-long contracts: unlike coffee, where you can choose to switch to a "fair trade" brand, there is no other source for that music. Mobile phone manufacturers lock in customers by controlling where we can get our apps. Facebook and Google do it with news publishers by controlling all sides of the market for ads, as does Live Nation with the market for live music. And Google does it by using its search engine to funnel users toward YouTube instead of competing video platforms, and by subsidizing its operations so it's harder and harder for anyone else to compete.

The more users or customers a corporation manages to lock in, the more power it gets over suppliers. Creative producers—whether they are book publishers or newspapers or record labels or screenwriters or game developers—can't survive unless they're able to reach the people interested in the products and services they have on offer. That's why, once Amazon captured the ebook market by locking its readers in to Kindle, publishers had no choice but to keep supplying it with books, even though they were convinced its pricing model was going to drive their industry off a cliff. In a world without legal prohibitions on circumventing DRM, they could have started their own ebook store, offered readers incentives to migrate over, and offered software to let them remove the DRM from books they'd already bought so they could convert their libraries. The very anticircumvention provisions that are meant to protect their interests have been co-opted by Amazon to strip away their power to do so.

Everyone wants Amazon-like power. That's why the Big Four talent agencies rearranged Hollywood so writers, directors, and actors would be sold to studios as a package, rather than individuals. That change made the agencies critical to closing most deals and positioned them to extract an ever greater share for doing so.

It's also why Spotify is investing so heavily in playlist culture. Its most promising route to riches is if it manages to train subscribers to delegate the work of deciding what they hear. If it manages to do so, it will be the one to decide which musicians, composers, and podcasters get heard. As its power to do so increases, so too will the toll it can extract in exchange. It's already flexing that muscle to drive down royalties to desperate artists and labels.

Users and suppliers aren't locked in if some upstart can simply come along with a better deal and start peeling them off. That's why dominant businesses devote some of their rents toward making their markets hostile to new entrants. They love raising switching costs, as when Amazon makes it impossible for customers to take your bought books to another provider, or when record labels lock artists into inexorable contracts. When everyone's locked in, a better product or deal won't be enough to win them away.

As we saw, regulation can also act as a tool to entrench the dominant players. Consider music streaming, for example. Global music licensing rules are mind-numbingly complex—the kind of complex that makes you want to gnaw your face off. This makes streaming markets incredibly expensive to enter, keeping out hordes of talented, passionate, idealistic people who genuinely want to make the music industry work better for creators and producers.

But it doesn't particularly bother the biggest players—the Spotifys, Apples, Googles, and Amazons of the world. Sure, it slows down the pace at which they can innovate, but it also acts as a powerful moat to keep out new entrants. It's cheaper for them to pay the costs that flow from this insanely complex system than to have to actually compete. It's the same when the GDPR forces smaller ad-tech players out of the market, or when the EU's internet filter mandate all but guarantees YouTube will continue its reign over video. Regulation can be a good friend to powerful corporations, second only perhaps to regulatory capture—like when Big Radio in the US uses its purchased influence to avoid any obligation to pay recording artists at all.

And, of course, if all that isn't enough and a new player is somehow able to enter their kill zone, these behemoths know exactly what to do. Venture capitalists know that too, making them cautious about where they invest, and thus making it even more difficult for nascent competitors to get a toehold. All this explains why supracompetitive profits (like Google's with YouTube) aren't enough to attract new entrants like the Chicago School still insists they will.

This shows that simply blaming Big Tech for bankrupting culture workers is too blinkered a view. *All* large firms with excessive power use it to divert maximum value to shareholders and executives: it's the chokepoints that are the problem. If we really want to make a difference to what ends up in creators' pockets, that's what we have to target.

SYSTEMIC PROBLEMS NEED SYSTEMIC SOLUTIONS

For the past forty years, regulation has been in decline as a means of fixing problematic corporate behavior. Rather than seeing ourselves as *citizens* who deserve a say in how our society is structured, we've been urged to view ourselves as *consumers*, a kind of ambulatory wallet whose influence on society extends only to a series of buy/don't buy decisions.

The story of the consumer rights movement isn't just about neutralizing the power of the public—in its early days, when markets were more competitive, boycotts and bad press could successfully drive a company to change its ways. But the early promise of "consumer rights" became hollow once industries began to consolidate. Instead, consumerism became a way to shift the blame for harms caused by large, profiteering firms onto their customers: if you don't like climate change, get rid of your car! (Which would be great, if the monopolized auto sector hadn't used its excess profits to lobby against public transit.) If you're worried about landfill, just switch to a brand that uses recyclable packaging (never mind that both brands are owned by one of three companies, which simply charges a premium for the "green" alternative while continuing to manufacture the high-waste version).

When the system is working—when firms are competing for both suppliers and customers—individual choices really can make a difference. But once the system is busted, your individual choices cease to matter to firms' bottom lines. Now that Apple and Google completely control the market for mobile apps, you virtually *cannot* decide to go elsewhere while still participating in our online society. We're near that same point with Amazon for ebooks and audio titles, with Live Nation for big concerts and ticketing, with Spotify for streaming—on and on, ad infinitum.

Systemic problems can't be solved with individual actions alone. Your individual purchase decisions, which services you do or don't create accounts on, whether you recycle, and whether you drive or take the bus make almost no difference to our social outcomes. If we want to change the world, we have to fix the system. We need social solutions. Political solutions. The most important individual action you can take is to join a *movement*. And what we need right now is a movement against chokepoint capitalism—one that finds new tools to cut through the roots of monopolistic and monopsonistic power.

ANTITRUST IS VITAL—BUT IT ALONE WON'T SAVE US

Our recent ancestors practiced a lost art of maintaining a pluralistic society, where monopolies were prohibited *because they were monopolies*, not because they might raise prices. Robert Bork and the Chicago crew forced upon us a great forgetting, shattering our capacity to rein corporate power in.

It was a breathtaking trick: convincing us that monopolists are good, regulators are bad, and that captured markets are "free." For forty years, we've lived in the Chicago School's funhouse upside-down land, where greed is good and hourglass-shaped markets make us all better off.

By focusing enforcement on "consumer harm," Borkian antitrust explicitly exempts harms to everyone else from consideration: harms to workers, suppliers, and the environment are all more or less out of scope. And since consumer harm is calculated with incredibly complex (and functionally useless) economic models that can only be created and interpreted by experts in a narrow (and functionally useless) branch of mathematics, we have all been excluded from the debate over market concentration and corporate power for forty years.

Thus insulated from outside criticism or the need to formulate policies that make even glancing contact with reality, the antitrust establishment has created a series of rules and laws that have piled concentration on concentration, a self-feeding machine whose positive feedback loop has revved its engine so high the whole thing is ready to fly apart.

But after generations of neglect—antitrust was not even *mentioned* in the Democratic Party platform between 1992 and 2016—it has roared back onto the agenda.[1] Citizens are sounding the alarm about how the richest people and corporations are blocking responses to society's most urgent problems, including climate change, police brutality, wealth inequality, weakened democracy, and regulatory capture. The Chicago School's "consumer welfare" standard is increasingly being challenged, most no-tably by the New Brandeisians, who compellingly argue that America's core antitrust statutes were always intended to address the broader dangers of excessive market power—not just its consumer effects.[2]

We're getting better at recognizing that antitrust can actually hurt smaller players in their dealings with bigger ones, as when it prohibits atomized companies or workers from banding together in support of their common interests. And we see how it's actually driving corporate concentration: when you act in concert with rivals it makes you an illegal cartel, but if you *buy* your rivals, you can do what you like.

Regulators are also starting to take a more hands-on approach. For the first time, Congress has begun seriously investigating the dominance of Big Tech, particularly its power over suppliers. While Facebook's ac-quisitions of Instagram and WhatsApp were waved through by the Jus-tice Department, in 2020 the Federal Trade Commission and more than forty states took action to challenge them. In the EU, regulators are busy with multiple investigations into apparent violations of its com-petition law, including Apple over its App Store and Amazon over its self-preferencing.[3]

The Biden administration has broken with decades of antitrust con-sensus and looks set to reverse the tide. Three key appointments—Lina Khan as FTC chair, Tim Wu as special assistant to the president for technology and competition policy, and Jonathan Kanter as antitrust boss at the Department of Justice—embody the political aphorism that "per-sonnel are policy." All three advocate for a return to a more muscular, interventionist form of antitrust enforcement.

In July 2021, the Biden administration published a ground-breaking seventy-two-part executive order on antitrust, setting out highly specific measures that US administrative agencies can take right away, without any further congressional action. These seventy-two policies ran the gamut from meatpacking to Big Tech. What's more, the memo explicitly rejected the "consumer welfare" framework for antitrust enforcement and promised a much wider set of antitrust action that would take into account the fortunes of workers, suppliers, and the public.

The heads of the agencies implicated by the memo are not under the president's orders, though: they are nominally independent, and the ex-ecutive order only matters to the extent that the agency chiefs choose to do as they're bid. Within hours, many of those agency chiefs had issued public statements promising to do just that.

The hits keep on coming. In September 2021, the FTC jettisoned the Trump administration's "vertical merger" guidelines—the rules for when a company is allowed to acquire firms that compete with its suppliers. The 2020 guidelines were a Trumpian disaster, but they were not much better than the guidelines they replaced. Happily, the FTC isn't reverting to the earlier version, either—instead, they're reconsidering the whole matter, with an eye to preventing chokepoints. These developments are all welcome, and antitrust will certainly play a role in extricating us from the mess we find ourselves in. But it alone can't save us. In part, that's because its remedies are so limited, particularly when it comes to addressing the insidious problem of excessively powerful buyers.

Antitrust mostly relies on two kinds of remedy—"structural" and "conduct." Conduct remedies are about changing *behavior*. An example is when Live Nation was legally forced to pinkie swear it would not use its power over events to grow its ticketing dominance.

Antitrust expert Peter Carstensen says conduct remedies are particularly limited when it comes to dealing with monopsonies. In a capitalist system, the freedom to set the conditions of a purchase is central to the competitive process, and that makes it "difficult to construct meaningful rules that address abusive exploitative conduct of suppliers by buyers" in the first place.[4] And, even where buyer abuse is indisputably made out, antitrust regulators struggle to figure out how they can protect suppliers without distorting the market further.[5] Attempts to do so can actually raise barriers to entry, making markets even less competitive. And, even if good rules *could* be formulated, it can be really tricky to get powerful companies to actually comply with conduct-based orders. We saw this with Live Nation too, when it consistently violated the consent decree that was supposed to protect competition in ticketing.

Structural remedies are more powerful. They force companies to change their structure—maybe even breaking them up into different entities so they no longer have the power to distort their markets.[6] The American Antitrust Institute says that separating out Live Nation's events and ticketing businesses would have been more effective than the conduct-based remedy that was actually used.[7] We can also see that songwriters would have a much better chance of getting a fair deal if the three biggest music publishers were separated out from the leviathans that also own the three biggest record labels: that would eliminate the incentive for shuffling cash from one side of their ledgers to the other.

Structural remedies can be especially useful where there's no practical way to make companies comply with conduct remedies. Take Google, for example. Regulators can make Google promise not to preference YouTube in its search results, but it's almost impossible for them to tell the difference between "YouTube is at the top of the search results because the algorithm thinks they're the best" and "YouTube is at the top of the search results because Google tweaked the algorithm to think they're the best."

As neoliberal economists like to say, "incentives matter"—which means that taking away Google's incentive to big-up YouTube (by making Google spin off YouTube as a standalone, competing business with different owners) would be the most reliable way to make sure conduct remedies are actually honored. Structural separation can also make markets more attractive to new entrants, since they have the effect of making the leviathans' kill zones smaller.

As we grow more aware of how giant corporations use their power in one area to lock in hegemony elsewhere, calls for structural separation are growing louder (enunciated particularly elegantly and urgently in Zephyr Teachout's *Break 'Em Up*[8]).

However, structural remedies are no panacea. As exemplified by a case against IBM, they can be almost unfathomably complex and expensive to bring about. As Tim Wu recounts, the Justice Department brought monopoly charges against the company in 1969, after a lengthy investigation uncovered widespread evidence of unlawful predatory and exclusionary practices aimed at maintaining its dominance. To fix that, the government wanted to break it up into smaller businesses. But as Wu marvels, the trial required six months of discovery and then a further six years of hearings. IBM reputedly spent as much as a billion dollars on its defense—a staggering amount in 1970s dollars, but less than it could have cost the company to compete fairly in the market. And finally, after all that, Reagan was elected and the case was dropped![9]

Breakups are so costly, lengthy, and uncertain that they've been used very sparingly even in the EU, which takes a much stricter approach to regulating competition than the US. Many of today's behemoths have reached a point where there are good reasons to pursue them anyway. However, even with all the will in the world, this will only work if the wannabe breaker-upper is strong enough to actually enforce it. This is a bar smaller countries might not be able to hurdle. While it's primarily America's antitrust failures that have resulted in so many of these companies' getting out of control, the whole world has to live with the consequences.

These limitations are why even antitrust specialists look toward other forms of regulation, especially for reining in abusive buyer power.[10] We should absolutely be using antitrust and its remedies to their full capacity, but we shouldn't rely on them to do *all* the heavy lifting. And we don't need to! As historian Gabriel Winant points out, antitrust was far from the only factor that helped labor improve its share in the early twentieth century: "Whether or not you rate antitrust as important, it still beggars belief to see it as a more significant force in the remaking of American society in the 1930s than the insurgency of millions of industrial workers and the wave of reforms they won: the National Labor Relations Act, which established union rights; the Social Security Act, which created the eponymous program as well as family assistance and unemployment insurance; the Fair Labor Standards Act, which established the 40-hour workweek and the minimum wage and banned child labor; and, indirectly, legislation touching on housing and urban development, veterans' policy, and more."[11] Considered through this more expansive lens, we have plenty of tools to help brake those anticompetitive flywheels and start taking back the value of culture.

There are three core ways interventions outside of antitrust can help: by encouraging new entrants, by directly regulating buyer power, and by building up countervailing power in workers and suppliers.[12] If we're serious about fixing the chokepoints that allow so much value to be siphoned away, we must address all three.

This second half of the book explores what such responses might look like. We investigate how we can leverage tools like copyright, contract, and labor law to do the new-entrant-encouraging, buyer-power-regulating, producer-power-building work necessary to brake Big Business's anticompetitive flywheels. The solutions we describe range from adversarial interoperability to minimum wages for creative work to collective ownership and action.

Rather than treating the symptoms of excessive power (and risk baking it in), these tactics cut at the sources of excessive power and offer new defenses against its abuses. And they do so without sacrificing the good things in the current system—like Creative Commons licensing, amateur and commons-based production, and the public domain. The idea is to get at the root of the problem, eliminating excessive power so everyone keeps some money for lunch. In setting out these ideas, we canvass a broad swathe of creative industries. Some of you reading this book will know far more about their specific intricacies than we do and have thoughts about how our proposals might be improved—or even entirely different ideas about how to brake the anticompetitive flywheels that plague them. That's terrific. The ideas we set forth are intended to be the beginning of a conversation, not the end. The best solutions will come from those with the deepest knowledge of each sector's specific chokepoints and those they most intimately affect. So please read this critically. Build on our ideas, or come up with your own, and help change your world.

While our focus is on stopping the shakedown in culture industries, we hope to provide some inspiration for how tools outside of antitrust can be enlisted to deal with chokepoints—particularly those caused by insidious monopsony power—in other fields too. Agricultural workers and delivery drivers and the primary care doctors whose practices have been bought up by private equity firms are all part of the same fight—one that's becoming harder and harder to win. When buyers get too much power, workers are the ones who get hurt worst. Although creative labor markets have some distinctive characteristics thanks to humanity's innate drive to make art, they're not *that* distinctive. All people in straitened circumstances are vulnerable to exploitation because their circumstances make them so. As monopolies and monopsonies suck up ever more money and opportunity, more and more of us are being shaken down. What's been happening in the creative industries presages what's coming for everyone else if chokepoint capitalism is allowed to reign unchecked.

IDEAS LYING AROUND

Transformative change isn't easy. We tend to talk about watershed moments—the US Civil War, the burning of the Reichstag, the collapse of the Berlin Wall, the election of a politician or the passage of a law—as if they were the moments when everything changed. But in retrospect, of course, we see that they were just milestones marking longer-term transformations. The New Deal commemorated a change that had been brewing for more than a century of labor organizing, striking, street fighting, orating, singing, and weeping over the dead. The vision that became the New Deal started off an absurd fantasy, but when the crisis struck, FDR and his advisors found the idea lying around, much-handled and much-debated, and pressed it into service.

No less a person than Milton Friedman—the archduke of neoliberalism—recognized the transformative potential of ideas ready to be used. Friedman began his project to force low wages and unsafe working conditions on 99 percent of the world and shower wealth on the rest at an inhospitable moment. Friedman was pitching his ideas to the second generation of New Deal beneficiaries, trying to convince them that a society where only a few could afford the necessities, experience leisure, and exercise self-determination would be better than the more pluralistic (if still racially and gender-discriminatory) world of FDR's policies.

When Friedman's acolytes bemoaned the impossibility of their task and the irrelevance of their movement, he would comfort them by reminding them that their mission was to create "ideas lying around" that could be picked up and pressed into service when a crisis arose.[13] There will always be crises: even the best-run society is subject to exogenous shocks—pandemics, extreme weather, earthquakes, invasions. When crisis strikes, the order crumbles, and in a flash, ideas lying around can move from the fringe to the center. Naomi Klein calls this idea "the shock doctrine" and describes it as "one of Friedman's most lasting strategic legacies."[14] Monopolists and monopsonists create their own crises as they extract ever more profit and opportunity, which they predictably wield to make things ever better for themselves, until there's not enough left for everyone else.

Forty years of Friedmanism has produced the inevitable. The struggles for racial justice and gender equality are being fought in the streets, exacerbated by the climate emergency and the COVID-19 pandemic. Political processes—regardless of which party controls Congress or the White House—exist to funnel ever more wealth toward the already wealthy, aided in the US by *Citizens United*, a Supreme Court decision that demolished campaign donation restrictions, giving corporations and special interest groups the ability to buy as many politicians as their coffers afford.[15] Corporate monopolies and monopsonies have become so powerful that there's ever less profit and opportunity left for everyone else.

Forty years is a long time. It's been so long since we even aspired to a pluralistic society, a humane nation grounded in care and mutual aid, that the ideas behind such a society sound outrageous. They are outrageous. They're outrageous the way that Friedman's ideas once were.

Cory once helped draft a UN treaty, the Access to Knowledge (A2K) Treaty. Written at a weekend-long meeting at the Médecins Sans Frontières office in Geneva, Switzerland, it called for a bold agenda of universal access to all human knowledge and set out how to make that happen in the international legal framework. But as the assembled representatives from multiple NGOs gathered in MSF's cold basement meeting room that weekend, there was a sense that they were merely fantasizing, dreaming up policies that had no hope of finding their way into law.

Hearing these complaints, the meeting's convenor, James Love, of Knowledge Ecology International, addressed the group: "Not that long ago, a group of people no smarter or better than you met in a room within a kilometer or two of this one; sat down on a weekend like this and drafted the World Trade Organization agreement. If they could change the world, why can't we?"

The Access to Knowledge Treaty never passed in the form in which the group drafted it that weekend, but a section of it became the Marrakesh Treaty to Facilitate Access to Published Works for Persons Who Are Blind, Visually Impaired or Otherwise Print Disabled. The parts of A2K that made it into Marrakesh are important, long-neglected, and have made a transformative difference to the lives of the print-disabled.

You never know what might happen to the ideas you have lying around. Here are some of ours.

CHAPTER 13

TRANSPARENCY RIGHTS

S usan May, a successful speculative fiction writer, could feel in her gut that something was wrong with her Audible sales. She had invested heavily in creating high-quality audiobooks, spending $6,200 on her most recent edition, and the reviews were great. But the sales posted to her daily Audible sales reports were lower than they should have been, and declining. Some days they were actually negative—she would be told she'd sold *minus* one or two copies.

Audible said those negative sales reflected returns. Its publishing platform, ACX (the Audiobook Creation Exchange), is what independent authors like May and small publishers use to get their books to Audible listeners. But ACX reported only net sales—that is, the number of sales after returns, instead of listing sales and returns separately, and Audible stonewalled authors who asked them to break down the figures. May discovered it was pointless to even ask: "They deflect and stall and refuse to connect you to anyone who has any real power to help you. Half the time they don't even answer. Then exhaustion sets in and you give up and go away."[1] The upshot was that nobody knew how many books were actually being sold and returned.

But in October 2020 an ACX reporting glitch saw three weeks of returns processed in a single day. Authors suddenly found themselves dozens or even hundreds of sales into the red, with Audible clawing back royalties for every one. As May puts it, "the veil was lifted." Before this, she'd suspected that perhaps 30 percent of her sales were being canceled out by returns, but the glitch showed her it was more like half. She was stunned, calling it "probably the single worst royalties grab by an Amazon company so far."[2]

It turns out that these independent authors were subsidizing another one of Amazon's anticompetitive flywheels. As we've seen, Audible heavily dominates the audiobook market. It keeps suppliers locked in via its royalty structure, which pays higher rates to those who agree to be exclusive to Audible, combined with a draconian requirement that books stay on the platform for at least seven years (more on this below). They lock in customers with monthly memberships, discounts, and DRM— oh, and an extraordinarily generous exchange policy that gives subscribers a full year to swap titles with the promise of no questions asked. Because this only applies to ongoing monthly subscribers, it's a key tool for keeping customers tied to the platform and paying every month.

In case it didn't occur to subscribers that they might want to return their books, Audible's marketing emails actively encouraged them to do so, even popping up a screen offering the possibility of exchanging them the moment they reached the end. Readers bragged on discussion forums about using Audible in much the same way as they would a library, repeatedly exchanging one title for another. Audible support representatives assured customers it was fine to return as many books as they liked, even if they had enjoyed them, "just because."[3]

Every independent writer who licensed books to Audible via ACX was affected by this scam, as were the narrators who worked on royalty share deals, and sources have confidentially told us that some trade publishers had contracts exposing them to unreasonable royalty clawbacks too. Audible created its returns policy to lock in its customers and keep competitors out of the market, and forced the most atomized and powerless people in the system to subsidize it. It was good for consumers, good for Audible, and disastrous for independent writers. You could not ask for a better example of how the "consumer welfare" test—the idea that we only fight monopolies when consumers suffer as a result of their actions—turns artistic audiences into accomplices to programs that destroy creative workers' lives.

Nobody knows how long Audible was forcing its writers to let people listen to their books for free—at least nobody outside of the Amazon/ Audible complex, where they're keeping mum. It might have been years.

Without that glitch, it would have been even longer, because it's almost impossible to fight an opponent if you don't know what it looks like. By preventing authors and their advocates from understanding what was being done to them, Audible successfully muted resistance.

Once that accidental data dump shone a spotlight into this very dark corner, however, change became possible. May, whose background is in franchising and marketing, began organizing: "I understand legal documents, contracts, how to deal with difficult, international companies, and how to create an organization from scratch. Sometimes, it's not about a negotiation. If they won't play fair, you find other ways to negotiate. Public ways."[4] A pressure group she'd set up when she first suspected something amiss, Fair Deal for Rights Holders and Narrators (FDRHN), ballooned to thousands of members after the glitch unexpectedly gave away the extent of the con.

One member, Colleen Cross, was initially reluctant to get involved: "You know when you're in an abusive relationship and you don't want to acknowledge what's happening? That's what it's like to work with Audible." But when she saw May trying to move mountains all by herself, she jumped in to help. And she was uniquely placed to do so: a former forensic accountant and CFO turned writer of fraud thrillers, she found herself in the midst of just the kind of tangle she's delivered to hundreds of thousands of readers.

Since then, she has spent hours poring over Amazon's financials and writer pay statements trying to figure out how much Audible's policies might have cost independent writers. The more she looked, the more red flags she saw. Audible advertises royalty rates of 40 percent for independent authors who agree to be exclusive to Audible, Amazon, and Apple (helping lock listeners into those platforms), and 25 percent to those who distribute their books "wide" via other platforms too. However, for revenues generated by members' monthly subscriptions (i.e., most revenue), rates are supposed to be based on net sales instead, following a complicated calculation based around total monthly membership revenues.

This should have meant authors received a different amount each month. But Cross noticed they were always being paid the same: just 21 percent of retail for exclusive recordings, and 13 percent for those made available on multiple platforms. That simply wasn't possible if author earnings were being calculated the way the contract said they should be. After weeks of analyzing statements, Cross discovered that Audible seemed not only to be paying independent writers differently from the formula set out in their contract, but also to be charging them *twice* for returns: "You start with net sales (which already has returns taken off it), and then they do it again. That's their strategy in a nutshell: they try to steal margin from everywhere."[5]

Although Audible doesn't invest a penny in creating these audiobooks, Cross estimates its total take from independent authors ends up being an extraordinary 79 to 87 percent of revenue.[6] We asked her how much money the returns policy might have cost the independent sector, and her answer came fast: "Hundreds of millions of dollars for the last couple of years on the returns alone—that's the conservative estimate."[7]

Orna Ross, founder of the Alliance of Independent Authors, told us that, before 2014, Audible had the best terms in the business: "Looking back, it looks like those fantastic terms that were there from inception to 2014 were all about getting people in. Digital audiobook publishing was up and running very quickly, with Amazon controlling the market— that gave them the power to introduce unfavorable terms and practices later on."[8]

Audible has provided various (inconsistent!) explanations for how payments are calculated, but independent authors aren't satisfied. One of May's group's early responses was to try to remove their books from the platform in protest. That drew attention to yet another abusive practice: that Audible's contract with independent writers forced them to keep their books on the platform for at least *seven years* after upload—even though ACX doesn't even contribute to the costs of production! Citing this policy, Audible flatly refused to release nearly all the authors who sought to quit in protest.

That was the final straw. Those independent authors—who must have seemed so powerless when Audible drafted its contracts and hid returns and creamed off its usurious margin—began *really* baying for blood. They were "angry enough to stay involved," May told us. Like so many other workers and suppliers, these writers and narrators had been forced to sign contracts waiving their rights to bring class actions or other litigation as a condition of accessing the platform. But they have found other fronts on which to do battle. They've organized into a tight-knit network that is gathering evidence, recruiting new members, and formulating strategies for getting their share. May describes a "hive brain," closely monitoring Audible and reporting back: "We know when anything happens such as different boilerplate emails coming from Audible customer service or changes in policy or website or behavior by their customer service reps. This way we know how high we are raising the temperature in Audible Executive land."[9] They've mounted far-reaching social media campaigns, marshaled global author rights organizations to their cause, and exposed the issues via wide coverage in the mainstream media. And they've contracted antitrust lawyers to build a case to take to regulators in the US, UK, and Australia as a start to prompt investigations into the company—just as Amazon's unethical treatment of suppliers and crushing of competitors was finally beginning to draw serious scrutiny.

This is the kind of spotlight Amazon's share price–sensitive executives most want to avoid. Thrown on the back foot by the writers' coordinated fury, it offered concessions meant to deflate their movement: committing to making returns data available, promising not to claw back the author's share for books returned after more than seven days, and giving participants a one-time chance to withdraw titles within the seven-year term. But the writers insist that's not good enough. They're demanding no royalty clawbacks on books that have been listened to more than a quarter of the way through, access to historical data to understand how many returns they've been hit with, and compensation for what they've lost from Audible's misuse of their books.

On top of that, they're organizing to decamp altogether. Having looked around and realized that every other dominant platform is charging 45 to 50 percent commissions for just hosting their books and processing payments, they want to create a new author co-op platform with much lower fees that lets them not only more fairly share in the fruits of their labor but offer readers lower prices as well. And the ultimate goal? To be the catalyst that forces an Amazon/Audible breakup.

Audible's writers have a long way to travel before they get justice. But their story so far shows the possibilities that open when light is shone into dark corners. The glitch that accidentally exposed Audible's returns scam transformed atomized exploitation into powerful solidarity, unleashing a furious wave of collective action that's rebalancing power relations between lowly creators and one of the most powerful companies on the planet. May marvels over what they've already been able to achieve: "I was just sitting on my veranda one day and I said to my husband, 'I think we're going to change the publishing world.' If we win, we'll be an example to everyone of what you can actually do when you say 'no, not good enough,' and you follow through and fight."

More transparency elsewhere would do much to help widen out cultural industry chokepoints. Audible is by no means the only one with things to hide. Publishers sometimes screw up their accounting, and authors only find out if they smell a rat and can afford to hire an auditor to figure things out. Even where they do, though, secrecy gets in the way. We know of one example where a big-name author audited their publisher and found a *six-figure* error, but the publisher refused to pay up unless they signed a restrictive NDA. That meant they couldn't let other authors in that stable know about the problem (and why we can't tell you who it was). Professional organizations like the Science Fiction Writers of America conduct random audits on behalf of their members, but only a tiny fraction of books benefit from such treatment.

Publishers also routinely fail to report on whole income categories in the royalty statements they give to authors—like the revenues that are paid by libraries who license ebooks for digital lending. These are licensing revenues, which should be paid out to authors at a much higher rate than sales revenues, but almost never are—a detail that gets obscured when they're not broken out in the statements.

Amazon, for its part, is on record opposing publishers' licensing books to libraries *at all*, claiming it's bad for their sales. But Amazon has an obvious interest in removing libraries from the equation to promote its own sales and subscription services, and it refuses to make available the ebook sales data authors and publishers need to see to evaluate the giant's claims. And don't even get us started on the opacity around Kindle Unlimited, its book subscription service that is once again largely populated with material by independent writers. These writers have been locked in grinding trench warfare with Amazon since the program began, trying to find a way to maximize their revenues: publishing lots of short books, or repetitively long books, or books with hundreds of keywords in the tag fields, and so on. Predictably, the prime beneficiaries of Amazon's opacity about its payments and recommendations are scammers, who can devote endless resources to generating and posting different kinds of word salad junk books that siphon up large amounts of the Kindle

Unlimited payment pool shared out to all participants in the program, scammers and writers alike. Ironically, Amazon justifies the opacity of the program as part of its ongoing war against scammers, endorsing a nonsensical "security through obscurity" model that not only fails to thwart outside predators with their scam "books," but provides cover for Amazon's own accounting scams as well.

And that's just trade books. Netflix doesn't tell composers how often the films their music appears in have been streamed. Streaming music platforms don't publicly report on their per-stream payouts, and individual deals are subject to strict nondisclosure agreements. As a result, only the platforms and the biggest labels have any clue where the billions brought in by music streaming each year actually go. The Future of Music Coalition points out just how ridiculous this is: "Can you imagine having a job where you get an unpredictable paycheck and no one is allowed to tell you how it's calculated?"[10] There is evidence of widespread manipulation of streaming numbers, with *Billboard* suggesting it could be costing artists perhaps $300 million each year.[11] Jay-Z's platform Tidal has been accused of fraud, with forensic investigators at the Norwegian University of Science and Technology finding its data had been manipulated to add hundreds of millions of streams to Kanye's *Life of Pablo* and Beyoncé's *Lemonade*, massively inflating their royalties at the expense of other artists.[12]

Record labels don't report on how much their books are cushioned by "breakage"—revenue unattributable to specific use of catalog, but still paid to them only because they control so many artists' rights. Composers had no idea how much money was sloshing around in unmatched royalties until the streaming services handed over almost *half a billion dollars* to the Music Licensing Collective. This was required under the Music Modernization Act—an important reform we talk more about in our chapter about minimum wages for creative work. Without that, songwriters may never have seen that money at all. There are deep suspicions that YouTube underreports the number of music streams played on its service to avoid having to pay royalties, and it has been accused of paying lower rates to artists not signed to major labels. Is that true? Nobody knows, because they can't access the data to check.

Every chokepoint business knows that restricting access to information is a powerful weapon to wield against workers and suppliers.

Keeping deal terms secret deprives producers of access to information about their treatment relative to others. When you know someone else is getting a better deal, that gives you leverage to demand more yourself. In other words, knowing you are being underpaid is a prerequisite to doing something about it. The International Music Managers Forum understands this power: "We don't just want artists to be paid fairly, we also want them to get the relevant usage data. It is impossible to prove fair remuneration is occurring without transparency. . . . Labels and publishers are our 'partners' but we don't always have the same interests."[13] The UK parliamentary inquiry into the economics of music streaming similarly blames the "systematic lack of transparency from both music companies and the streaming services" for "exacerbat[ing] the inequities of creator remuneration by creating information asymmetries and preventing them from undertaking their right to audit."[14]

The lack of data stymies collective action too. If nobody knows how bad their deal is or their contracts ban them from sharing the details, it's hard to organize to collectively demand better. It's no coincidence that Susan May's activist group took off only after the Audible glitch showed how badly indie writers were being exploited. Artist Molly Crabapple is blunt about opacity's effects: "Not talking about money is a tool of class war. A culture that forbids employees from comparing salaries helps companies pay women and minorities less."[15]

If secrecy makes anticompetitive flywheels turn, transparency can help unwind them. Transparency over revenues, pay, and conditions can empower workers and suppliers to refuse to accept unsustainably low prices, not only by giving them the data they need to negotiate, but by facilitating public shaming. In a world hyper-fixated on stock prices, that's a useful lever for change. We saw how effective shaming was with Susan May's stunning campaign against Audible, but that's far from the only example. Remember when Sony's contract with Spotify was leaked? Artists had been asking their labels to commit to sharing breakage for years, but it was not until that contract provided proof of all the ways deals were being structured to avoid having to share with artists that the two biggest, Sony and UMG, finally gave in (even if the precise terms on which they do so are *still* unacceptably opaque today). The same thing happened when the Science Fiction and Fantasy Writers of America and Alan Dean Foster went public about Disney's ceasing to pay science fiction writers and its radical insistence that it had acquired the rights to their work but not the responsibility to pay for it (we talk more about this shameless heist in chapter 17). This triggered the humiliating public shaming campaign #DisneyMustPay, which finally forced Disney into settling with Foster and some of his fellow writers. When we chip away at the secrecy with which Big Business controls its empires, it's not just that workers and suppliers get leverage to negotiate better deals; markets also become friendlier to new entrants, who get a better idea of what they need to do to compete. That creates alternatives for suppliers and customers who would otherwise be locked in, and *that* has the knock-on effect of making them less susceptible to abuse.

Disclosure requirements are commonly imposed on publicly listed companies to protect shareholders, and, in the US, the Federal Communications Commission, Federal Trade Commission, and Securities and Exchange Commission all already have power to force corporate disclosures. In the same spirit, we should be demanding appropriate divulgement of information to help widen chokepoints out.

The European Union has already taken action on this. In a 2019 directive, it ordered all twenty-seven member states to make sure their authors and performers would receive relevant, comprehensive, and timely information about how their works are being exploited, the revenues they generate, and the remuneration that is due. Creators must also be given the right to demand that information from sublicensees, like the platforms that sell books and stream music and video.[16] Implemented well, such laws would leave far fewer dark spots for businesses to hide their predations.

Laws like this would make it much harder for rapacious corporations, but we could and should take transparency much further. Chokepoint-busting transparency requirements could be designed to protect suppliers and creators all along creative distribution chains. After all, labels don't have the power to make YouTube hand over accurate information any more than artists do. Platforms and rights holders should have new, auditable obligations to publicly report basic information that affects creator outcomes. Suspect YouTube underreports streams? Force it to provide accurate data, with penalties for failure to do so. Record companies and music publishers seem to be maximizing breakage? Make them report how much there was, where it came from, and whether and how it will be distributed among makers—and make those figures auditable by not only individual artists, but organizations representing their collective interests as well. Are we finally ready to demand justice for the recording artists who are still being held to decades-old contracts with pitiful royalty rates? Demand labels publish pseudonymized data showing the range of rates being paid, and how long acts have been paying off their recoupment debts. Disney wants to change the system by which it pays creators for future uses of their content, like streaming? Mandate transparency around the profit pool and how it's shared out and require that to be independently audited too. Shining a spotlight on what's going on is a key way of creating countervailing producer power, putting pressure on companies to do the right thing by artists.

If we're going to make transparency requirements a reality, it helps if opacity really *hurts*. The accounting fraud of the Enron collapse led to the passage of the Sarbanes-Oxley Act, imposing personal, criminal liability for executives who knowingly signed false financial statements. *That* certainly changed the way execs thought about fiddling the books.

In other situations we need information on a more ad hoc basis. One option for extracting it might be to give regulators additional powers to disclose information where it would promote competition within concentrated markets, and demand that they actually exercise the powers they already have. Consider the user-centric payment model that Deezer, a French music streaming app, has been trying, fruitlessly, to introduce for years against the majors' intractable obstruction. By paying out each subscriber's revenue based on what they actually listened to, advocates argue it will increase the rates paid for more complex and sophisticated music—the kind you can't possibly listen to all day on repeat. But we don't know this for sure because the streaming platforms and major labels refuse access to the data that would enable it to be accurately modeled. If such access could be ordered—with appropriate confidentiality safeguards—independent researchers could cast light on the matter once and for all. Once the results of any such analysis were available and being debated in the public sphere, it would move the debate forward—and make it far harder for powerful corporations to defend their chokepoints.

ENFORCEABILITY IS KEY

New transparency rights will only help combat chokepoints to the extent they can be enforced.

In considering whether to act, creators need to factor in the chances of being locked out of future jobs in their professions. Where industries are highly concentrated, as is the case for so many creative markets, that fear is often justified—and it might help explain why various European laws that are supposed to guarantee fair payment have so little effect in practice.[17] One solution is to mandate rights, as the European Union has done with regard to provision of payment data. If the law requires transparent payment data to be provided to everyone, there is no single troublemaker to single out and punish. Another option is to give unions standing to enforce compliance failures, saving any individual from having to put their own neck on the line, or even to give regulators audit powers. Music critic David Turner has argued that "even light government auditing of streaming services could go a long way towards combating the issues of fraud."[18]

Another way of addressing this is by taking measures to normalize transparency. Right now, lots of creators have the technical right to audit their book publisher or record label, but restrictive contracts make those rights all but impossible to enforce. Record labels in particular are notorious for incorporating artist-hostile terms, like prohibitions on using auditors who are already auditing the company (and thus know what to look for), restricting the data they can access (defeating the point!), and preventing artists from sharing what they discover with their colleagues (something we saw happens in the book industry too). Accounts also tend to be highly complex, which works to the advantage of companies who don't want you to understand what's going on. That makes audits expensive (they can easily reach $100,000), putting them out of reach of all but the richest artists.

Accounting errors tend to flow in one direction. One accountant whose firm had conducted thousands of royalty compliance audits, recovering more than $100 million in unpaid royalties over thirty years, recalled just one instance where it was the artist who owed money to the label.[19] Legendary guitarist Nile Rodgers told the UK's economics of streaming inquiry something similar: "Every single time—and I am not making this up for dramatic or comedic purposes—I have audited a label, I have found money. Sometimes it is staggering, the amount of money. That is because of the way the system was designed right from the beginning."[20] But still, because of all the barriers we described above, audits are only rarely used in practice.

If creators had inalienable rights to band together to collectively audit their publishers and labels, it would make it much more affordable and lessen the chance of any one participant being targeted for revenge. They should also have the right to hire auditors on a contingency basis—something that's commonly barred by contracts, but which would help sniff out discrepancies, poor accounting practice, and bad behavior. Auditors must be able to access all relevant data (with appropriate assurances of confidentiality), and contracts that say otherwise should be unenforceable. And, when errors are found, creators should have the right to make them public, which would improve incentives for companies to get it right and further reduce enforcement costs by pointing other creators and auditors in the direction of what to look for.

Making contractual terms unenforceable is a powerful weapon indeed, and it's a measure that in the US can take place at the state (not federal) level, where lawmakers are typically more responsive to voters. Take California, where noncompete agreements are unenforceable "as against public policy." This means that tech workers can abandon companies whose founders turn out to be toxic and found competing companies without worrying about lawsuits from their former employers.

That one legal quirk is the reason California has a tech industry: the first Silicon Valley company, Shockley Semiconductor Laboratory, was founded by the Nobel laureate William Shockley, who invented the method for making semiconductors out of silicon (without Shockley's work, we'd still be using gallium arsenide in our electronics, and "Gallium Arsenide Valley" doesn't have quite the same ring). Shockley established this lab to make the first silicon computer chips, but around the same time he suffered some kind of breakdown and became obsessed with eugenics, touring the nation to debate biologists and spend his Nobel money to subsidize surgical sterilizations of women of color. He also became paranoid and erratic in his personal dealings, wiretapping family members and employees.

Finally, his eight most senior engineers quit in disgust, realizing they would never manage to make a chip while working for Shockley. They founded another company, Fairchild Semiconductor, and then spread out to create a whole bunch more. They included Intel, AMD, and Microchip Technology, to name just some.[21]

The vast majority of entertainment companies are concentrated in just two states: California and New York. Legislation in either or both states about which contractual and audit transparency and accounting practices measures are enforceable in contracts entered into with companies headquartered within those states would be a powerful check on abuses in the creative industries. Throw in Washington State, home to Amazon, and you'd go far toward effecting real change for creative workers. And if such interventions were effective? There would be a strong case for similar protections being rolled out nationally or even worldwide.

The same rights should govern relations between investors and platforms too. Labels should be able to audit YouTube's claims about the number of music streams. Publishers should be able to confirm that Amazon is accurately reporting its sales of ebooks and audiobooks. Such rights would help to normalize transparency. At first it would be the most powerful and best-resourced creators and labels who would find out what's going on. But if they were allowed to share that information, and if accessing it in the first place became easier, that knowledge would filter through to others, and soon enough the big companies who have relied on darkness to maximize their profits would come to accept that now there is light. If everyone came to know what was going on, there would be no point singling out any one of them for punishment.

Enforceability also means managing costs. Litigation can be hugely expensive, especially in countries like the US, where successful litigants usually have to pay their own costs. Even if you win, those fees can eat up all you're awarded in damages, and then some. That's a real barrier to creators and small businesses enforcing their rights, and one that powerful companies use to their advantage. In 2002, a Californian Senate Committee found that record companies force artists to sue so they can settle those lawsuits at a discount.[22] Country music star Merle Haggard experienced this for himself: "[My auditor] catches them cheating me out of hundreds of thousands of dollars and then the company offers to pay me half of what they owe—with no interest. What's wrong with this picture?"[23]

There are plenty of ways around this. The European Union's solution is to ensure that disputes under the transparency obligation may be submitted to a voluntary alternative dispute-resolution procedure. For something like this to work, however, it must only be voluntary for creators and their representatives—not for the behemoth businesses they seek to take on. Another solution could be to force businesses over a certain size to bear the litigation costs in the event of substantial breaches of creator rights, like underpayments of at least 10 percent of the amount that was owing. That would transform those high litigation costs from bug to feature, giving companies a proper incentive to get their numbers right. However, such rules should only apply to dominant corporations. Applying them to small players would make it too risky for any but the most deep-pocketed corporations to participate in the market—another way of baking chokepoints in.

While creators and small business shouldn't be *forced* into expensive litigation, equally, they shouldn't be barred from seeking redress. The independent writers going up against Audible found it hugely difficult to get legal representation because their contracts mandated that disputes be resolved via arbitration, barring class actions. Weighing the costs of going up against a giant like Amazon versus the likely returns from individual mediations, most lawyers simply couldn't take the case, and that's making it much more difficult for them to get justice.

Transparency rights are one of the most promising ways of resisting shakedowns, and of being able to actually enforce the rights that workers and suppliers already have. They're key to unleashing the power of collective action, and to making concentrated markets more welcoming to new entrants. In deciding where to focus reform efforts, creative laborers and their allies could do worse than campaigning for light in dark corners.

CHAPTER 14

COLLECTIVE ACTION

In 2020 and 2021, some sixty thousand drivers, fifteen thousand couriers, and five thousand riders began arbitration against Uber, Postmates, and DoorDash. Arbitration is a kind of private court, but with arbitrators making decisions instead of judges. There are other differences too: the process and outcomes are hidden from public scrutiny, and there are usually caps on the amount that can be recovered and no right of appeal. Unlike a court, an arbitration doesn't produce a precedent, so you can't leverage the victory of someone like you who has already achieved a successful verdict. Two people with identical cases might get different outcomes, and since the whole thing is secret, they probably won't even find out.

Workers use it because they have no choice: a growing number of companies compel their workforces to give up the right to have disputes heard in court as a condition of doing business. Usually, this works out well for big business. Jurisdictions like California require them to pay the costs, which can be around $60,000 per arbitration, but it's proven that arbitrators tend to find in favor of the powerful corporations that pay their invoices.[1] The fact that outcomes are so unfavorable to workers keeps the number of claims low.

But these drivers, couriers, and riders flipped the script. Realizing how their companies had trapped them, they organized to spring the trap in the other direction with a coordinated deluge of claims. At $60,000 apiece, DoorDash's liability in arbitration fees alone would be $300 million—probably far more than they would have had to pay in any class action lawsuit. All three companies found themselves scrambling to get out of this disaster of their own making, ironically begging courts to rule that their workers' mass arbitration claims should not be allowed. Uber ended up settling with most of its drivers for at least $146 million. Postmates and DoorDash were ordered to go ahead with thousands of individual arbitrations they can't afford, putting their vulnerable, low-paid workers in a sudden position of power.

This jujitsu from some of America's most disempowered workers inspired us to think about how creative workers might themselves take better advantage of their collective power to claim a greater share of the value they produce. If we think of collective action as a theory of change, what are the most promising levers that can be pulled, and to which fulcrums should they be applied?

One huge advantage of authors, musicians, screenwriters, and artists is that they are highly visible—collectively, and (the most famous of them at least) individually too. When they speak, the media reports. Starstruck members of Congress pay attention. Dedicated fans amplify their messages. Stock prices tremble. Change can be made—as when recording artists worked together to roll back a change the recording industry had snuck into law to steal away their rights. (Keep reading—we dig into that incredible story in the chapter that comes next!)

But while top creators use their political and media platforms to support any number of important causes (world peace, world hunger, climate, Black Lives Matter) it's less common for them to throw their weight behind improving conditions for their less-advantaged brethren. There are plenty of examples where the interests of famous artists happen to coincide with the less well off, like when Bryan Adams advocated for a new reversion right in Canada, but these have an obvious whiff of self-interest. Maybe that's why so many creators decide not to weigh in at all.

But it's also possible to make the case for reforms that would *only* benefit others, as Taylor Swift did when she made it a condition of that new UMG deal that the label would share its Spotify gains with artists on a non-recouped basis. Before that, it had committed to share, but there was a risk that it would have followed Warner's lead and offset payments against recoupment debts, with the result that few artists would have received even a penny.

Swift has also sometimes been credited with forcing Apple Music to pay royalties to artists for music played during extended unpaid trials, though that reversal is much more likely to have been the result of a much broader coalition of collective action. Labels representing about a quarter of the global recorded music market refused to do further deals with Apple until it reversed its stance.[2] Standing together, *plus* the highly visible additional pressure from Swift, *plus* other artists' speaking out was, cumulatively, enough to get even Apple to back down.

Artists—like all workers—have been subjected to forty years' worth of propaganda about the importance of the individual in economic and political situations: if you get a good contract, it's because you've earned it by producing a catalog that has publishers or labels bending over to please you and by being represented by a cunning and ruthless manager or agent who only takes on the most promising clients. But there's another, countervailing force in artistic lore: the story of the mentor, the person who lifts up others, the musician who starts a label to feature obscure acts or the author who funds an imprint to showcase underappreciated writers.

Everyone who's worked in the arts has wallowed in the toxic stew of comparison, treating some other artist's success as your own failure. We all know, deep down, that comparison is the thief of joy, and celebrating and lifting up other artists isn't just a favor we do for them—it's a kindness to ourselves.

We aren't suggesting that even the most powerful artists could fix the broken system we've described in this book—but they could certainly help. What if fifty of the best-selling authors on the planet politely refused to let Audible host their audiobooks unless it removed DRM? It would be gone in a month. What if two dozen of the biggest composers in TV and movies refused to work with any studio that was requiring its less powerful colleagues to give up their rights to ongoing performance royalties? The practice would be replaced with a more sustainable option before it had a chance to fully take hold. And what if two hundred leading recording artists refused to make their music available on platforms that didn't meet minimum ethical standards and begged their fans to boycott them too? We could quickly see the popularization of fair trade–style certifications like the one created by Fair Trade Music International, which would help make small acts of solidarity easier.

In the US, there's also an urgent need to reform antitrust law's limits on the kinds of private coordination that are permissible. Labor law scholar Sanjukta Paul explains that under current rules, actions that have economically identical outcomes are treated very differently: "Let's say you have a market where there are 100 different truck drivers and five firms of 20 truck drivers each. Each firm sets the prices for the loads that their truck drivers are carrying. And it just seems very obvious that of course the firms set the prices. But [if] 20 of those truck drivers decide to be independent and agree on the prices together, that is going to be prohibited by antitrust law as a price-fixing cartel."[3]

In the EU, by comparison, unions have more power to help atomized individual workers enforce their rights. For example, the recently formed App Drivers and Couriers Union was entitled under the GDPR to help thirteen drivers sue Uber and Ola, demanding that they provide drivers with greater access to data held about them. One purpose of the action was to improve their ability to collectively bargain against the rideshare giants, causing the companies to complain that it was an abuse of the data protection rights. However, the court ruled that that purpose did not disqualify the action and ordered the companies to provide drivers with anonymized ratings by passengers and some other data used to profile and surveil them.[4]

The US rules prohibit smaller companies from banding together to collectively negotiate rights against bigger ones. Remember how much trouble those big publishers got into for colluding with Apple to try and break Amazon's grip on ebooks? If they had been one gargantuan firm instead of a few extremely large ones and made the same decision, it would not have raised an eyebrow. It was irrelevant that their action was motivated by Amazon's ever downward ratcheting of their prices—which meant they had less to pay their workers, authors, and suppliers—or that Amazon might eventually drive them out of business altogether.

Even more limited sharing can make businesses fall afoul of the law. A2IM's President Richard Burgess told us how much independent labels "have to be concerned about breaching antitrust by discussing nonpublic deal terms, or any implication of a boycott, and they cannot collectively negotiate." These rules are supercharged by the lack of transparency in culture industries: with so little information public, and such strict limits on sharing it (even if it's for the purpose of gauging how badly they're getting screwed!), creators and producers are at a ludicrous disadvantage compared to the massive corporations they're forced to deal with. Burgess's frustration is palpable: "Antitrust law has been turned on its head in this country. Where it was designed to protect the little people from gigantic corporations, it now protects gigantic corporations from the little people. We're really in another robber baron era."

Ironically, this drives the very shift toward excessive concentration that antitrust should be trying to prevent. When publishers band together against one big corporate foe to fix prices they are an illegal cartel. But when they merge with one another and then use their own monopoly might to do exactly the same thing, the DOJ looks the other way. Producer integration is actually *forced* by these rules, but that just makes things worse for all the suppliers and workers downstream. Who could possibly want to live in a world that ends up with just one trade publisher battling against a single book retailer? Worse still, what happens when they make peace by merging? This isn't entirely hypothetical: AMC Networks was in bad shape after three rounds of private-equity debt-loading and looting. Then the pandemic hit, even as Disney (unimaginably large thanks to its merger with Fox) set up Disney Plus, a massively popular distribution channel that bypasses theatrical exhibition, meaning that a majority of blockbuster films will now be released into a channel that competes directly with AMC. With AMC at death's door, there's a good chance that it could end up a subsidiary of Disney—or of Universal, which also owns its own streaming service (Peacock) and the largest cable operator in the US (Comcast). Failing that, AMC might end up a division of Time Warner/HBO/AT&T—that is, WarnerMedia. The "synergies" are amazing—and terrifying—to ponder.

We're not saying the price-fixing those publishers engaged in against Amazon should necessarily have been permitted. But one of the most notable things about the deal they struck with Apple was how desperate it was—they colluded to *be paid substantially less* out of fear of where Amazon's dominance was leading. That they reached such a state of desperation is a sign that the balance is seriously out of whack. So long as excessively powerful buyers exist, there should be better mechanisms to promote collective bargaining by weaker ones. Sometimes, anticompetitive conduct can actually have pro-competitive effects.

One solution might be limited protection for producer cartels. Antitrust scholar John Kirkwood doesn't think the publishers' collusion against Amazon was warranted, but the case did get him thinking about the need for antitrust reform. He argued that suppliers *should* be allowed to collude to offset the power of a large customer where that customer has durable and substantial buyer power, where their action is pro-competitive, and where the collusion does not itself create downstream market power of the kind that would harm consumers.[5] Such rules would at least put a ceiling on the abuses smaller firms are obliged to put up with from bigger ones.

As we flagged earlier, US antitrust law similarly stops independent workers from organizing—if those truck drivers were to try to get together and unionize, that would effectively be treated as illegal price fixing too. The laws enacted to distribute power more equally not only affected John D. Rockefeller and J. P. Morgan but also some of the most vulnerable workers in the nation, giving contract labor fewer rights than employees even though their more precarious conditions make them actually need *more*. That's why some parts of the labor movement are so suspicious of antitrust; while it's supposed to promote competition, when it promotes the interests of Big Business over workers it very often has the opposite effect. We would have been much better off if we'd followed economist Joan Robinson's lead right from the beginning and viewed "competition policy as a labor-rights issue."[6]

As we saw in the previous chapter, Susan May and Colleen Cross did an incredible job in their campaign against Amazon's Audible. But they're just two people and a handful of volunteers up against one of the most powerful and ruthless corporations in the world. Imagine how much stronger such campaigns would be if writers organized to combine their influence. Unions are an important tool for creating the kind of countervailing producer power necessary to counterbalance the excessive corporate concentration that leads to chokepoints. We know that because, where creators *are* classified as employees, unions have helped them achieve much better conditions than they could have individually bargained for.

Take the Writers Guild of America, for example. Film and television writers are enormously vulnerable to exploitation: the work is seen as hugely desirable, so there's an inexhaustible supply of people offering their labor, which drives down pay and conditions. Not only that, but screenwriters often have to sell their work before anyone knows what it's worth, which makes it harder still to enjoy a fair share of the proceeds. And many of them work as freelancers, not employees.

That would usually disqualify them from organizing. But studios have always insisted on a high degree of control over their writers. Screen-writer turned scholar Leo Rosten wryly describes what it's like to work as a writer for hire: "He is handed collaborators whom he dislikes. He is ordered to introduce a tap dancer into a story about an African safari. He is asked 'to add a few jokes' to the scene he fought to keep poignant; or to 'speed up the story' at precisely the point where he wanted to develop the characters."[7] Legally, that looks a lot like the kind of control an employer has over an employee. And studios have also long called writers "em-ployees," since that has allowed them to claim that the studios themselves were the authors of the scripts under US copyright law.

Writing under these conditions brought on a great deal of creative despair, but then along came Roosevelt's New Deal, giving employees (but not independent contractors) those strong new labor protections, and Hollywood writers realized the status they had so begrudged was the key to unlocking greater protections for their profession. The studios backpedaled, trying to argue that their writers were freelancers after all, but the control they maintained over their writers doomed that argu-ment.[8] The upshot? Hollywood writers are employees and entitled to all the labor protections—including the right to organize—that flow from that status.

We're told that powerful unions will devastate their industries, but of course that's nonsense. Like other workers, Hollywood writers and directors and actors and so on want to preserve their industry, which means it has to be sustainable for everyone in it. And the TV industry is thriving, all while powerful unions have been collectively negotiat-ing minimum pay and conditions and taking industrial action to protect member interests.

That's not to say there haven't been ferocious battles between capital and labor along the way. One of the biggest began in 2007, when Net-flix pivoted away from DVD rental-by-mail and into online streaming. The Guild, which had no jurisdiction over internet distribution in its existing agreements with studios, quickly recognized the threat. When its contract with producers expired, it demanded members be entitled to a share of digital distribution revenues similar to the residual payments they received via other channels. This issue—coverage over a market that didn't even exist yet in any meaningful form—was the single biggest at the negotiating table.

WGA West president David Goodman told us the studios knew exactly what was at stake and were willing to go to any lengths to retain their advantage: "We knew that if we didn't get it then, we would never get it."

Realizing a strike was the only way forward, writers took their fingers off their keyboards and shut down production on almost every scripted show in the country. It was an enormously stressful and expensive time, with the writers grinding out a hundred straight days on the picket line. But they held their ground and eventually reached a new deal that gave them what they needed. Goodman still marvels over the achievement: "We won. I'm just so impressed with the forethought, the research and the guts it took to do this. And thank God—because 20 percent of our members work in those streaming shows today."

More recently, the WGA has been fighting another huge battle. Earlier, we wrote about how the Big Four Hollywood talent agencies were threatening the viability of writing careers via packaging fees and other conflicts of interest that were diverting money away from their clients and into their own pockets. Although we're in the so-called Golden Age of television, with record profits and an unprecedented number of scripted shows in production, writers' compensation has been in decline even as executives and agents have been getting big raises. Writers were having their pay driven down as a result of being hired on shorter shows with contracts that demanded they remain exclusive for most of the year, preventing them from taking on other shows to make up the difference. Another downward pressure came from the major agencies starting up their own production companies. That meant that when they put shows together, they were increasingly bargaining with *themselves*.

Collective action was the Guild's main tool to turn this around. Recall that in 2019 the WGA adopted a new code of conduct abolishing packaging fees and prohibiting agencies from holding more than a 20 percent stake in any production house, then directed members to terminate relationships with any agents who wouldn't comply. Within days, more than seven thousand writers had done so—including some of the industry's best paid stars, like *Grey's Anatomy* showrunner Krista Vernoff: "I . . . understand that my deal is made, that I am in a position of privilege, and that this action does not hurt me in the short term because I have a lucrative job right now."[9] But she, and others like her, still risked relationships, future jobs and income for a chance at putting the industry on a more sustainable footing.

It took twenty-two months to grind it out, but on February 5, 2021, it was done—all the major talent agencies had agreed to the new code, returning the industry to a commission model for the first time in decades. WME and CAA, the largest and most conflicted, had been the final holdouts. Their business models depended on packaging and in-house production, and with those activities prohibited or curtailed under the new agreement, their private equity owners have much less chance of a successful exit. And yet even they could not withstand the power of Hollywood's writers standing together.

The relief of WGA leadership at finally getting over the line was palpable, with David Goodman saying nobody had wanted the agency campaign win more than him: "The agencies who represent us now have their financial interests aligned with their writer clients, and the agencies' problematic business practices such as packaging fees and agency-owned production entities are at an end." The victory, he emphasized, was owed to the members, "who understood what we were fighting for, and were willing to make personal sacrifices for the greater good. I'm proud and lucky to be one of them."[10]

While the strike was still under way, in 2020, the writers' studio deal came up for renewal. The WGA was able to negotiate new protections over span (the amount of time a writer can be kept on a show without additional payment) and exclusivity, including specific limitations for short-run shows. They did not get everything they wanted, with uncertainty over the COVID-19 production shutdown hampering their ability to negotiate. But they nonetheless managed to plug the drain and claw back some of what their agents had given away.[11]

The WGA is effective because its members believe in their shared mission enough to put relationships and income on the line. As Slack told us, "As a union, solidarity is the only thing you have." That's why they have collectively agreed to punish one another (and accept to be punished themselves) if they depart from the baseline minimum protections that are intended to protect the whole sector. The WGA actively chases down any writers who break their strikes, and those who do risk being shunned or even banned from future projects.[12] The companies they work with know about those protections and consequences, and that puts a floor under pay and conditions. Hollywood's directors and actors band together in much the same way, and with much the same effect.

This kind of enforcement power has to be taken seriously by the other side, making it an effective lever for change. Creator unions that lack the legal protections that accompany the employee status of members (like the recently formed Union of Musicians and Allied Workers) can use tactics like public shaming to try to get companies like Spotify to raise their rates. But without the ability to strike, they have less power to effect meaningful change.

Even with the WGA's power, it is a constant struggle to hold this line. Studios have consolidated just like in every other industry we've looked at. And they've figured out that by banding together (they negotiate collectively as the Alliance of Motion Picture and Television Producers, or AMPTP) they can divide and conquer the various unions that represent different creator interests. In 2020, however, Hollywood's various worker unions—the directors, actors, writers, technicians, teamsters, and those providing basic crafts—themselves combined forces to create an historic agreement with the AMPTP on worker rights during the COVID pandemic, including new quarantine and sick pay and safety measures for their protection. If that solidarity stands, it might herald a new era of these workers combining forces themselves to advocate, even more strongly, for each other's needs.

Labor conditions have changed greatly since Roosevelt's New Deal, but the outdated idea that only employees can organize persists. Sanjukta Paul argues that "we ought to view coordination rights as a public resource, to be allocated and regulated in the public interest rather than for the pursuit of only private ends."[13] If we follow that reasoning, all workers should have the freedom to organize where it's in the public interest for them to do so. That doesn't just mean stopping abusers like Uber from misclassifying what are really employees as independent contractors, but enabling genuine freelancers, like so many creative workers, to band together to create countervailing producer power. Sandeep

Vaheesan of the Open Markets Institute says that giving *all* workers the right to organize is what we need if we're ever "to transfer firm and market governance away from the privileged, mostly white few to the multiracial."[14]

That right won't be given easily. We have to demand it.

While we're currently living through a gilded age that shares many characteristics with the 1920s—rampant inequality, massive market concentration, a political class that is disconnected from the concerns of working people—there are key differences when it comes to labor organizing, for better and for worse.

Some things never change: workers both today and in the 1920s faced the threat of being replaced if they complained. In the Gilded Age, bosses would pit different groups of immigrants against one another, using German Americans to break a Polish American strike, then throwing Italian Americans against the Germans when they walked out. Today, workers can face replacement threats from around the world, with both digital and physical workplaces easy to relocate to low-wage zones with fewer workplace protections. This includes many white-collar workers who previously felt insulated from these realities. But now that the COVID-19 pandemic has demonstrated that many of their jobs can be done remotely via video links, they are beginning to realize that they, too, could be replaced by the lowest bidder, anywhere in the world.

Gilded Age workers turned the tide by creating solidarity between different ethnic groups, recognizing that their different national origins were a trifle compared to their shared economic interests. So far, twenty-first-century workers have struggled to replicate this feat, with Detroit car workers demonizing their Mexican brethren working for the car companies that fled south after NAFTA, and Silicon Valley computer programmers doing the same thing to Indian workers in Bangalore and Pune who took over "their" jobs.

It needn't be that way. While it's true that it's harder to meet up with a replacement worker in person when that worker is halfway around the world, by the same token it's never been easier for scattered workers to communicate, thanks to digital media and digital organizing tools. The gig workers—who are living the future of all workers, if things don't change—pioneered the use of social media groups to compare notes and make common cause, coordinating action around the world.

Of course, even with the *right* to organize, creative workers would still need the *will* to do so. That requires belief that organizing really could achieve better outcomes than what they're getting alone. Screenwriters and directors and actors have this because they have decades of proof. In other sectors, it would have to be built.

Our worker forebears faced violence from thugs working for their bosses: Pinkerton skull-breakers and their mercenary competitors tormented and murdered workers and their families for having the temerity to demand decent working conditions. The Pinkertons are still around, staffed up with ex-NSA, CIA, and FBI creeps, and they're working for Amazon and other Big Tech firms to spy on and neutralize union organizers. Today's worker-organizers don't have to worry (much) about skull-breaking, but the Pinkertons and their digital mercenary competitors will hound them through cyberspace.

That's yet another reason that every artist—and every worker—needs to be concerned about how the internet looks: a centralized internet, instrumented for total surveillance, is a death knell for all justice struggles. But a pluralized, decentralized, human-centric internet is a place where workers everywhere can organize and fight back.

CHAPTER 15

TIME LIMITS ON COPYRIGHT CONTRACTS

L ots of creators end up with terrible deals. Some are so bad they've entered into folklore: like that first Beatles contract, which gave the band a penny per record, from which they had to pay their manager and then split the rest four ways. Jerry Siegel and Joe Shuster sold the Superman rights to Detective Comics in 1938 for just $130—only for it to go on to generate hundreds of millions while they were left destitute. It was not until Siegel took their plight public shortly before the release of the first Superman film that the rights holders were finally shamed into giving them credit for their work, a pension of $20,000 a year, and healthcare. The movie grossed $300 million at the box office.[1]

The worst deals are reserved for people of color. In the 1950s, white recording artists usually received royalties of about 4 percent. Black artists, including Muddy Waters and Bo Diddley, commonly got paid low flat fees and no ongoing royalties at all.[2]

Artists don't take such terrible terms because they want to, but because they have no choice—they're in the same boat as the warehouse, factory, and fast-food workers obliged to sign away legal protections and work under arduous conditions with little security and few benefits for minimum wage because every employer in town is offering the same deal.

The unfairness of artists' deals is made much worse by the fact they literally outlive the artists themselves, since the most powerful record labels and music publishers routinely extract creators' rights for the entire copyright term. Authors can usually get theirs back when books go out of print, but the advent of print-on-demand and digital mean that, for many, there's no such thing: they're stuck in those contracts indefinitely, even if their publisher is no longer promoting or investing in their book.[3] Many contracts do give artists an ongoing right to royalties, but that does no good if the works stop being exploited—which regularly happens, because most copyrights far outlast investors' commercial interests.[4]

Some deals become more unjust over time. The standard 4 percent royalties paid to recording artists in the 1950s became 10 percent for artists signed in the 1980s, and closer to 25 percent for artists signed today. Much popular music, including jazz, R&B, disco, soul, and hip-hop classics, is still being paid at those outdated rates, even though it sells and streams right alongside the newest releases. Worse, many of those artists and their heirs don't actually get a single penny in their bank accounts, because their labels insist they still haven't paid back their recording debts. At a 5 percent royalty, with a $40,000 advance and recording and tour costs of $110,000, a record would have to generate $3 million in revenue before that original $150,000 debt would be erased. But although they've known about the issue for decades, the firms who profit most from that exploitation have mostly failed to do so.

The ability for powerful buyers to take rights for the whole copyright term also contributes mightily to their outsized control over their industries' futures. We saw this most clearly with streaming: in order to get established, Spotify had to get into bed with the major labels, giving them the sweetest deals and biggest freebies. As Liz Pelly reminded us, they also got to decide the terms of engagement: streaming "was shaped *by* the majors *for* the majors." It's bad for progress when corporations whose interests are based on the model of the past can dictate the future. In the words of Audre Lorde, "The master's tools will never dismantle the master's house." Just look at digital photography: invented by a Kodak engineer in the 1970s, it was killed in the egg over the company's fears it would cannibalize the lucrative film business. For the same reason, we shouldn't rely on ExxonMobil and BP to come up with the best solutions to climate change. The biggest beneficiaries of existing ways of doing things will never be interested in curtailing their own power.

The ability to take rights for the entire copyright also gives the biggest players compounding advantages over smaller rivals. As we've seen, three record companies, three music publishers (owned by those same record companies), and five book publishers have industrially aggregated the copyrights of most of the world's most valuable sound recordings, songs, and books. All that backlist generates passive income, which translates into bigger margins than their independent rivals. They use it to lobby for more advantageous regulatory treatment and to outbid competitors on the most lucrative new projects. It also gives them the muscle to negotiate the best deals with distributors. Though all book publishers and record labels have been ground down by Amazon and YouTube, it's the independents that have lost the most: they're the gazelles targeted to bleed out bigger and bigger discounts.

Reining in Amazon and YouTube and their ilk is necessary to fixing the culture industries, but it's not sufficient. If Big Content still has the power to block alternative business models, siphon off value that should have been shared with creative workers, and get an unfair leg up on smaller competitors, too much value will still be transferred from makers to owners. That's a problem time limits on copyright contracts can help solve.

Critics may scoff at this suggestion. After all, such limits have been around in various forms forever, and yet here we are—copyright's buyers have more power than ever. When you look more closely, though, it becomes evident that they have never actually been enacted in a way that would give meaningful power to creators.

The world's first modern copyright law, the 1710 Statute of Anne, gave authors exclusive rights for fourteen years. If they were still alive after that, they got fourteen years more. This dual term system was intended to benefit authors by giving them a chance to sell their works twice. Occasionally it worked: for example, Adam Smith sold the copyright in *The Wealth of Nations* for £300, and his publishers later paid him the same amount again to renew the copyright. But such instances were rare. In practice, most books stopped selling, or the author died, before the first term expired. Book and music sellers also routinely drafted contracts that claimed to extract rights forever, trying to stop authors reclaiming their rights once the first term was up.[5]

Even in the unlikely case where the author survived, and her book was still selling, she understood her rights, and had enough bargaining power to prevent the second term from being wrested away: she *still* might not have benefited from the second term. That's because the most powerful publishers formed a cartel called the Conger to enforce their own system of "tacit" or "honorary" copyright, bullying and shunning other publishers to make sure each publisher maintained control of books they saw as theirs—even after the statutory protection expired.[6] In such a market, even if the author legally owned the copyright, they might have been unable to persuade any competing publisher to print it.[7] As early as 1737, new legislation had been proposed to curb the publishers' power by limiting transfers to ten years apiece, but it never became law. Although the Statute of Anne was supposed to improve the lot of authors, they ended up being paid about the same as before the copyright system was introduced.[8] The real beneficiaries were the most powerful publishers, who kept growing stronger as they accrued ever bigger catalogs of rights.

US copyright law has also included reversion rights from its inception, but they too have been designed in ways that do little to reduce publishers' power. The first US federal copyright law, in 1790, imported the UK's structure of two successive fourteen-year terms, but publishers insisted they could simply use contracts to extract rights to both up front. It was by no means clear that the law actually entitled them to do this, since that would defeat the purpose of authors having a reversionary right at all. However, despite amending the law several times over the next 150 years, Congress failed to resolve the ambiguity—perhaps deterred by substantial pressure from publishers and other investors not to.

The Supreme Court eventually ruled that contracts with creators could indeed take both terms upfront, though separate contracts would be necessary to bind heirs.[9] Subsequently, creators were routinely obliged to sign over not only their own rights, but make their families sign over what would have been their inheritance too. Jay Morgenstern, a former general manager of Warner Chappell Music, recounts one instance that shows just how systematic investors became in capturing these rights, and how seriously they took that mission: "The studio demanded all of the signatures and we were able to comply. [Then] the author died while his wife was expecting. Everybody at the studio went into cardiac arrest thinking that the new heir could renege on the license at reversionary time."[10]

Creators in the US finally won unambiguously inalienable termination rights in the 1976 Copyright Act. However, in the lead-up to their enactment, record companies, movie studios, and music and book publishers fiercely fought every proposal to make these protections meaningful, disingenuously arguing that they were paternalistic and went against freedom of contract. So these rights ended up being neutered too.

Freedom of contract is a key plank of laissez-faire capitalism. It's the idea that people should be able to do what they like without interference from government regulation, including the right to decide whether to contract with one another and the terms on which to do so. In reality of course, we limit contracts all the time. The law won't enforce illegal contracts (like murder for hire or attempts to pay below the minimum wage), impaired ones (where a party wasn't capable of consenting or was tricked into doing so), or unfair restraints of trade. And you'll find that those who insist on the sanctity of freedom of contract when it suits their own interests are quick to change their tune when it doesn't: the very publishers who cited freedom of contract to resist authors getting new rights under the 1976 act were at the very same time trying to secure laws that would let them dictate to retailers the prices at which their books would be sold. Copyright lawyer Irwin Karp pointed this hypocrisy out during industry discussions on the draft termination bill: "Each of us will object to certain interferences and support other interferences, depending on whether we are the owner of the ox who was gored or whether we want to gore somebody else's ox."[11]

That hasn't changed. Rights holders still lobby policymakers to preserve freedom of contract when proposals to protect creators are raised, while railing against it when Amazon and Google and Facebook are the ones getting ahead. Blue-collar workforces see the same double standard when their employers—members of vast industry associations who advocate for their mutual benefit—insist that unionization deprives workers of the right to strike their own bargains with their employers.

Rights holders succeeded in both watering down the author protections that were enacted and making them far more complex. The original proposal had been for a reversion right that would operate automatically, kicking in twenty-five years after the transfer of rights. The eventual law (in 17 US Code § 203, for transfers executed after the law came into effect in 1978) ended up not applying until thirty-five years after any transfer. It also requires creators to follow complex and costly procedures to recover their rights; they risk losing their entitlements if they get it wrong. Rights holders also managed to secure substantial car-veouts preventing the creators of works for hire from terminating them at all. "Works for hire" is defined inclusively to cover those works made by employees as part of their employment, those specially commissioned for use in collective works, and those used as part of films and other au-diovisual works.

These victories weren't enough for the record industry. The record-ing lobby had fought for sound recordings to be listed as one of the works for hire that can't be terminated but had failed to get it onto the list. They could at least make the argument that some albums fell within the cate-gory of "specially commissioned collective works," but they had no way of preventing artists from reclaiming their rights to singles, which were often the most valuable songs. In order to do so, record label lobbyists would have to get the law changed to expressly include sound recordings as a category of work for hire.

They attempted to do so for years without success. So, incredibly, they decided to steal those rights instead. In 1999, a congressional staffer surreptitiously inserted four little words into the unrelated Satellite Home Viewer Improvement Act, which had the effect of adding sound recordings to the Copyright Act's list of works for hire. There were no hearings or publicity around the last-minute change. The bill became the appendix of a mammoth, thousand-page appropriations bill, which was passed and then signed into law. Only then did the alteration come to light. An investigation discovered that it had not been sought by any member of Congress but was instead made at the behest of the Record-ing Industry Association of America (RIAA)—a lobby group represent-ing the biggest record labels.

The register of copyrights at the time, Marybeth Peters, decried the amendment for having come "in the middle of the night" and "without any input from performers." The RIAA played innocent, insisting that the change was a mere "technical amendment." US law permits techni-cal amendments to statutes to bypass some of usual lawmaking processes, but this is limited to fixing obvious mistakes like typos   not changing the substance of what Congress has deliberately decided. Hilary Rosen, the RIAA's then-president and CEO, who later went on to be a signif-icant Democratic Party operative and political director at the *Huffing-ton Post*, falsely claimed that "in everybody's view this was a technical issue," because "record companies have long registered recordings with the Copyright Office as works-for-hire." As one legal writer caustically retorted, "Rosen's idea of 'everybody' . . . must not include the artists, their attorneys, Intellectual Property professors and authors, top officials at the Copyright Office, or the courts for that matter, because all believe differently."[12] Adding to the stink around the surreptitious dead-of-night maneuver, the congressional staffer who had clandestinely slipped in the amendment, Mitch Glazier, was hired by the RIAA just a few months later. He is now its chair and CEO.

Although the RIAA's sneaky change should never have happened, it still became law. This was a huge blow to musicians' interests. Labels had already been aggressively using the "specially commissioned collective works" category to try to prevent artists from reclaiming rights to albums. With the stolen amendment, those claims suddenly became much stronger, and labels finally had a way of preventing artists from even reclaiming rights to singles. After being hollowed out by rights-holder opposition from the get-go, this heist swept away the final vestiges of benefit the termination law had intended for recording artists.

But it didn't stay that way. When the theft came to light, artists erupted with a collective fury, organizing like never before. The RIAA tried to brazen it out, but after almost a year of fierce, coordinated lobbying, artists finally succeeded in having the amendment rolled back. Today, creators are still excluded from reclaiming their rights over the enumerated categories of works made for hire. But thanks to the dogged efforts of leading stars in fighting against the RIAA's maneuver, the category of sound recordings isn't one of them.

Despite that victory, the US termination law, at least as currently drafted, poses little threat to the power of Big Content. The law's complexity makes termination expensive and time consuming, and, as a result, very few creators actually use it. Rebecca (with Joshua Yuvaraj, Daniel Russo-Batterham, and Genevieve Grant) investigated just how many, finding that in the eight years since the first transfers under USC § 203 became terminable, just sixteen thousand performing arts works have been subject to termination notices (mostly songs), fewer than ten thousand sound recordings, and just eight hundred books.[13] That's a tiny fraction of the works that are actually covered by copyright.

The paucity of book terminations is particularly striking. Just ten authors (including Francine Pascal, Debbie Macomber, Nora Roberts, Stephen King, Ann M. Martin, and Piers Anthony) are responsible for about 70 percent of the total terminations. Pascal alone, with her vast catalog of *Sweet Valley* titles, terminated over three hundred.[14]

Another reason the US termination law is used so little may be because it takes so long to kick in. Rebecca (with Jacob Flynn and François Petitjean) published another study in 2019, this time investigating the availability of older, culturally important, English-language books across the US, Canada, Australia, and New Zealand. This investigation found that many important books were unavailable for libraries to access, suggesting that copyright terms—even for culturally enduring works—can far outlast their commercial lifespans.[15] Such findings suggest that thirty-five years for the right to terminate may well be too long for creators to wait.

Record companies continue to resist even the eviscerated version of the termination law. The majors have made it clear all along that they would "not relinquish recordings they consider their property without a fight," claiming that "the termination right doesn't apply to most sound recordings." While their ploy to add sound recordings to the Copyright Act ultimately failed, they still claim albums are "specially commissioned collective works" or alternatively "compilations" and thus works for hire anyway.[16]

This claim has still never been authoritatively tested, and the lingering uncertainty about whether it would succeed makes it risky and expensive for recording artists to assert their rights. Where big-name stars attempt it—that is, those with sufficiently deep pockets to see the process through—their claims have been settled out of court, which means there end up being no precedents to help those with less money or power. It also means they might have to settle for less than they're owed. When the termination window opened for Prince's first albums with archnemesis Warner, it was announced that he would regain that long-coveted ownership of his catalog—but with strings attached. In exchange, he agreed to return to the label, issue a new album, and authorize *Purple Rain*'s rerelease. If creators' rights under the termination law were clearer, they could be exercised without the need for any such quid pro quos.

Class actions are currently under way to clarify these claims, but they're still far from being resolved—and have plenty of hurdles still to leap. Sony and UMG are fighting them with all the firepower they can muster—including by counterclaiming that the artists who believe they have terminated lawfully are in fact liable for copyright infringement for selling "pirate" versions on their own websites, and even accusing artists of copyright violation because their attorneys used their own album artwork to recruit others to the litigation.[17]

These rights certainly have helped some artists: like the creators of iconic cult film *This Is Spinal Tap*, who used the law to win back exclusive global rights. Overwhelmingly, though, the US termination rights have not lived up to their potential for reclaiming lost culture and getting creators paid.

Time limits also exist elsewhere, but they're unsatisfactory too. One of the most interesting is a 1911 UK law, exported throughout the Commonwealth, that auto-reverted copyrights to authors' heirs twenty-five years after death. It's still on the books in Canada and one or two other former British colonies, but has been repealed for spurious reasons elsewhere.[18] It was most prominently applied to South African composer Solomon Linda's "The Lion Sleeps Tonight"—"the most famous melody ever to emerge from Africa"—which you probably know from Disney's *The Lion King* or one of the other 170 recordings made by artists including American folk singer Pete Seeger and the doo-wop group the Tokens.[19] Linda had been obliged to transfer the rights for almost nothing. His daughters saw almost none of the proceeds, and, while his song was making millions for Western corporations, they were living in shacks and working as domestic laborers. But then it was discovered that under the old British imperial law, the copyright had automatically reverted to them—and Disney's use was therefore infringing. Disney initially resisted paying up, but after Linda's daughters secured a dramatic ruling attaching its lucrative trademarks in South Africa, a settlement was reached. The exact details aren't public, but it's believed to include compensation for past uses of the song, plus provision for future royalties. Like the US law, however, this old imperial copyright law is inadequate. In most cases, it kicks in too late to have much impact: often sixty or seventy years after the work first hit the market. Since few works still have any value that long after release, the law has little effect in practice. And because it has little effect, few people know about it—even in Canada, where it still operates. That includes rights holders, who often continue as if they still own copyrights that have actually transferred to someone else.

Placing time limits on copyright transfers like those we've talked about here can certainly help achieve justice in individual cases. But if we want them to have the kind of structural impacts that will curb excessive buyer power, we need to take a more radical approach.

We're not the only ones thinking about this. Policymakers have begun understanding reversion's broad potential for helping creators get paid and culture get accessed, and it's becoming a hot topic in copyright. The UK parliamentary inquiry into the economics of music streaming recommended that creators be given a new right to recapture works after twenty years.[20] Similarly, Canadian lawmakers are currently considering a recommendation to create a new reversion right that kicks in a flat twenty-five years after transfer (in addition to their existing law, which would still apply twenty-five years after the author's death). Unfortunately, though, early signs suggest the new Canadian right might import many of the US version's shortcomings, including complex "formalities" (the copyright lawyer's term-of-art for "red tape") for reclaiming rights.

South Africa came close to implementing a much more radical reversion right as part of its new Copyright Act in 2019: it would have seen copyrights automatically revert twenty-five years after transfer. It was derailed, however, when President Cyril Ramaphosa declined to sign the new act into law. That derailment was largely spurred by deplorable interference from US officials and corporations who were trying to prevent the nation from introducing a fair use exception—something that already exists in the US, and which was sorely needed to help address access problems faced by South Africa's struggling schools, universities, and libraries.

In the case of the proposed reversion law, however, the halt was also motivated by concerns that automatic reversion could increase the number of orphan works—works that are still in copyright but whose owners are unknown. This was more warranted. Automatic reversion, particularly to people who might not know they now held the rights or what they might do with them—and who might be difficult to find— would indeed be less than ideal. Instead of returning those works to their creators, orphaning them could remove them from culture altogether, since no one could reproduce them until their copyrights expired, which could be decades. Any automatic reversion system needs safeguards in place to ensure that it doesn't cause new problems in its wake.

So what could we do instead? If we were to dream big and envisage a time-based reversion law that could make a meaningful difference to the ability of creative workers to share in the fruits of their labors, to promote access, and to maintain incentives to invest in creative content, what might it look like?

Here's one radical possibility. Start by automatically boomeranging rights over books, music, sound recordings, and visual art back to creators twenty-five years after transfer. Those creators could then re-exploit them however they wished—including by licensing right back to the original investor ("Okay, Universal, you can still publish this but I want my recording debt wiped clear so I start actually receiving royalties"). Alternatively, they might choose to license it to an investor using a different business model ("What's that, Spotify? You'll pay me more than Universal? Yes please!"), or even keep hold of the rights and exploit it themselves ("Hello, Bandcamp? How do I set up a seller account?"). If the parties wanted to invest more and there wasn't long enough left on the contract to make it worth their while (say, they wanted to make a movie, but there were only three years left to run on the film rights transfer) they could mutually agree to end the deal and enter into a new one for twenty-five years more.

We propose twenty-five years because that would maintain incentives to invest in the initial production and distribution of knowledge and culture. Every economist that seriously considered this question has found twenty-five years of exclusive rights is more than ample to incentivize even the most lavish investments in producing content and bringing it to market.[21] Additional years beyond that add little to investors' decisions whether to invest *today*. In large part, that's because of "the time value of money": the fact that, the further away in time a benefit will be received, the less it is currently worth.

We all intuitively grasp this concept. Imagine you're interviewing potential housemates: both offering the same amount in rent, but one promising to pay weekly in advance, and the other ten years after they move out. The dollar amount is the same, but one is worth more than the other. For the same reason, rights that might generate income far in the future have little additional incentive value *at the time an investor decides to invest*. And the fact that most books, songs, movies, and sound recordings depreciate quickly makes the current value of those future rights less still.[22]

Thus, reversion after twenty-five years would maintain the incentives necessary to get works produced in the first place. That isn't changed by the speculative nature of copyright investment. It's true that investors will typically invest in a number of works, expecting that some will make losses and others will generate profit enough to make the whole enterprise worthwhile. But since the vast majority of most of those works' commercial value is still typically extracted soon after release, the calculus doesn't change. That's why new record labels, movie studios, and book and music publishers can start up and make money even without the big backlists enjoyed by their bigger and older competitors. Naturally, investors *want* to hold the lottery ticket that turns out to win the jackpot, but they don't actually *need it* to incentivize their investments.

For time limits on copyright contracts to achieve the kind of structural change necessary to make a meaningful difference, it's crucial that reversion be automatic. That's the only way to get enough rights regularly coming back onto the market to genuinely change the power dynamics at play. Take a moment to imagine how automatic reversion twenty-five years after transfer would change the recorded music market. For one thing, there'd be fewer unfair contracts. If rights reverted to creators every twenty-five years, the artists who were signed to those 4 percent royalties in the 1950s would have been able to secure 10 percent rates by the 1980s, and then 20 or 25 percent rates in the 2000s.

That would mean the biggest labels would get less of a profit edge from their backlists than they do today, meaning less to spend on rent-seeking. It would also give newer competitors an opportunity to compete for that older catalog. Artists could choose companies offering fresh marketing investments, new exploitation opportunities, or higher royalties instead of just being stuck with the company that happened to sign them decades earlier (or more likely—a giant who swallowed up their original label). New creator-friendly business models would have more scope to emerge, since, if rights were guaranteed to be regularly coming onto the market, the legacy players would have less ability to steer the industry away from structures that could threaten their interests.

But of course, automatic reversion could create its own problems: particularly around orphan works, as we saw with the South African fight. Safeguards—like registration, so we know who owns what—would be needed to prevent this. International copyright treaties limit individual countries' lawmaking power in this space (starting with the Berne Convention in 1948), but it is possible to navigate those rules in a way that gives us most of what we need. For example, we could require that all copyright transfers and exclusive licenses be registered, which would make it clear who owns them and when those transfers end. After all, as the RIAA reminded us during the bitter fights over the scope of the US termination right, they routinely register copyrights on albums and songs anyway. On top of that, each country could ask its own local authors to register their ongoing interest in *all* works once those works reach, say, twenty-five years of age. That would result in a central register along the lines of the one that governs domain names, from which potential licensees could easily locate owners to negotiate access.

What about all those local works whose owners don't indicate their ongoing interest? We'd propose that all works that are more than twenty-five years old but don't appear in the registry—every abandoned book, song, sound recording, painting, sculpture, drawing, photo, computer program, and so on—be looked after by a cultural steward, tasked with preserving them, licensing them, and promoting access.

It would be crucial to get the governance of this right. But there are *tons* of uses to which those works could be put if it were all properly managed. They could be bulk-licensed to universities and schools and cultural spaces. Books could be made part of a digital public library. Galleries and museums could create new online collections to shine new light on the shared human experience and challenges we all face. Existing works could be licensed by creators for remixing into new ones. And of course if a creator at any point wanted to reclaim a work they'd previously left unregistered, they could do so, and even be entitled to the revenues their works had generated during their orphanhoods. Some of the orphan money should also go to tracking down missing creators and getting them paid.

All this would open up tremendous new investment opportunities for smaller players. Letting investors take rights for the entire term of copyright, even if they soon stop making the work available, is tremendously wasteful. Study after study has demonstrated that works under copyright are less available and receive less investment than similar ones in the public domain. One study by Paul Heald, a professor at the University of Illinois, examined the availability of books by age on Amazon and found availability drops sharply soon after release and then spikes again as they enter the public domain. Remarkably, more books originally published in the 1880s were available than books originally published in the 1980s.[23] Another study, by Rebecca with collaborators Jacob Flynn and François Petitjean, looked at the relative availability and price of important English-language books in the United States and Australia (where they were under copyright for life plus seventy years) compared to Canada and New Zealand (where copyright was life plus fifty). The data showed that books were much less available and much more expensive in the countries with the longer terms (and that those higher prices far exceeded the additional amount that was payable to authors of in-copyright works).[24]

The widespread problem of orphan works further demonstrates that, just because someone holds the rights, it doesn't mean that they'll exploit them. Rather than improving availability then, long copyright grants can actually stand in its way.

You wouldn't buy a car at a price that factored in a century of ongoing maintenance without any obligation for the seller to actually provide it. But we're effectively doing just that when we let investors take copyrights for the whole term without any obligation to continue making those works available to the public. Under the alternative we've sketched here, we'd pay by instalments instead. Returning rights to creators twenty-five years after transfer (or to a cultural steward if the creator no longer has any ongoing interest in them) would free works up for new investments, new opportunities, and new access.

In our vision, creators would benefit not just from being able to negotiate new contracts and find new partnerships to make their work available on an ongoing basis, but also from those neglected works that end up under the care of the cultural steward. We would propose that all licensing revenue generated from cultural works whose owners were no longer interested would go directly toward supporting creators via fellowships, grants, pensions, and prizes, as well as tracking down creators whose works were experiencing a renaissance under the scheme. In other words, our proposal is to generate new revenue for creators by reclaiming culture that is currently lost. It would take advantage of copyright's non–zero sum nature to make the pie bigger. That would, in turn, help those creators make more of the stuff we love—and more fairly reward them for their contributions to knowledge and culture.

It would be vital to get the governance right. Collecting societies can easily get addicted to collecting and forget the social and cultural aims they are intended to serve (we talk more about this in the chapter that follows). The license arrangements would need to be calibrated carefully too. It would sometimes be appropriate to zero-rate licensing fees, for example in the case of noncommercial uses by public-serving institutions like libraries and archives. That would facilitate a rich range of public interest activities that wouldn't otherwise be possible, while simultaneously opening up a vast number of new paid uses.

Big copyright buyers will tell you that, if rights reverted after twenty-five years, the system of cultural production would collapse because they could no longer reinvest their windfall profits into producing more works. But that's just the same debunked trickle-down economics that oligarchs always insist really is true . . . *this time*. In the model we've sketched, the money would still be there—just allocated a bit differently from how it is now. So long as they have access to cash or capital markets, copyright buyers will continue funding the investments they think will make a profit and continue rejecting those they think will flop. If anything, *more* new works would be produced, because this system would deliver more of the proceeds from existing works into the hands of the individual creators and independent producers who actually need it to fund new production. If you want to dig further into the detail of this proposal, and especially if you're enough of a copyright wonk to wonder about its compatibility with international treaties, check out Rebecca's work in *A New Copyright Bargain*.[25]

While we're talking about reversion, we'd also urge careful consideration of use-it-or-lose-it rights. Returning rights to creators after twenty-five years would fix many of our current problems, but too often, investors stop making works available long before that. Book publishing contracts routinely contain clauses allowing authors to reclaim rights after their books go out of print, but these sections are often outdated, ambiguous, or missing altogether.[26]

Other artists don't even have that. Recording artists sometimes have their albums "shelved," with record labels refusing to release them, rarely leaving artists any way of doing anything about it unless an alternative release label steps up to fund the recording. Jane Weaver found herself in this situation in the 1990s: "Sorry, the album you've been working on for months isn't happening. We're shelving you and you can't release it anywhere else unless they pay out a load of money for the recording."[27] Rights holders aren't concerned about scooping up dolphins in their tuna nets—they insist on taking broad rights just in case this is the Next Big Thing, even though it's almost always not. But locking culture up without using it is another way of avoiding competition. The EU's 2019 Copyright Directive requires member states to implement laws giving authors and performers the right to revoke their transfers of rights where there has been a lack of exploitation.[28] Countries elsewhere should consider following suit.

You can readily imagine how much more hospitable a world with time-limited contracts would be to creative workers. The biggest buyers wouldn't be able to count on forever having passive income from their backlists or catalog, because if they didn't treat their creators well, they'd risk losing them to competitors. New business models would find it easier to emerge. There would be less freedom to strong-arm creators into unfair deals, and less freedom to avoid fixing outdated or unfair terms. And there would be more *genuine* freedom of contract, with the freeing up of rights creating more options for creators and independent producers.

CHAPTER 16

RADICAL INTEROPERABILITY

Physical lock-in is easy to understand. In Australia, a combination of would-be nineteenth-century robber barons and chaotic governance among the then-independent Australian states resulted in the "middle-gauge muddle": regional rail systems chose different track-widths, which means that, even today, you can't get a single train all the way across the country. Instead, its freight or passengers have to be unloaded at the intersection of each rail system and reloaded onto a train that's compatible with the next segment of rail.

The middle-gauge muddle has proven nearly impossible to undo. Over some 150 years, hundreds of designs for multitrack railcars have been tried and discarded, as the mechanical complexity of retracting one set of wheels and dropping another has frustrated all efforts to engineer a reliable, low-cost system. In the end, Australia "solved" this problem by embarking on a decades-long project to tear up thousands of kilometers of rails and replace them with standard gauges.

But *digital* lock-in is an entirely different matter. Digital computers are possessed of a nearly mystical property of universality: all of them can run every formally correct program. The very earliest digital computers can run the same programs as your laptop (albeit those early monsters might take billions of years to complete the work your laptop does in an eyeblink). Your smart coffee maker can run the same programs as your printer, which can run the same programs as the processor in your Wi-Fi router, which can run the same programs as the processor in a five-dollar no-name Chinese "TV playback device," the size of a pack of gum, for sale at your local flea market (albeit at very different speeds).

This universality explains the rapid expansion of digital technology into our lives. The research and development that goes into improving a particle accelerator's computer ends up benefiting all kinds of computing, bequeathing improvements in power, reliability, and cost to the processors in your car, HVAC system, and mobile phone. Digital technology gets faster and better and cheaper because everything we do to solve problems in one corner of the digital world makes things better everywhere else.

But this universality can also be a curse. We know how to make universal computers—computers that are Turing complete, a concept named for the British wartime computer science pioneer Alan Turing—but we don't know how to make *almost*-universal computers. It's easy to make a train track that only supports one kind of railcar: it's *impossible* to make a phone that only runs apps from one app store.

When you encounter a digital product that has a restriction like this—a video service that won't let you access its streams without logging in or using its app, an ebook that only plays on one kind of reader or an ebook reader than only displays one kind of ebook, a gaming console that only plays games that were approved by its manufacturer, or even a coffee-pod machine that rejects third-party pods—you're not dealing with a computer that *can't* do what you've asked of it. You're dealing with a computer that *won't* do it.

That computer was programmed to check whether its owner was doing something that the manufacturer disliked, and, when necessary, defend the manufacturer's shareholders by disobeying its owner. This is a powerful weapon for would-be monopolists. Imagine if you could lay tracks of the same width all across the country but program the tracks to refuse to carry railcars unless they'd paid you rent for the privilege of rolling down your rails.

But there's a problem with this: the program responsible for this refusal—a restriction built into the low-level firmware or BIOS, or into higher-level systems like operating systems and apps—is running on a universal computer. It can be replaced, rewritten, or fooled. Computers are universal, stubbornly so, and that makes this kind of lock-in transcendentally technically complex.

For example, take the problem of virtual machines (VMs). All computers can run all programs. "All programs" includes "a software program that pretends to be a hardware computer." You've probably seen retro video game systems that play old games that were designed for obsolete hardware that hasn't been sold in decades. These retro systems often run VMs, which are programs that pretend to be the processors and input and output of those long-extinct arcade systems and home game consoles. As far as the game can tell, it's running on an old ColecoVision or stand-up arcade system from the 1980s. But it's not; it's running in a VM, like a brain in the Matrix, trapped in a simulation it can't detect or break free from.

VMs pose serious problems to digital monopolists. Consider how VMs interact with "streaming." We put streaming in scare-quotes because streaming is a consensus hallucination. There is no such thing as a video stream (as distinct from a "video download"). If there's a video stored somewhere on the internet and you want to watch it on your computer, you have to download that video to your computer. Every video you've ever streamed is a video that you downloaded.

When Netflix or Spotify claim that they're letting you "stream" a video but not "download" it, what they actually mean is, "We scrambled this file and we gave the descrambling keys to a program we trust. It is designed to throw away the file after it is descrambled, so you'll have to re-download it if you want to hear or watch it again."

These streaming programs (apps or browser modules) take all kinds of precautions to ensure that their user isn't saving the video for later playback or sharing. But all of these measures ultimately depend on asking the computer they're running on about how it's configured: "What operating system are you running? Are you running any video-capture programs?" Many operating systems are designed to faithfully answer these questions, even if the owner of the computer they're running on would rather they didn't. But the operating system, too, depends on the computer's being a faithful reporter of its own technical characteristics and configurations.

What if the computer isn't actually a computer? What if it's a program pretending to be a computer, running inside *another* computer, this one more responsive to its owner and happy to falsify the answers to questions like, "Is there any video-capture software running right now?"

Universality is the downfall of anyone hoping to wield a computer against its owner. A savvy computer owner can always trick the programs they run, which is a good thing if we want them to take orders from us (instead of giving *us* orders). VMs aren't just how people rip Netflix streams, they're also how computer virus researchers safely study malicious software, trapping it inside virtual machines they can slow down or stop at various points in the virus's execution cycle, examining its memory and instructions in detail to unravel the virus's techniques and methods for attacking its prey.

This foundational, flexible character of computers has bedeviled the entertainment industry's attempts to control media use since the earliest days of consumer digital technology. It turns out that if a computer owner does not acknowledge the legitimacy of a digital control, then the digital control will fail. It's simply too easy to make tools to bypass and defeat it.

As we saw earlier, though, the tech and entertainment industries hit on a solution to this conundrum in the dying days of the last millennium: to simply make it illegal to bypass a digital lock. Starting with Section 1201 of the US Digital Millennium Copyright Act, the world's governments adopted rules that felonize distributing tools to bypass digital locks. Sometimes these laws are framed so expansively they even criminalize disclosures of how those locks work, and what their flaws are.

These laws are said to be about protecting copyright, but in the US and many other countries, they prohibit circumvention even when no infringement occurs. They're what lets printer companies charge more per liter for ink than Chanel does for perfume.[1] HP doesn't make its profits by selling the best ink at the best price, but by rigging the system: buying out all its competitors until it dominated the industry and then jacking up prices on consumables while relying on laws that were designed to address very different problems to keep cheaper alternatives off the market.

Anti-circumvention laws also deliver Apple and Google their stranglehold over app and game developers.

If we write an app for your phone, and you want to buy it from us, the creators, instead of via Apple's official store, Apple won't let you. And we can't give you a tool to force your phone to run our official, licensed, paid-for app, because that tool would bypass the locks that keep your phone tethered to the official app store operated by its man-ufacturer. It's incredible but true. As we noted in a previous chapter, Apple can and does use a copyright law to make it a crime for a creator to sell their copyrighted works to an iPhone owner without Apple's permission. You own the phone, an independent developer made the app, and individual creators made the content, but the DMCA makes it a crime for you to buy those works without Apple being in the loop, which is what enables them to extract a whopping cut of the revenue from news, music, and book publishers, record labels, and other sellers of creative work.

The anticircumvention law is not the only way tech and entertain-ment giants lock in suppliers and customers and lock out competitors—it's just one of a whole bestiary of similar laws that each help preserve corpo-rate chokepoints. In the US, one is the Computer Fraud and Abuse Act (CFAA).[2] This Reagan-era cybersecurity law has been distorted through high-priced cases brought by the likes of Facebook, which has argued that violating its terms and conditions should be viewed as a criminal act of hacking. Then there's noncompete agreements, which lock up tech workers who might defect from a controlling company to a liberating one; trade secrecy, which lets companies sue rivals that rely on "secrets" to make compatible products; and binding arbitration, which deprives customers and suppliers of a day in court to object to these practices. New dirty tricks are also always on the horizon: *Oracle v. Google* was a bizarre copyright case that threatened to make it illegal to make a new product that can use the apps or commands from an existing one—like a non-Android phone that can run Android apps, or even a smart TV that can understand commands from any of the remotes you already own. Thankfully, after more than a decade of litigation, the Supreme Court eventually knocked this claim out on its head.[3]

All these tools are used to lock in customers and suppliers, and ulti-mately contribute to creative workers getting such a small share.

The Big Tech companies (and in many cases Big Content, which are allied with them on this issue) argue these measures are reasonable. After all, don't the companies already use industry standards to make it easy for users to enjoy their devices? Your Chromecast and your Fire Stick and your Roku will all plug into your TV's HDCP interface, and your Mac and PC can both run Chrome or Firefox and access all the same sites.

Standards work, and the managed interoperability they represent delivers real dividends to consumers and industry alike.

But this focus on voluntary interoperability erases a far more significant type of interop: the "adversarial interoperability" of plugging something into an existing product or service against the wishes of the company that made it.

When you buy a third-party ink cartridge, you're practicing adversarial interoperability: doing something to your own printer that its manufacturer is opposed to. Some companies allow their customers and suppliers to have some interop that doesn't harm their bottom lines. But if that's all we're allowed, we enter a bizarre world where everything not forbidden is mandatory, and our priorities are sidelined in favor of manufacturers and their shareholders.

The last half century of technology shows how disruptive radical interoperability can be to chokepoints. IBM, whose abusive monopolistic practices had mired it in a twelve-year US antitrust investigation, was not able to make its own PC operating system because of fears of further antitrust investigations, and instead turned to an unknown startup called Microsoft to make DOS and then Windows. But IBM didn't just lose control over the software that ran on its machines—it lost control over the machines themselves! A tiny startup called Phoenix Computers hired a hardware virtuoso named Tom Jennings to reverse-engineer the IBM PC ROMs—the chips that gave IBM's machines their distinctive technical capabilities—and then cloned those chips, selling them to yet more startups with names like Compaq, Dell, and Gateway, who quickly eclipsed IBM's PC business with their PC clones.

Meanwhile, Microsoft quickly grew to monopolistic stature and started to put its rivals out of business, leveraging its dominance over different parts of the market to squeeze competition. Microsoft launched its Excel spreadsheet in a market dominated by the industry standard, a spreadsheet program called Lotus 1-2-3. Each version of DOS was subtly tweaked to favor Excel over Lotus, and the company's unofficial motto was "DOS isn't done until Lotus won't run."[4]

But Microsoft, too, fell victim to adversarial interoperability. The company incorporated Excel into the Microsoft Office suite—Word, Excel, and PowerPoint—and used these to put the squeeze on Macintosh computers. Microsoft's Mac versions of Office were farcically unreliable, unable to consistently read the files created by users of the Windows versions of these programs, prone to crashing and irretrievably corrupting their users' files.

It got so bad that the sole designer in an engineering shop would grow ever more isolated from their Windows-using colleagues, unable to exchange Mac files with them and vice versa, to the point where the superior graphics performance of the Mac didn't outweigh the workflow liabilities created by endless hassles of exchanging documents.

Apple's answer? Adversarial interoperability. The company reverse-engineered the Microsoft Office file formats and launched a rival productivity suite (iWork), whose Pages, Numbers, and Keynote could perfectly read and write the files created by Windows users. In one stroke, Microsoft's walled garden was transformed into an all-you-can-eat buffet for Apple, which launched its aggressive "Switch" campaign to inform Windows users that they no longer had to choose between a superior operating system and access to the files they and their colleagues had spent decades creating. All of this was only possible because Microsoft had originated the Office suite without any DRM (Office launched long before personal computers and the internet were reliable enough to support a DRM system for personal documents), so Apple didn't need to "circumvent" DRM in order to make iWork. Today, most vendors (including Apple) add a thin skin of DRM to every product, solely so they can invoke the DMCA against competitors who reverse-engineer and improve their products.

The flexibility of computers means adversarial interoperability is always in the mix, a possible escape-hatch for suppliers and users who are locked into this or that walled garden. In fact, the pro-competitive nature of the concept—combined with the unwieldiness of saying or typing "adversarial interoperability"—prompted Cory and his colleagues at the Electronic Frontier Foundation to search for a better term of art to use when discussing it. They hit on "competitive compatibility" or "comcom," which is not only a lot more fun to say, but also more directly highlights its relevance to braking those anticompetitive flywheels.

If we were living under the same rules that applied when Apple and Microsoft were as they built themselves up against the industry giants that dominated the field in their early days, comcom could be used to circumvent many of the ways in which tech and entertainment lock in and abuse creative workers. For example, Audible authors who were getting ripped off by Amazon could give their listeners the tools to move Audible books to a rival service—one that deals honorably with creators—and invite their listeners to follow them there. They could make a plug-in that would search for authors' books from providers other than Audible first, *even on Audible's own website*, and direct users to buy the books from Audible only if there were no other option. YouTubers and other video creators could offer fans alternative video players that would remove the ads they were forced to carry as part of YouTube's Content ID system, and instead display better ads from more honest brokers that paid creators larger shares and spied less on their fans. Independent creators could distribute their videos, games, books, and sound files direct to Android and Apple mobile devices through apps that bypassed the mobile duopoly's app stores—and the huge tolls they exact on content. Those 30 percent vigs are maintainable only because DRM law makes it illegal for competitors to enter the market.

Even if many of these things never came to pass, the fact that they *could* would seriously alter the dynamics of digital creative markets. Today, the only thing that stops Apple and Google from raising their app tax is the fear of bad publicity, or maybe angry regulators. In a comcom world, both companies would have to reckon with the possibility that artists themselves—or co-ops, nonprofits, and startups out to get artists a better deal—would use technology to bypass these abusive arrangements. That in itself would go far to moderate abuses.

Big companies spend enormous fortunes to create consumption habits among audiences, convincing customers to download apps, create accounts, enter their credit card details, and put the icon on their desktops or home screens. Those habits represent powerful inertia that aids their ongoing domination. Right now, breaking a consumption habit requires active change: downloading a different app, moving your media and playlists and preferences over, changing the icon on your home screen. That's a *lot* to ask of busy people who just want to relax with a good book or play some music while making breakfast or driving to the grocery store.

Comcom offers a gentler slope from the world of concentrated chokepoints to a world of pluralistic, decentralized, fairer creative markets. Imagine overlaying "Buy with Bandcamp" buttons on Spotify, iTunes, and Amazon Music—or "Get this ebook direct from the author," on Amazon pages and the Kindle app. Imagine an alternate YouTube player that automatically checks to see whether the same video is available on a fairer platform—hell, imagine if your Uber app could collude with the driver to cancel the ride you just booked and reestablish it with a rival app owned by a drivers' co-op.

There's yet a third kind of interoperability that's worth considering, which we call "mandated interop." Sometimes, companies are *legally required* to use particular interfaces or standards. For example, an FCC regulation requires US phone companies to offer standard interfaces to independent long-distance carriers, and a 2012 Massachusetts law requires automobile companies that do business in that state to supply mechanics with diagnostic codes and manuals so they can fix their cars.[5]

Mandated interop is gaining political momentum, and just in time. In the US, the 2020 ACCESS Act mandates interop for the largest social media companies (it failed but will likely come back); in the EU, the proposed Digital Services Act and Digital Markets Act goes further, mandating interop and fairness in app stores and other supplier-squeezing bottlenecks, like search results.[6] A 2020 report from the UK's competition regulator into online platforms and digital ads—a magisterial, four-hundred-plus page brick of literal chapter and verse on Big Tech abuses—recommends similar measures.[7]

Some of the most egregious shake downs, like the usurious cuts charged by Apple and Google via their app stores, are also being targeted. In August 2021, South Korea became the first country to outlaw app store operators from forcing use of their own payment systems, with similar interventions also being actively considered elsewhere.[8] Just days later, the US court charged with resolving the litigation between Epic Games and Apple issued a permanent injunction prohibiting Apple from stopping app developers from linking to their own purchase mechanisms. That explicitly widens out the chokepoint: sellers of music, video, and books will finally be able to offer users ways to subscribe and buy while bypassing Apple's cut.

Such laws could do a lot of good. They could also be terrible, if they get *too* specific about mandates: like if they stopped Facebook or Apple or Google from taking action to block identity thieves they just caught in the act because doing so might affect a mandated interface. But let's say for the sake of argument that well-constructed, thoughtful interoperability mandates become law in some of the largest tech markets in the world. Do we still need comcom if that happens?

Resoundingly *yes*—and the history of that Massachusetts automotive right-to-repair law shows us why. In our changing world, repair laws are increasingly important. As explained by Aaron Perzanowski in *The Right to Repair*, repairing goods doesn't just help us save money and reduce the environmental costs of the consumer lifestyle. It also "helps us grow and flourish as people. Through repair, we become better informed about the world around us, develop analytical and problem-solving skills, exercise greater autonomy, and build stronger communities."[9]

The Massachusetts legislature had been working toward a right-to-repair law in 2012, resisted fiercely by lobbyists for Big Car. The lobby's aim was to kill the independent repair sector, rendering all drivers completely dependent on official manufacturer repair depots, which could then charge their captive customers whatever they wanted. Those skilled independent mechanics who'd been fixing cars from North Adams to Provincetown could either retrain and go into another line of work—or go work for the manufacturers, who'd have a buyer's market for their labor.

A "compromise" bill was passed at the eleventh hour, watering down the car industry's responsibilities. Due to the delay in getting it passed however, Bay Staters still got a chance to weigh in on the matter via a ballot initiative. They voted in favor of a more stringent version, passing the measure ("Question 1") with an incredible 86 percent majority in favor.

Question 1 ordered car manufacturers to provide diagnostic codes for messages that traveled on the wired networks that are woven through modern cars. As Aaron Perzanowski recounts, the Massachusetts law "was soon adopted as a de facto national standard," with automakers entering into a voluntary agreement to operate under its terms nationwide.[10] But their ballot-box trouncing didn't kill Big Car's dreams of dominating the repair sector. Manufacturers regrouped—and redesigned. Cars that rolled off the line after 2012 increasingly used *wireless* signaling to communicate diagnostic information to mechanics. Since Question 1's mandate did not cover wireless interfaces, the people's will was flouted. Despite this flagrant undermining of the democratic process,

Massachusetts lawmakers were unwilling to close the loophole. Instead, voters were forced back to the polls in 2020 to vote on a new Question 1, a ballot initiative that Big Car threw millions into blocking.

The ads that ran against 2020's Question 1 beggared belief: they flat-out stated manufacturers had redesigned cars to gather so much sensitive information on their owners that allowing anyone to access that data would lead to women car owners being *stalked and raped*. (Somehow, the manufacturers did not propose solving this problem by gathering less data.)[11] Despite the fear campaign, the 2020 Question 1 sailed through with a 75 percent majority. Auto makers are still resisting the will of the people however, challenging the state regulation on the grounds it conflicts with federal laws. As we go to press, the law remains in limbo.[12]

A key lesson of Question 1 is that interoperability mandates are fragile. If we order Facebook to allow competitors to access the API it uses to connect the back ends of Facebook Messenger, Instagram, and WhatsApp, the company may comply—while simultaneously reengineering all three systems so that the API is slowly rendered useless, all its dataflows shifted to a different system that is *not* mandated. If Facebook subverts a mandate, we can create another one, and another, and another. But Facebook can reengineer its systems as quickly as it can write new code, while regulators can only revise their mandates after public notice, comment, and hearing periods. Each time, Facebook can throw hundreds of millions at gumming those new regulations up, so that by the time the government catches up with Facebook's last dirty trick, it's ready to move onto the next.

The fragility of mandates is why we need competitive compatibility, or comcom—the right to plug something new into something that already exists, whether or not the company whose product you're modifying agrees to let you do it. If scraping, bots, and reverse-engineering remain legally fraught, then the only consequence that Facebook faces if it subverts its mandates is a regulatory battle over the next one. But if the DMCA's prohibition on bypassing digital locks were abolished, then any competitor Facebook shut out of its system wouldn't have to wait for new regulations, but could immediately start working its way back in, using bots, scraping, and reverse-engineering to reconnect competing systems to Facebook and override its lockouts while users of rival services and their friends on Facebook cheered them on.

This cat-and-mouse version of interoperability is unstable, of course. Your path to your off-Facebook friends might work one day and then stop working the next day as Facebook changes its systems to block the comcom system. It's chaotic too. By definition, rivals that form their own interfaces to Facebook will do things Facebook doesn't expect, exposing and exploiting weaknesses in its systems that can be turned to bad purposes just as readily as good ones.

In other words, if we have comcom, then the penalty for shutting down the managed, orderly interoperability systems is to be plunged into a chaotic, unmanaged, disorderly fight to reestablish those systems. Facebook's security and product engineers—already fighting battles on multiple fronts—would be diverted to fighting a pointless Cold War that made its own users angry and miserable and more prone to leaving for a rival.

In other words, comcom shifts the equilibrium. In a world with interoperability mandates *and* comcom, Facebook's optimal strategy is to tolerate competition. If comcom had been legal in Massachusetts, then as soon as Big Car shifted its data from our cars' wired networks to their wireless ones, every body shop and mail-order catalog would have immediately filled up with unofficial gadgets to decode those wireless communications too. Shifting to wireless would become a full-time job of cat-and-mouse, with codes and locks changing all the time, creating support nightmares for the *authorized* mechanics who worked for the manufacturers, who'd have to cope with the ground shifting under them all the time.

We're not saying that every company will decide to play it straight if comcom is in the mix. Corporate greed often trumps common sense, especially when it's a company that's accustomed to using its monopoly to exploit, silence, and trample its customers, competitors, suppliers, and critics.

But that's the beautiful thing about comcom: it's not just a deterrent, it's a *remedy*. If Amazon kills a mandate to open its Kindle books, that doesn't just kick off a pointless war over third-party Kindle jailbreaking tools; it also allows those tools to flourish and find their way into readers' hands, so they can continue to unlock and move their libraries. Sure, those tools may not be as smooth as the mandated interfaces, but they're still available, and the longer Amazon fails to comply with a Kindle mandate, the more time developers will have to make their unlocking tools easier to use, and find new users, collaborators, and investors.

When there are alternatives, boycotts can be the impetus the public needs to try something new, and when it does, the new thing might just stick around (even after COVID-19 is under control, how many people will continue to wear masks when they feel sick?).

The point of radical interoperability isn't merely to provide "choice" or "competition" or "innovation," or any other empty Silicon Valley buzzword: it's to let people decide for themselves how to live their lives. It's to clear the way for the exercise of self-determination. You, the user of a product or service, know more about your needs than its designers ever will. A farmer with a hailstorm on the horizon knows whether she wants to trust her own tractor repair to bring in the crops to a degree John Deere will never be able to match. A person with a physical or cognitive disability knows more about how they need to adapt their tools than even the most empathetic design team. A person who is poor, or facing an emergency, or in physical danger, knows more about whether it's appropriate to change the operation of a product than the company that made it. Good products and services—like good art—routinely outlive their makers. You know more about how you want to use a computer program to recover your old working files than the company that made it ten years before.

The case for interoperability isn't about creating competitive markets in which the best products win. It's about creating a world of tools, devices, and services that are under the control of the people who depend on them.

So how do we get our comcom back? Remember that no one passed a law against reverse-engineering, scraping, and bots. No legislature banned third-party printer ink, independent repair, or refurbishing old parts. Indeed, many of the laws used to shut down these activities have explicit carve-outs for repair and interoperability, but these are so narrowly worded that no one trusts them to work when the case gets in front of a judge.

Some of these laws just need to be struck down. DMCA 1201—the anticircumvention law—shouldn't be on the books, period. We already have laws banning copyright infringement. We don't need a law that makes it super-duper illegal to violate copyright with a certain kind of general purpose computer program or device.

Since 2016, the Electronic Frontier Foundation has been suing the US government to overturn DMCA 1201 as unconstitutional, representing the eminent Johns Hopkins cryptographer Dr. Matthew Green and the legendary MIT electronic engineer Dr. Andrew "bunnie" Huang. The case is slow moving, but it represents one path to ridding the world of US anticircumvention law. (If successful, other countries that the US trade representative pressured into adopting versions of this law will then have to embark on the slow process of abolishing or reforming it in their own systems.)

Another path to fixing anticircumvention law is legislation: getting the US Congress to amend or repeal the offending clause. Getting rid of DMCA 1201 is the simplest fix, but it may not be politically feasible (though who knows—US politics are weird and growing weirder). One compromise measure would be to tie anticircumvention enforcement to acts of copyright infringement. So it would be illegal to remove the locks from a Kindle book in order to share it without authorization (a copyright infringement) but it would be fine to remove those locks to move them to another device (not a copyright infringement).

What about the Computer Fraud and Abuse Act, the Reagan-era cybersecurity law that has been used to criminalize violations of terms of service? Various US Appeals Court circuits have split on whether this is a valid interpretation of the CFAA, and better case law could substantially defuse the risk of CFAA's being used to block legitimate activity. A 2021 US Supreme Court decision left it ambiguous whether simple terms-of-service violations could violate the law.[13] Alternatively, we need legislation clarifying that the CFAA can't be used to criminalize terms-of-service violations, like "Aaron's Law" would have. Rep. Zoe Lofgren introduced this bipartisan bill in 2013 to honor the computer pioneer Aaron Swartz, hounded to death by CFAA threats when he was only twenty-six years old. But with so many corporations relying on the CFAA to maintain their chokepoints, the bill still hasn't made it into law.

Then there's all the other laws deployed to block interop: patents, API copyrights, nondisclosure, binding arbitration mandates, and non-compete clauses. All of these systems are harmful when abused and lack curbs against that abuse. Reforms that introduce safeguards to all of them would be most welcome.

But all of those fights will drag on for years and we need interop *now*.

We could have it if the US Congress would enact an "interoperator's defense" shielding people from *all* liability, under any cause of action, if they could demonstrate they were modifying an existing product or service to improve its security or accessibility, to repair it, to add otherwise lawful features to it, or to help bona fide users of the system shift legitimately purchased digital products to a competing service.

At the state level, legislatures could pass laws that make certain contracting terms "against public policy" and therefore unenforceable. If California banned binding arbitration or terms of service that prohibited security disclosures, independent repair, or accessibility adaptation, then startups and co-ops in the state could offer nationwide access to interoperability tools.

State legislatures have another powerful tool at their disposal: procurement. State and local governments buy a lot of stuff, and can set their own rules for who they buy that stuff from and on what terms. States could enact laws banning all levels of government from buying services from manufacturers unless they promise to allow interoperability. For example, no local school district should *ever* buy iPads without securing a promise from Apple to allow side-loading of apps not in the App Store: otherwise, what happens if Apple kicks out the app the district relies on and that its teachers have built their curriculum around? The same goes for Google Classroom. The effect of such a rule wouldn't end at the school gates: once Apple redesigns its devices to allow apps to be loaded from outside the App Store, *everyone* would get to take advantage of that, including independent authors, musicians, and filmmakers wanting to sell their work without being shaken down by Google and Apple.

Wise governments have long been wary of entering into contracts for tools they can't maintain themselves or repair with parts from multiple suppliers. Lincoln's Union Army required its rifle makers to standardize their parts and ammo so products and components from different companies could be mixed and matched in the field! Ironically, the monopolization of the US defense sector undid this bedrock principle, and today's Pentagon is utterly beholden to extractive service contracts with stateside manufacturers, leading to everything from generators to artillery being shipped back to the US for private-sector service rather than being repaired by military technicians in the field.

Blocking interoperators is key to how chokepoint capitalists extract the monopoly rents that they use to lobby against all other kinds of enforcement. Allowing interop alone won't win the war, but it *could* cut the supply lines that feed the war machine.

CHAPTER 17

MINIMUM WAGES
FOR CREATIVE WORK

A lan Dean Foster is a science fiction legend, having written not just a shelf of original novels but also film and TV novelizations—including for *Star Wars* and *Alien*—that have become beloved bestsellers in their own right. When Disney bought Lucasfilm, and then 20th Century Fox, it didn't just come to take over 40 percent of the US box office and acquire the copyrights to a huge amount of America's cinematic heritage; it picked up the rights to a bunch of Foster's books too. And then his royalties stopped coming.

Struggling with cancer and a wife who was also unwell, Foster eventually brought a private grievance via his professional association, Science Fiction and Fantasy Writers of America (SFWA), to find out where the money was. SFWA's grievance process nearly always results in a successful outcome for members, but not this time. In refusing to pay, Disney was relying on a radical theory: that when it bought Lucasfilm and Fox, it acquired the rights to Foster's books (i.e., the copyright licenses that enabled Disney to sell them), but not the liabilities (i.e., the obligation to pay him)!

This theory isn't just radical, but dangerous. Mary Robinette Kowal, president of the Science Fiction and Fantasy Writers of America, says that if it succeeds, it has the potential to affect *all* creators: "If we let this stand, it could set precedent to fundamentally alter the way copyright and contracts operate in the United States. All a publisher would have to do to break a contract would be to sell it to a sibling company."[1]

Having failed to get what Foster was owed, the only remaining leverage was to go public, relying on the obvious justice of Foster's claim and his legions of loyal fans to embarrass Disney into paying up. But Disney tried to take even that, insisting he sign an aggressive nondisclosure agreement *prior* to opening negotiations. Such deals get signed once parties have reached a deal—not before. Talk about cartoon villains.

Of course, Disney isn't the only big company that tries to minimize the share they pay out to creators. They all do, once they have the power to, as we saw throughout the first half of this book. Since the only thing worse than the deal on the table is not being on these platforms at all, creators and producers find themselves accepting the pittance they're offered. That's one reason why, of the billions generated by creative work, so much gets siphoned off before reaching the people who contribute the time, money, and inspiration that makes it worth listening to, performing, looking at, or watching.

For decades, acolytes of the Chicago School have been telling us that "mere wealth transfer away from producers is not a competitive concern."[2] But of course it is. By ratcheting down the rates they pay, investors make it difficult for creators to continue producing high-quality work. It also ensures that creative people—the very ones who are most devotedly interested in cultural products and services—have an ever reducing capacity to pay for books, magazines, visual art, films, performances, and lessons in their craft, further distorting markets for culture. Floors under the prices of creative work would help put these industries on a more sustainable footing.

We control prices in all kinds of situations where pay would otherwise be forced below sustainable levels—like minimum wage laws for workers. Unfortunately, most creative workers, like an increasing number of precariously employed gig workers (people delivering, driving, cleaning, teaching) fall outside the shelter offered by these laws, and an ever growing number of those who *should* be protected are having their wages stolen anyway.

Sometimes we also put floors under the price of commodities, like milk. Historically, these came about because farmers were being ground down by powerful buyers in much the same way as creators are now. But there's no floor on cultural commodities like streamed sound recordings or online video or self-published books: Spotify and YouTube and Netflix and Amazon get to decide what they pay. Given their excessive power and fixation on maximizing short-term shareholder value, it's no surprise that turns out to be very little indeed.

Minimum wages for creative labor won't fix all of the market abuses that place downward pressure on prices. But by putting floors under the cost of creative work, they *can* reduce how much value gets creamed off by those who had nothing to do with its making. In thinking about how to introduce them, we might draw inspiration from the European Union, which recently required its twenty-seven member countries to make laws to give creators the right to "appropriate and proportionate remuneration" whenever they license or transfer their exclusive rights.[3]

This kind of law has been around for years in Germany and the Netherlands, and those countries have acted as labs for figuring out the kind of interventions that actually succeed in raising creative wages. According to leading expert and law professor Raquel Xalabarder, the most promising is "residual remuneration rights." The concept is simple. Creators transfer their copyrights just as they do now, and their labels and publishers decide how to exploit them—again, just as now. The difference? That creators keep an inalienable right to "appropriate and proportionate" pay for the use of their work. Most significantly, those rights *can be enforced directly from licensees* like Spotify, Amazon, Netflix, and YouTube. The new EU law applies even over contracts that have already been decided, which means creators won't have to wait generations to take advantage of the improved protections.[4]

Residual remuneration rights in the EU mimic the hard-won WGA-negotiated rights to residual royalties in the US screen industries. As we saw earlier, those rights are under attack by both streaming platforms and studio giants changing the system so they don't have to pay creators based on the market value of their creations. A statutory right would shore them up. Beneficially, new residual remuneration rights could also be introduced in sectors where unions are currently too weak to win them. As an added benefit, residual remuneration rights could *strengthen* creator unions if they were tasked with enforcing them on behalf of members and increase solidarity across diffuse creative classes.

Such laws would also help creators like Alan Dean Foster. Even if Disney's bizarre and radical argument that it had acquired rights over creative work but not the liability to pay for it was somehow valid in contract, a residual remuneration right could give writers like Foster ongoing claims in copyright—even against subsequent licensees, like Disney.

This kind of protection would also help protect against other shakedowns too, like Discovery Networks' recent insistence that composers sign away their rights to ongoing public performance royalties—even *royalties they were already entitled to under past contracts.* Losing said rights would reduce incomes by an estimated 80 to 90 percent, threatening the viability of film scoring as a career. Composer David Vanacore says it's those "back end" payments that make the work viable: "There's no way I can support what it takes to do a show based on what they're offering. . . . I don't think they understand the amount of time and energy that goes into the creative process."[5] Composers who refused to agree to the new terms were told their scores would be stripped out and replaced with generic music the network already owns.

Netflix is also asking composers to agree to buyouts, though it insists they have a choice about whether to sign. But industry sources say these terms mostly target "young composers or those who aren't as much in demand . . . and can't afford to pass on the work or complain about the terms for fear of being blacklisted."[6] One award-winning composer told the *Hollywood Reporter* he felt obliged to agree to a buyout because it was the only way to score a Netflix documentary—and, in a world where Netflix is spending substantially more on programming than the entire US box office, that's a market that cannot be ignored. While these companies are powerful enough to insist on contracts assigning these rights, well-drafted and inalienable residual remuneration rights could put a floor under wages.

Such rights could also be useful where one player takes over almost the entirety of a market—as Amazon has done with self-publishing. At time of writing, it still pays authors 70 percent of revenues on most self-published sales: much more than its Audible subsidiary pays out on self-published audiobooks. That generous split is not motivated by altruism. Rather, it's designed to weaken publishers by building up an alternative market that cuts them out altogether. Once that end is achieved, and it has enough readers locked in, it will start to turn the screws on those authors too. An ongoing right to fair remuneration could hold it in check.

But while residual remuneration rights hold promise for delivering more money to creative workers, they also have dangers. If it's only the biggest players that end up able to make those additional payments, such reforms could bake their dominance in. A creative ecosystem reliant on making sure Spotify and Amazon and YouTube continue being rich enough to pay won't necessarily be better than the one we have now.

There is a risk too that these rights might not actually result in any net dollar gains for creators. Remember, residual remuneration rights entitle creators to payments *on top of* contractual rates: they don't do anything to control the base price that's paid. It's easy to imagine a situation where the monster platforms cough up a few pennies on the dollar to give to artists, but make it back by squeezing labels and publishers, who then have to make *that* back by squeezing . . . creators! To avoid this, we need to also strike directly at the roots of their power.

Remember, also, that minimum wages for creative work are about addressing the exploitation that comes from negotiating imbalances between creators and intermediaries. The web and the internet have been a source of fantastic creative output and distribution by creators who found ways to go direct to their audiences, or who were remunerated through other means, from house shows to short story commissions to direct, voluntary payments. The point of this exercise is to enable redress when giant companies make tons of money while the artists who supply them make a pittance—not to supplant or undermine voluntarily, partnership-oriented relations between artists and their audiences.

Another limitation of remuneration rights is that they won't do anything to encourage new entrants. Anyone who wants to set up a new music or video streaming platform would still need to negotiate access with the major rights holders in just the same way as now—with all the conflicts of interest caused by their market power and equity stakes in the dominant platforms. When you factor in the extra transaction costs a residual remuneration system could create, these markets might become even *less* attractive to new entrants. That would be truly disastrous to the broader project of dispersing control more fairly across creative ecosystems.

A NEW WAY OF THINKING
ABOUT STATUTORY LICENSES

Rethinking the way we use statutory licenses is one way we might achieve the benefits of residual remuneration rights while putting a genuine floor under the prices paid for creative work *and* encouraging new entrants.

Statutory licenses give providers the right to use copyrighted material without getting the owner's permission in exchange for paying a fee and complying with any other license conditions. They're widely used around the world, usually where transaction costs are too high to license every little transaction like when books are being photocopied by teachers in schools, or music is being played on the radio. In the US, performing rights organizations like BMI (Broadcast Music, Inc.) and ASCAP (American Society of Composers, Authors and Publishers) issue licenses that permit restaurants, clubs, and other businesses to play music. They're obliged to grant a license to anyone who asks, which is crucial to the healthy working of this market. Imagine a world where only TGI Fridays was allowed to play music!

We've talked previously about the need to create a statutory license that would force US radio stations to finally join the rest of the world and start paying when they broadcast recordings. But we should go beyond thinking about statutory licenses as just a remedy for high transaction costs. Reconceptualized, they have real potential to safeguard creators and producers with minimum wages and protections that would apply no matter how much downward pressure comes from predatory players along the distribution chain. Warning: in this section, we're going to get into the weeds around music licensing, which is mind-numbingly complex. If you find your eyes glazing over, remember this: it's not hard to understand because it's complicated, it's complicated so it'll be hard to understand. The people getting rich from it while artists starve don't want you to know how it works.

The US already has a statutory license for noninteractive streaming services like Pandora, and some of its features illustrate why statutory licenses have such chokepoint-busting potential. This license was introduced to cover internet radio companies, but not services like Spotify, where users decide which songs to play and when. That distinction is increasingly a fiction: after all, users are delegating their decision-making whenever they listen to Spotify-generated playlists. But it is nonetheless successfully used to justify creators not getting the benefits of the non-interactive license.

The noninteractive license lets any internet radio company stream sound recordings to subscribers in exchange for royalties set by the Copyright Royalty Board.[7] Every play on every commercial service gets paid the same rate whether the song was written by Stevie Nicks or a waitress who has just arrived in Nashville, published by a micro-publisher or one of the Big Three. SoundExchange collects the money and has paid out over $7 billion in royalties since its founding in 2003.[8] Critically, the law requires half the money go directly to performers, *regardless of whether they have recouped their recording debts*, with the other half being paid to the copyright owner (usually a label).[9]

It's easy to see how this promotes a competitive playing field. Remember when Spotify and the majors reached that cozy deal to reduce royalties by three percentage points in advance of Spotify's IPO? The biggest labels had their concessions offset by overlarge advances, free ads, and all those other perks, plus a jump in the value of their equity. But they're also powerful enough to negotiate "most favored nation" clauses into their contracts, which guarantee nobody else gets a higher rate. Thus it was the indies that bore the brunt of the decision: when it was time to renegotiate their own contracts, they found a new lower ceiling than what had been there before. By making this deal, the majors shaved points off the indies' already squeezed margins.

The noninteractive license leaves no scope for the majors to use their massive catalogs to extract fatter margins than everyone else or structure deals in ways that prioritize their interests over those of their artists. It also makes it easier for competitors to enter the market, knowing they can get access to the music they need without having to negotiate individually with every label (and without needing capital to cover the bribes routinely demanded by the most powerful as a cost of doing business).

We don't want to paint too rosy a picture: there are *plenty of ways* to do statutory licenses badly. Sometimes they act as a ceiling on the rates creators can get, instead of a floor. This is the case with those US public performance rights licensed by BMI and ASCAP. In that system, licensees are allowed to bypass those collecting societies and enter into private deals instead—and when that happens, artists can lose out. Sony/

ATV Music Publishing once notoriously accepted royalties 30 percent below what would have been due under a blanket license in exchange for an oversized advance and a $300,000 "administration payment" it wouldn't have to share with its composers.[10] That also gave it the right to dip into the songwriters' share. Like the noninteractive streaming license, ASCAP- and BMI-issued blanket licenses make sure artists get half the money, even if they haven't recouped. When they're bypassed, the contracts between songwriter and publisher determine where the money goes. Almost always, they say writers don't share in any performance revenues the publisher receives directly.[11] Even if they *were* entitled to a share, those contracts would give the publisher the right to offset it against their recoupment account. If a statutory license is going to usefully set a minimum wage for creators in markets controlled by excessively powerful corporations, it needs protections against this kind of subversion.

Statutory licenses also fail when they get the price wrong, as happened under the old interactive streaming license for composers, something that has now been replaced by the Music Modernization Act. For years, music publishers and songwriters got a raw deal on rates, bringing in just 10.5 percent of streaming revenues compared to 52 percent for the labels.[12] By comparison, synchronization rights, which apply where music is attached to video, like in ads and movies, are negotiated in the free market. Industry practice is for the fees to be split fifty-fifty between publishers and labels.[13]

As we explained earlier, this disparity was probably compounded and prolonged by the gigantic conflict of interest caused by the industry's vertical integration—the fact that the conglomerates who own the Big Three record labels and the Big Three music publishers will be better off if revenue goes onto the record label side of the ledger. But the original sins were the deficiencies in how the old law required rates to be set, which asked rate setters to balance varied policy criteria like the need to minimize disruption to existing industry structures—yes, it was this blatant in favoring old business models over new![14]

The Music Modernization Act has now addressed these issues by requiring rates to be set at the amount a willing buyer would pay a willing seller, which songwriters think will substantially raise their pay.

All this shows that new statutory licenses will have to be designed with care if they're going to help allocate culture's proceeds more fairly between creators and platforms, publishers and labels. But if we think about them differently from how we have in the past, they have real potential to combat buyer power, provide more transparency, put a floor under prices, and create more equitable splits between creators, investors, and platforms.

Take music streaming, for example. It's convenient and hugely popular. Responsible for resocializing people to paying for music, it has started generating enormous revenues without which many creators would be worse off still. But the streaming market has been distorted by excessive corporate power from the get-go. We've seen the conflicts of interest that make the biggest labels side with the biggest streamers against the interests of their own artists, and the inequitable contracts that give heritage artists, especially the people of color who are disproportionately bound to the very worst contracts, a fraction of the pay for the same number of streams.

We don't want to contribute to what Mat Dryhurst calls "streaming fatalism"—the idea that streaming is all there is, and all there will ever be.[15] There needs to be room for other business models to grow, and policymaking needs to go beyond simply moving deck chairs around a business model that's proving disastrous for so many artists. But it *is* the dominant system right now, and there are things we can do to make it fairer. One, potentially, is a reconceptualized statutory license.

The first thing it could do is set a floor on payments. If we've learned anything from history it's that it's critical to get rates right. Too high, and providers can't afford to enter or stay in the market. Too low, and creators fall into a financial abyss. The Music Modernization Act's model of setting rates at the amount a willing buyer would pay to a willing seller is a good start, but this just approximates the market rate. If the market rate is distorted by overly powerful companies, creators could still end up with less than their due. So we'd suggest adding a rider: "so long as that amounts to fair remuneration." In deciding whether the market rate was sufficient, independent rate setters could take into account all relevant evidence including whether the market was highly concentrated (so concentrated that it might drive the "willing seller/willing buyer" rate below what's fair).

If streaming platforms had the right to license music upon payment of fairly set rates, it would encourage new entrants into the market. They wouldn't need as much capital to get started because they wouldn't have to pay the bribes the biggest players demand as a cost of doing business. To help diversify music's revenue base, new entrants—especially those trying out new business models—and smaller players might be given the benefit of more advantageous terms than the established giants, something the Future of Music Coalition has already advocated for in the webcasting context.[16]

This model could also help reduce the rush to ever greater consolidation. If the same rates were paid to small and big labels alike, and the biggest ones couldn't muscle their way to a disproportionate share, much of the impetus for producer integration would disappear. If labels could stay small, recording artists would have relatively more power in their dealings with them.

Then there's the question of how royalties should be divided up. One benefit of statutory licenses over private contracts is that they can mandate the shares that go to creators and investors, overriding unfair contracts. Many of the heritage artists signed up to those terrible deals in the 1950s and 1960s have *still* never recouped their recording debts, even though their records have been making money for their labels for decades. They probably never will. Although they've had every opportunity to do so, the majors have moved incredibly slowly in response to calls to give justice to the heritage artists who are filling their coffers. Of the Big Three, only Sony has so far made any meaningful move, announcing in mid-2021 that it would no longer offset earnings against unrecouped balances for artists signed before 2000. This may have been triggered by pressure by the UK parliamentary committee on the economics of streaming, which was deeply unimpressed to discover its artists were having royalties offset by decades-old debts, long after the labels had themselves written those debts off.[17] At the time this book went to press, Warner and UMG were yet to follow suit.

This meanness should surprise no one. The primary concern of these record industry giants is to maximize (short-term) shareholder value, and they won't reduce their margin unless and until they're forced to—either by law or by a grassroots audience uprising that makes it more costly for them to continue to rip off artists than to finally pay them fairly. Competition from new distribution options has improved the terms on offer to artists today but doesn't help contracts signed in the past. If record labels continue to refuse to fix this injustice, a set statutory rate that applies to all plays regardless of the terms of the contract would do it for them.

Currently, label-signed artists receive anywhere between 5 and 50 percent of the streaming revenues attributable to their records, depending on when they signed their contract and whether it's with an indie or a major. International licensing expert Amanda Harcourt argues there's a strong case for revenues to be split fifty-fifty between artists and labels, since labels don't have to assume the risk and cost of physical sales.[18] Rate setters should be able to hear evidence from artists and labels and settle on something that is sustainable for all.

Should those royalties be subject to recoupment? Some music industry insiders have told us they'd need to be, to incentivize the high upfront investments some artists need to put out records. At the very least, though, the exercise of coming up with a suitable statutory license would provide an opportunity to regulate the costs that can be recouped (surely not the label receptionist's subway fare to the office?) and how long those debts should be recoupable *for*. In the EU for example, recording artists already have their recoupment debts written off after fifty years,[19] but we can do much better than that. Leading independent label Beggars Banquet cancels recoupment debts after fifteen years.[20] That sounds much more like it. Such a change would instantaneously put older artists on a more sustainable footing.

As well as setting a floor on payments, a rethought statutory license could help protect new players from the hegemons' kill zones. Remember those twentieth-century farmers who, after being squeezed by the owners of the grain elevators that controlled access to the rail network, organized to build their own? The Chicago grain merchants who had been luxuriating in the profits that came from being able to buy grain at exploitatively low prices tried to mobilize a boycott of the grain that was being shipped by their new co-op rivals. But because grain is a commodity, and thus has a fixed price in the market, the boycott failed and the farmers were able to wrest back control.[21] A statutory license that would allow anyone to sell access, so long as they satisfied the kind of creator-protective standards we've outlined, could help do the same for music.

Of course, the streaming model will never work for all musicians. As Holly Herndon has pointed out, there's something fundamentally broken about the idea that a song's sole measure of value is the number of times it's listened to: we also need models that finance the kind of music that's important and challenging and that you can't just cycle through infinitely on repeat.[22] Music like 75 Dollar Bill's album *Live at Tubby's*, during which one song masterfully builds and breaks tension over an exhilarating twenty-four minutes. It's complex, challenging, and was one of Rebecca's favorite albums in 2020—but there's no room for it in a world that values music purely by the number of times it's played.

Fortunately, streaming isn't the *only* game in town. Alternatives, like Bandcamp's direct sales model, allow this kind of music to find audiences who are willing to pay for it. Bandcamp is a user-friendly, low-fee venue for artists to promote and sell music, merch, and show tickets, and it generated $625 million for artists in its first ten years. *Live at Tubby's* was released as a Bandcamp exclusive pay-as-you-want release during the COVID-19 pandemic, bringing in $4,200 from almost seven hundred buyers in two days—more than the band had made from streaming via Spotify, Apple Music, and YouTube *combined* for the six years before.

Simply saying any platform could stream any recording on payment of a flat fee would risk digging up this one healthy plant in the garden. Fortunately, it's not necessary to do so. The US already has a blanket license entitling anyone to make a cover version of a song *if* it has previously been lawfully recorded and sold.[23] A statutory license for streaming sound recordings could create its own eligibility threshold—say, covering only those that have already been licensed to at least one streaming platform. In other words, if an artist or label has licensed its catalog to Spotify or Apple or Amazon for streaming, it would be subject to the statutory license. If not, it wouldn't, and its creators would be free to continue exploiting it however they pleased.

RAISING THE RATE

Both residual remuneration rights and statutory licenses would probably need collecting societies to take in the license money and pay it out. That will be enough to convince some people this is a bad idea. Although well-governed and efficient societies do exist, there are enough nightmarish tales about the others to fill their own book. The chapters would be titled Corruption, Embezzlement, Mismanagement, Unfair Distributions, and Excessive Overhead. If we were writing that book we'd tell you about

Spain's SGAE, which stole up to €87 million from its members, and about the Bahamian CRO that didn't pay out a cent in royalties *for over eleven years*, and the 60 percent tariff skimmed off the top by one in Romania.[24]

We'd also tell you about the way some societies use revenues set aside to invest in new culture—one of the few remaining sources of arts funding—as a lever to silence critics. We know this one works because when *we've* criticized those societies, creators have sometimes slid into our DMs to say thanks, admitting they were too fearful to speak up themselves.

But it's perhaps the sheer *wastefulness* of the current system that hurts artists most. We've talked before about the mind-numbing complexity of music licensing, especially across borders. Critic David Turner describes "the number of mental hoops it currently takes to explain how a single song stream makes it into the pockets of artists" as "almost bizarrely cruel."[25] Each use gives rise to a payment, perhaps just a fraction of a penny, which must be portioned out between publishers, composers, producers, labels, featured artists, session musicians, and more.

When the play occurs in one country and the rights holders are in another (or worse—several others!), the complexity and cost of getting those penny fractions to their rightful owners blows out incredibly. Each nation has at least one music collecting society, and—we can't emphasize enough how ludicrous this is—*nearly every one maintains its own massive database of songs, recordings, artists, and owners.* Just take a moment to sit with that. Not surprisingly, they're often out of date, incomplete and riddled with errors, making it difficult (and expensive!) to match songs to artists and composers. Want to know how bad it is? Collecting societies regularly fail to correctly identify and pay *Beyoncé.*[26]

Music licensing expert Becky Brook has observed that "even the most efficient PROs don't process all the data they get, because it's too inefficient. But it's too inefficient because we're processing it in silos."[27] The result? Up to 75 percent of music royalties can get swallowed elsewhere before copyright owners see a dime.[28] And, because matching uses to owners is so difficult, an estimated 20–50 percent of what's left won't make it to the correct hands.[29] In the US, for composers alone, over $424 million of unmatched money was sent to the new Mechanical Licensing Collective as required under the Music Modernization Act.[30] That's almost *half a billion dollars* that composers were shortchanged in just a decade of streaming.

With the system in this much of a mess, it's no surprise that royalty checks can take *years* to arrive, that they're so small when they do, and that so little of the money paid out by way of streaming royalties trickles down to the people who actually made the music. Annabella Coldrick, CEO of the Music Managers Forum, is clear about the deficiencies of the current system: "If you were starting from scratch, no-one would invent the current territorial licensing framework for online streaming."[31]

Everyone knows the solution: to transition to a global, multi-language database with high quality metadata about who owns what sound recordings and songs in which countries. However, repeated attempts to create such a system have failed.[32] That's not because we lack the technology, but because we lack the right incentives.

The only reason it was possible to reform the (terrible) statutory license for songs via the Music Modernization Act was because it didn't work for *anyone*. Not only were songwriters desperately unhappy but the platforms were too—the requirements were difficult to comply with and they faced statutory damages of up to $150,000 each time they got it wrong. This meant those with the power to change it were motivated to do so. It was still difficult, but eventually the old system was swept away in favor of a new statutory blanket license enabling any digital distributor to use the musical compositions in any sound recording they are licensed to distribute, powered by a new database that will make it much easier and cheaper to match songs to composers and publishers.

Remarkably, it's not even going to be all that expensive: the budget is for $33.5 million in startup costs, plus a $28.5 million operations budget for the first year, funded by Amazon, Apple, Google, Pandora, and Spotify from the savings they make from not having to use the creaky old system it replaces. We don't love this model, because it depends on those companies staying big and wealthy enough to keep paying. But it does show reform is possible if you have the right incentives.

It will be much trickier to fix the broken global system. Individual collecting societies don't want to transition to a centralized database because it means losing money and power. The dominant streaming platforms can live with it too—it's costly and complex, but that keeps competitors out, thus solidifying their chokepoints. It even works for the biggest labels and publishers. As explained by John Simson, former head of SoundExchange, "By not having great data and not having a worldwide database . . . it just makes it easier for money to go to the black box."[33]

While it's the independent artists and songwriters who are most likely to be misidentified, unallocatable money is usually distributed by market share—with the effect that the biggest players enjoy a disproportionate amount and get a competitive leg up on their indie rivals. The cherry on top? Because it's not attributable to any specific use, for a long time it didn't even have to be shared with artists or songwriters! (As we saw earlier, this is finally changing, although we *still* don't have any transparency around how much is shared or on what terms.)[34] The problem is not that there's insufficient copyright. It's that so much of music's value gets stolen before it reaches the artists who make it.

Meaningful reform means changing the incentives. The UK parliamentary inquiry into the economics of music streaming demanded regulatory action on three urgent matters: requiring labels to provide accurate metadata whenever they license recordings to streaming services; forcing industry to finally adopt viable data standards; and ending the practice of pro-rata distribution of black box revenues, which it found encouraged continuation of this wasteful and unfair system.[35] Virtually every nation's artists could benefit from similar interventions, making this an area where a new international copyright treaty would actually be useful. What if there was a new global system to replace the hundreds of poorly curated databases that payments flow through right now? To nudge the most powerful players toward supporting it, we might start by changing the way unattributable royalties are treated. What if they had to be paid straight to artist- and songwriter-hardship funds instead of bolstering corporate bottom lines? Major labels and publishers would immediately find new enthusiasm for ensuring royalties were correctly matched.

Any international treaty reform should also mandate governance changes to weed out collecting-society corruption and get these organizations managements' interests aligned with what we want to achieve. This includes introducing rigorous transparency and reporting processes and eliminating the temptation for societies to use their members' money to further their own interests. Crucially, any "cultural fund" revenues should be handed over to independent arts organizations for distribution so collecting societies can't use them to further their own interests over those of their members.

We could design any centralized global database not just to facilitate matching and payment, but to act as a licensing layer too. Imagine if creators and labels were able to upload their music directly to the system, ticking a box to say if they were licensing it for streaming and where. This would greatly facilitate the kind of statutory license we envisaged above. Any qualifying streaming service could then rapidly add that new music to their catalogs and have all the information necessary to pay the rights holders quickly, accurately, transparently, and with much less leakage.

If something like this worked for music streaming, maybe it could for video too. A statutory license set up as a minimum wage for creativity (a floor, not a ceiling), with licensing facilitated by a centralized database, could mean anything that gets licensed to YouTube would become available on other platforms too. The result of thinking about statutory licenses differently? More diverse and sustainable cultural ecosystems, each with more players, and less power in the hands of any single one.

Cory once provocatively argued for a universal statutory license over music, hoping to spark new conversations about what we could do to neutralize the advantages of the biggest players and get more money to creators. It certainly did that, with music industry experts enthusiastically wading in to dunk on the idea. They agreed with Cory about the problem but had different ideas about how to solve it. Some assumed he envisaged a ceiling, not a floor, which they feared would give YouTube even more power (we agree—this would be a bad idea!). Others (persuasively) pointed out that not all musical uses have the same value, so a one-size-fits-all approach wouldn't raise all boats. Those contributions welcomely helped us sculpt the statutory license proposal we set out above.

Cory's prompt led some of those experts to make some reform proposals of their own. Licensing expert Becky Brook made it clear that *something* had to be done to fix the current licensing mess: "I've spent my life licensing [rights to] companies. Let's not pretend it's not an absolute nightmare. . . . The current situation is stifling innovation—massively." The complexity means that clients with great ideas simply aren't able to ever get them off the ground. "It's death for a startup. It's slower innovation for a big tech company."

What we need, Brook argues, is a license to innovate, in order to encourage the experimentation necessary for creating new revenue streams, particularly in developed markets. She called for a global innovation license that would make it possible for start-ups to "take out a license like they buy Amazon services, . . . and on a multi-territory, hopefully global basis, but also covering both recorded and publishing rights." She'd like to see it happen willingly but suggests the *threat* of a statutory change might be what it takes for the industry to come together and find solutions.[36] And if it doesn't? Then, we think, an appropriately drawn statutory license for innovation might just be the solution here too—not only to create new revenue streams, but to smooth the path for the kind of new entrants that could dig away at the mega platforms' hegemony.

CHAPTER 18

COLLECTIVE OWNERSHIP

" "Why is it acceptable for a small and elite group of entrepreneurs to position themselves to capture the wealth generated by our collective creativity?" Why is it that, despite their "devotion to collaboration and 'social production,' technology gurus never raise the possibility that the platforms through which we access and share culture should belong to people whose participation makes them valuable?"[1] Astra Taylor asked these questions rhetorically in 2014, and of course we all know the answer: naked self-interest.

But just because tech gurus don't explore collective ownership doesn't mean it's not a viable option for reclaiming some of the culture's value for makers. We know that employee-owned firms are more productive, less likely to fold during downturns, and reduce economic inequality.[2] The Platform Cooperativism Consortium lists some five hundred platform co-ops around the world that deliver telecommunications, food, cleaning, healthcare, insurance, community organization, and a whole lot more. But cooperatively owned firms and platforms are not particularly common in the creative ecosystem—and certainly not at the kind of scale that might allow their artist members to hold their own against the tech and content giants.

One exception is Stocksy, a multi-stakeholder stock photo platform co-op in which the staff, governing board, and members all own shares. Founders Bruce Livingstone and Brianna Wettlaufer sold their original stock photo platform to Getty Images but found themselves unpleasantly surprised by the new regime's poor pay and conditions. Stocksy was their response.

Membership is limited to about a thousand, but it's exceptionally diverse, with members spread across some sixty-five countries. Stocksy pays out royalties of 50 percent on one-time sales (the industry standard is 15 percent) and 75 percent for extended licenses (compared to the usual 45 percent).[3] For these photographers at least, Stocksy is dechickenizing stock photography, letting creators participate effectively in the market while bypassing the dominant player.

Why has Stocksy been able to do what so few others have managed? The biggest challenge to worker cooperatives is raising the capital they need to start up.[4] In a satisfying irony, Stocksy was financed by the proceeds of its founders' earlier sale to Getty. But other creator co-ops will need to find the money elsewhere—an increasingly difficult task given how thoroughly they have been shaken down over the last years and decades.

This hurdle is not insurmountable. We write this during a time of historically low interest rates, and with economies in desperate need of stimulus. The US government has been pouring cash into corporations, much of which has then been funneled directly to investors and executives via share buybacks, resulting in very little actual stimulus. Instead, some of that capital could be loaned or granted to creator groups with a strong vision for alternative distribution models. Further resources could be put to raising awareness of cooperative ownership and supporting efforts to put it in place.

But this is where we butt up against the reality that, even if the capital problem is solved, entry into markets dominated by the giants will still be fraught. As Nick Srnicek reminds us in *Platform Capitalism*, "Even if all its software were made open-source, a platform like Facebook would still have the weight of its existing data, network effects, and financial resources to fight off any coop rival."[5]

NEW NEWS

Despite those challenges, there are some areas where culture producers, by working together, could reclaim value. Take news, for example. As we saw, Google and Facebook profit hugely from their monopolies over online ads, achieving returns of 40 and 50 percent respectively on their costs of capital. But very little trickles down to the people who produce the knowledge and culture to which those ads are attached, including news.

Earlier, we covered how the ad-tech scam allows advertisers to reach *Washington Post* readers without paying *Washington Post* prices. By participating in the behavioral ad markets that have become so prevalent, news outlets slowly erode their own rate cards, while at the same time enabling the middlemen to pocket more profits.

But there is an alternative: contextual ads. That's when publishers sell off the right to advertise to you based on the subject of the article you're reading, your location (based on your IP address), and other metadata, like which browser and OS you're using.

Contextual ads are gaining ground, thanks, in part, to laws like the EU's GDPR, which have simultaneously made it harder to do behavioral advertising *and* imposed compliance burdens that wiped out most of Europe's smaller ad-tech firms.

Triggered by the GDPR's privacy protections, which require affirmative opt-in for behavioral ads, the Dutch public broadcaster NPO ditched Google Ad Manager for a new custom contextual ad system that doesn't rely on surveillance. Instead of bidding on the user, advertisers target the material they're looking at or reading. The idea is that someone reading a restaurant review might be interested in your new online reservation service. A person reading about training for a sport might be a good candidate for ads promoting gym subscriptions or exercise bikes.

In early trials, NPO discovered that contextual ads "did as well or better than microtargeted ones" when it came to conversions. Encouraged by those results, NPO eliminated tracking entirely at the start of 2020. In January and February, its digital revenue skyrocketed—by 62 and 79 percent, respectively, on the previous year.[6] Even better, they get to actually keep that money, rather than being forced to hand over up to 70 percent to useless, creepy, spying, ad-tech middlemen.

Other big publishers, including the *New York Times*, *Guardian*, and *Washington Post*, are also moving away from behavioral ads, building their own platforms for serving up contextual ones. In the US, support for this hasn't come from GDPR–style privacy protections, but from browser developers. Safari already blocked third-party cookies, which are the ones that let advertisers track you from site to site, and so did Facebook—and

Google has promised to follow suit on Chrome from 2022.[7] Google and Facebook have good reasons to do this: they'll still be able to track everything you do within their ecosystems, while their smaller ad-tech competitors will be frozen out.

While a shift back to contextual advertising could help news publishers wrest back control, they aren't evenly placed to take advantage of the opportunity. Journalism and platforms expert James Meese cautions that these developments have the potential to create a "two-lane online advertising economy" in news, since it's only the largest and most powerful news publishers who have the resources to create contextual ad systems and who have the kind of customer bases that are likely to interest advertisers enough that they'd bother using a separate platform to access them: "Premium news brands can continue to rely on customer data, now collected in house, and can also expect to collect revenue from online advertising." But smaller publishers are unlikely to be able to gather enough first-party data to interest advertisers. "This could further accelerate the decline of local news . . . and harm local and regional news ecosystems, challenging efforts to ensure a diverse media landscape."[8]

The Bezos-owned *Washington Post* has not only created its own ad-serving technology but is offering to license it to other media companies, with the ultimate ambition of building the kind of news network that could one day rival Facebook. But handing power from Google and Facebook to a Bezos-owned machine would be a classic leap from frying pan to fire. A better solution could be for news publishers to prioritize their collective health by creating their own, cooperatively owned network. It could be run on a not-for-profit basis, funneling maximum proceeds back to participating news media organizations. With the right governance, designed to fairly balance the interests of the smallest and largest members, a cooperative approach would disperse the costs of creating the system, maximize the share of advertising dollars that go to the people creating the content, and re-intermediate publishers with their content. There's already industry precedent for this kind of cooperation: the Associated Press is a nonprofit cooperative that has been operating successfully for over 150 years.

This mission would be assisted by mandates for better transparency over online ad markets, which would put news publishers, advertisers, and platforms on a more even playing field. One of the clever things in the draft of Australia's News Media Bargaining Code was that it required the tech giants to provide information about how ad space was priced and allocated—which would have given producers some countervailing power against the platforms. Fierce lobbying from Google and Facebook succeeded in having this struck from the final version, showing their fear about what this kind of transparency might lead to. Regulators *everywhere* should be insisting that this kind of data be made public, with independent watchdogs tasked with monitoring for abuses.

While news co-ops have real potential to help journalism, we don't think advertising should be the main funding source going forward. We alluded to its failures earlier—like the way brands, trying to avoid having their ads associated with "controversial" content, blocked terms like *Black Lives Matter, protest,* and anything involving queer and trans communities. A *Vice* investigation found news content relating to George Floyd's death was monetized at a rate 57 percent lower than other news.[9] In this environment, anodyne content pays much more than reportage on vital social issues, making the latter even harder to sustain.

Subscriptions can't provide the whole answer either. As *Current Affairs* editor Nathan Robinson has pointed out, paywalls have been inadvertently contributing to the fake news epidemic: "The truth is paywalled but the lies are free."[10] One alternative is to squeeze news funding out of the platforms themselves. But as we can see from existing attempts in the EU and Australia, such attempts can easily become Faustian pacts.

The EU's 2019 "press publishers' right" is directly aimed at getting companies like Google and Facebook to pay up. While the right was granted to publishers, journalists and authors have an express entitlement to a fair share of the remuneration it generates.[11] France was the first nation to implement the new right. Google responded by announcing it would no longer preview European news extracts, infographics, photos, or videos—unless the publisher authorized them to do so for free. Google knew this would drastically cut traffic to news sites, which would make it difficult for publishers to withhold agreement. And indeed, that's exactly what happened: most publishers capitulated and agreed to let their content appear without charge.[12]

This time, Google's strategy of relying on its extreme dominance to bully publishers into submission now seems to have been a mistake. European competition regulators tend to be less shy about wielding their powers than their American counterparts, and the French authority ordered Google to negotiate with publishers in good faith. Google appealed, but the appeals court sided with the competition regulators, ruling that its behavior was likely an abuse of its dominant position.[13] Thanks in part to that intervention, deals are starting to be struck by platforms and news publishers in Europe.

Nonetheless, it's by no means clear the law will achieve its aims. Ula Furgal, a leading expert on the press publishers' right, told us she doesn't think it's going to work—and that it, too, risks entrenching the dominance of the biggest players: "The deals that we see being struck in Europe are never just about payment for using content pursuant to the new right. They always involve Google's new product, News Showcase. This makes the new right just an accessory, and further enhances press publishers' dependency on platforms." A better strategy, she believes, is to go to the source of the problem: advertising. "We need better regulation of online ads, or an additional tax on ad revenue. Plus, there needs to be more thought put into what we do with the money once we get it, which media organizations benefit from it, and how."

Beyond this concern, people who care about the news should be leery of attaching a "compensation right" (the right to get paid) to "a right to exclude" (the right to stop someone from linking to the news). Even the best newspapers make mistakes, and those mistakes can have consequences, as when the *New York Times* published false claims about Iraqi weapons of mass destruction and helped propel the world into decades of conflict that cost millions of lives. There's no reason that France's "link tax" (or the similar, EU-wide regime in Article 13 of 2019's Copyright Directive) needs to create a new right to decide who gets to link to— and thus debate, discuss, and criticize—the news. The right to link to a newspaper article, and the right to reproduce short snippets of text from it, should not be compromised by an economic arrangement intended to rebalance lopsided negotiating power.

Australia has also used competition law as a lever to direct some of those mega ad profits from platforms to news organizations. As we've alluded to earlier, the Australian competition regulator found a significant power imbalance between news businesses and the tech giants, and responded by creating a news media bargaining code obliging platforms to carry and pay for Australian news content.[14] This triggered embarrassing public meltdowns by the ad platforms (Australians call this "chucking a hissy fit"). Google threatened to withdraw its search engine from the country altogether. Facebook cut off Australian users from all news access, blocking posts from public health agencies, weather sites, and nonprofits devoted to helping victims of domestic violence for good measure.

Eventually, however, they both capitulated, signing deals with Rupert Murdoch's News Corp Australia and two other powerful news networks. Veteran Australian journalist and editor Alan Kohler says Google and Facebook got off lightly, since "their core operations of Google search and Facebook news feed have been quarantined, and their monopoly rents untouched." Platforms expert Jake Goldenfein goes even further: "More than getting off easy, I think the platforms got exactly what they want. They got to buy their way out of being regulated." Kohler decries the outcome for doing "nothing to address the dominance of Google and Facebook," or to support the kind of public interest journalism that most people are thinking of when they hear the rallying cry to "fund news!"[15] And, unlike the European solution, there was nothing requiring them to share it with their journalists, photographers, and cartoonists, or obliging them to hire more staff. All it really did was shift cash from tech giant ledgers to news giant ledgers. As Public Knowledge's Harold Feld persuasively argues, such solutions risk making chokepoints even worse: "In an effort to ensure the continued production of news—an important public interest goal—France and Australia have created a structure that will both preserve the existing market power of dominant platforms and the market position of the largest news publishers by requiring negotiations between the two."[16]

By addressing the symptom (too much money for platforms, not enough for news) rather than the cause (that the platforms have created chokepoints that enable them to capture an unfair share of value), these solutions risk exacerbating the problem: if news' survival becomes reliant on those giants remaining rich and powerful, it will be all the harder to wind them back to a manageable size. That's a real danger.

Meese points out that the link between advertising and journalism may well have come about through sheer historic accident and told us there's no need to limit ourselves to such models in the future: "It may well be that a sustainable cultural economy doesn't include journalism (or can only provide some revenue), leaving governments and philanthropists to pick up the slack."

Governments could do a lot, if they had the will to do so. For one thing, nations could work together to end the tech giants' successful multiyear run of international tax avoidance, tax them, and pay some of the proceeds into an independent trust to fund journalism. This would have the same broad effect as the Australian and EU solutions—more money for reporting—but in a way that is less dependent on individual corporations remaining powerful, and more targeted than simply pouring money into Rupert Murdoch's coffers.

European news organizations have a long history of substantial public funding. That has been less of a tradition in the US, although the postal service did successfully subsidize newspapers by charging enormously high prices for letter delivery in the nineteenth century, and more recently taxpayers have contributed substantially to funding broadcasters like NPR and PBS. There are also emerging signs of government willingness to intervene more directly. New Jersey, for example, funded a Civic Information Consortium in 2020, with the aim of improving the quantity and quality of civic information, engagement, and dialogue within its communities.[17]

A 2019 report of the Oxford University–based Reuters Institute suggests that, to be successful, any such government interventions must preserve press freedom, promote the public interest, and work toward putting the industry on a more sustainable footing.[18] Journalist Will Oremus says tax-and-reallocate proposals raise obvious questions, such as "on what basis to tax the platforms, who should oversee the resulting funds, exactly what types of journalism they should subsidize, and how to decide who gets those subsidies."[19] With appropriate governance, however, they're all surmountable.

There's also some low-hanging fruit: some countries—notably Canada—do not allow news entities to structure themselves as charitable nonprofits, meaning that crowdfunded Canadian news sources like the *Halifax Examiner* and *Canadaland* can't offer tax deductions to their supporters the way that US public-interest news nonprofits like ProPublica can. Granting tax deductions on donations to genuinely public interest news organizations is one alternative to direct government funding.

There's no doubt that the platforms are profiting excessively from their monopolies—or that they have cost our societies enormously via algorithms that radicalize us and spread fake news. Taxing them and re-allocating some of their profits to high quality, independent news would go some way toward addressing these problems without cementing in current inequalities.

PROTEST PLATFORMS

While news has perhaps the most immediate potential to co-operatize against the giants, co-ops in other culture industries are also managing to carve out niches in the gaps left by Big Business in ways that hint at a different kind of future. Scholar-activist Trebor Scholz argues that plat-form cooperativism's importance comes less from destroying "the dark overlords" and more from "writing over them in people's minds, incor-porating different ownership models, and then inserting them back into the mainstream."[20] Liz Pelly has a similar view. In the context of music, she calls alternative distribution means "protest platforms," arguing that *"the means through which music is created and distributed* carries as much po-litical weight as the content of the songs—by subverting the status quo, making their own platforms, and creating alternative worlds."[21]

Resonate is one such protest platform. Its mission is to create a sys-tem built on fairness, transparency, and cooperation that treats music as art rather than content, that enables sustainable careers for artists and that lets everyone own their platform and data.[22] Co-op executive Rich Jensen is motivated by the insights of Brazilian educator Paulo Freire: "You're either providing the tools for oppressed people to liberate them-selves from their oppression, or you're not."[23] As we write, Resonate hosts some 1,900 artists and 13,000 songs, and it's owned by 1,700 artist and listener members—each with one share, and one vote.

The payment model is radically different from the "all you can lis-ten" model of Spotify and its ilk. Listeners pay per stream. To encourage listeners to find new music, the first listen of any song costs less than a penny. Then it doubles for every subsequent listen. By the time you've streamed a song nine times, you've paid the equivalent price of a down-load. And, thanks to its unique "Stream2own" feature, at that point you *do* own it, so future plays are free. Compare that to Spotify, where it takes *hundreds* of listens before royalties equal those on a download. Despite paying higher rates, because Resonate's costs are lower, and because listeners consume music more mindfully, the overall cost to listeners ends up being similar to a traditional monthly subscription.[24]

Resonate has found a successful niche, but there are plenty left for others to fill. Even with first listens priced at under a penny, some music listeners will find the "mental transaction costs" too much to bear and eschew new artists. Just as Kickstarter spawned a group of crowdfunding competitors with slightly different models suited to different causes, someone might come along and offer a Resonate competitor that gives listeners their first listen for free. Or even their first three listens. There's no single right way to distribute and pay for music, or for musicians and audiences to find one another.

Mat Dryhurst sees enormous potential in co-operatizing music, and, instead of selling it as a commodity, would focus on generating revenue from its peculiar ability to offer connection and community: "Rather than pursuing the sisyphean task of imploring listeners to pay for files they already receive for free, why not invite people to become cherished members of an interdependent international network of venues, labels, publications and studios? Rather than corporate brands lining the pockets of individual artists under the guise of supporting the culture, why not collectively bargain for them to support the spaces and scenes that create it?"[25]

We need protest platforms for other forms of culture too. As we described in chapter 16, it's particularly easy to envisage one for ebooks, owned by and showcasing local authors and frequented by customers who want an alternative to Amazon—at least if we can strip away the DRM stranglehold that keeps publishers and readers locked in. We can imagine one for online video too, where popular YouTubers and Tik-Tokers jointly own their creativity via their own platform (though not in the EU, where that filtering law might require them to spend $100 million on additional start-up costs!). And it's even possible to imagine scaling up co-op music platforms like Resonate to a much larger number of artists and listeners, especially if new entry into this market could be facilitated by something like the rethought compulsory license we sketched out earlier. With such a structure, recording artists and composers could organize to form alternative creator-focused platforms—kind of like what Jay-Z did with Tidal, but owned by working-class artists rather than a handful of the very richest.

Game studios have huge co-operatizing potential too, according to Paris Marx, who has written and spoken extensively about labor issues in gaming. Game workers, including developers, designers, animators, artists, and translators, have begun pushing back against abusive practices like "crunch"—a phenomenon of mandatory overtime that can see some workers doing dozens of extra hours each week, for no extra pay. We explored some of the factors that drive this, like the 30 percent vigs being charged by Apple and Google on mobile and by Steam on PC, earlier in the book.

Game Workers Unite (GWU) is a new advocacy organization setting out to organize workers, and Marx is excited about its potential to achieve change—especially if workers manage to take over the means of production: "GWU Australia, in particular, has placed a focus on promoting worker cooperatives because its industry is primarily small studios, and organizers feel that's how they can make the biggest impact in the short term."[26] Bordeaux's Motion Twin is one small studio that has already co-operatized successfully. A self-described "anarcho-syndical workers cooperative," all eleven workers get paid the same amount, whether they are developer or artist, brand new or of longstanding tenure. If a game does well, the rewards are shared via cash bonuses. And their games *are* doing well: one recent release, *Dead Cells,* hit the 20,000 copies it needed to break even in a single week, going on to sell 730,000 units for PC alone during its first year on the market.[27] The system, says long-standing designer Sébastien Bénard, is "a direct challenge, not just to the exploitative practices you see at a lot of other companies, but also to tired old world corporate structures in general."[28] This might be just the beginning. Marx says GWU organizers see potential to convert large studios to worker ownership too: "It will just take a lot more work to get to that point."[29]

LOCAL PUBLIC OWNERSHIP CAN HELP TOO

Chapel Hill is the fifteenth-largest city in North Carolina. A college town with a major tech-center, it's known for its progressive politics. It also has a long history of supporting the arts. Its buildings are spectacularly decorated with murals by local artists, and its vibrant live music scene launched the careers of acts including James Taylor, Southern Culture on the Skids, Superchunk, and Ben Folds Five. So perhaps it's not surprising that it's at the vanguard of a movement to find a new way of making streaming work for local artists.

When we think about tackling major global challenges, a common first impulse is to look to federal governments to solve them. After all, they're the ones with the most resources, the broadest powers, and the right to enter into international treaties. That's why it can be so frustrating when those governments are immobilized on major issues like climate change—if they're not going to act, then who will?

Local governments are one obvious actor. While national governments have been disingenuously arguing over whether climate change really is being driven by humans, local leaders worldwide have collectively been organizing. Change at the local level doesn't look like federal initiatives, but it's still powerful. Local governments have been quietly converting their energy grids and public transportation systems to renewables, creating new rules around waste management, and insisting on sustainable development. Now operating at scale worldwide, such initiatives are making a real difference.

Local governments have long been big supporters of the arts. But now that the economic situation for creative workers has reached *this* stage of crisis, they are starting to think more deeply about how their resources can provide even better support to creative workers. In Chapel Hill, that includes taking a different approach to music streaming.

Tracks is a free curated music platform, featuring albums from over seventy acts local to the Chapel Hill region. Jointly funded by the local library and arts and culture center, the service seeks to connect local audiences to local talent. It's powered by a company called Rabble, which specializes in developing open-source software for libraries that reflects their values better than the big commercial offerings.[30] So far Rabble's streaming platform has been licensed to over a dozen library services—from Edmonton to Nashville, Austin to Multnomah County.

Not every band who wants to participate in Tracks makes it in: there's a curation process to ensure quality. Those who do are paid an honorarium of $200 per album. That might not sound like much to salaried workers, and the Chapel Hill group would certainly love to increase it if they could get the budget to do so. But still, it's the equivalent of the payout for about a million streams on Spotify's ad-supported tier,[31] and enough to support a small run of CDs or studio time for a new song.

As well as paying those stipends, the program works with local music leaders to facilitate new relationships and collaborations. This highlights something that's easy to lose sight of in all the angst around Big Streaming: the number of streams is not the only thing that's important. To support a vibrant arts space, we need projects that provide not just payment but form community and connection as well. Liz Pelly appreciates this element of Tracks, which directly counters her concern that corporate streaming platforms weaken the social connections between music communities: "Something like this is really pushing back on that by inviting artists to participate in the running of a platform." Tracks artist Rowdy (aka Joshua Rowsey), who curates the hip-hop collection, agrees: "I'm directly connecting with the Chapel Hill community, the people that support me the most. The people that know I'm a part of this foundation within the town of Chapel Hill."[32]

Participants license their music for at least five years; after that it will stay on the service unless they ask for it to be removed. According to other libraries that have been offering similar services for longer, such requests are rare to nonexistent. If that trend continues to hold, services like Tracks will end up creating ongoing public archives of local music. Given the ease with which music can be disappeared from commercial platforms, that's a very happy bonus.

Just as local climate interventions look different from national ones, local arts interventions do too. The libraries setting up services like Tracks aren't just hosting local music, they're actively promoting it to members. Since they're local, this kind of exposure is much more likely to translate into things that actually pay, like gig tickets, album sales, and merch. Services like Tracks aren't trying to be mini Spotifys—they're doing something much more intimate and local, something that Spotify simply can't achieve with its macro scale.

Similar initiatives are popping up in the book space too. In Australia for example, the indyreads platform lets some seven million people borrow ebooks and audiobooks via the New South Wales public library system. While its catalog is much smaller than that of the behemoth e-lending platform OverDrive, it contains more titles that are relevant to local readers, including titles from leading independent Australian publishers,

Australian literary classics, and the best home-grown self-published books.[33] Like Tracks, it isn't trying to compete with the big commercial services, and wouldn't have the resources or heft to negotiate the licenses it would need to do so. But with the promotional help of an army of passionate librarians, indyreads is making more local writing accessible to more local people, and opening up new revenues, readerships, and speaking opportunities for writers along the way.

Libraries are even helping to put independent film on a more sustainable footing, filling some of the void left by the demise of independent cinema. Their key partner has been Kanopy, which seeks to provide access to the world's most enriching, conversation-sparking, worldview-expanding films. Libraries, schools, and universities pay to subscribe and their patrons and students watch for free, with no ads, tracking, or waitlists. More than 50 percent of the revenue is paid back to independent filmmakers. Filmmaker Alicia Brown told us that "previously there was no real way to monetize the educational rights short of distributing to universities and libraries yourself. Educational was always just sold off as a job lot to the theatrical or ancillary distributor. Now filmmakers, in particular indie ones, are selling those rights separately and often seeing ongoing income from them."[34] But this market too is beginning to see the same problems as so many others we have looked at. Kanopy has become a big player, and libraries are increasingly reporting concerns about costs blowing out of control—to the point that in 2019, New York Public Library was forced to drop the service altogether.[35] And, in mid-2021, Kanopy was acquired by the library e-lending giant OverDrive (which had already recently gobbled up another rival, RBDigital, raising concerns about a lack of diversity in this marketplace too).

LARGER-SCALE PUBLIC OWNERSHIP

Sometimes smaller is better. Local initiatives can do things like build connection and community that the big commercial platforms just cannot. But of course, if national governments *do* want to get more involved in direct arts support, there's room for that too. One no-brainer in the book space is to introduce in the United States a public lending right that recognizes and rewards the educational and cultural value of books being available in libraries. Such rights already exist in more than thirty countries, including Australia, the UK, and Canada. There's an almost infinite variety of ways in which such schemes can be designed, but the most successful are centrally funded and administered—rather than coming out of individual library budgets—and inalienable, protecting the funding from being extracted from publishers in response to their squeezing by Amazon.

There's potential for grander-scale initiatives too—like entertainment lawyer Henderson Cole's radical proposal for an American Music Library. He envisages this as a government-financed digital public music library, which, like a public library for books, could be accessed by any American for free. Artists and composers would opt in by uploading their music and their labels and publishers would be barred from stopping them. As Pelly points out, "we don't currently conceptualize universal access to music as a public good, to be managed in the public interest with public funding. We should."[36]

In Cole's vision, a music library could also have a preservation role, keeping copies of uploaded music for future generations.[37] But what he is perhaps most excited about is the possibility of a new royalty system that bypasses the insane complexity and wastefulness of the one we have now.

Remember, the US federal government has the power to make copyright laws (subject to some international treaty constraints). That gives it a lot of flexibility to dictate the license terms that could govern this kind of public music library—including by mandating the shares that go to creators versus investors, and the rules around how much could be offset against recoupable debts and when. They could also ask participating artists to agree to caps as a condition of being involved: Cole suggests a monthly maximum of, say, $100,000 for recording artists and $75,000 for composers. This would leave more money for less commercially successful artists, smoothing out the music market's winner-takes-all effects.

Cole envisages a bare-bones service that doesn't have the fancy algorithms and shiny features of the commercial platforms. We like the sound of that. It's not all that difficult or expensive to stream music, especially since there are numerous open-source modules that are already ready for adaptation. Much of the major platforms' R&D investment is spent on figuring out how to surveil us better, persuading us to delegate ever more decision-making power to them, and finding ways to charge artists to access their listeners and generally promote the most powerful artists and labels over everyone else. That's the kind of investment we'd rather go without.

A platform like the American Music Library (or the Music Library of Canada, Australia, Mozambique. . .) would create a new revenue stream, strengthen creator power by setting an implicit price floor, and encourage commercial platforms to offer features that genuinely value-add for both creators and listeners.

What's more, once nations establish public service media within their territorial borders, they could augment them with multilateral agreements with other nations that have done the same: a Norwegian public music library could establish parity with a Senegalese one, and Jamaica could offer parity to Vietnam: "You let our residents into your library, and we'll do the same for yours."

Pelly isn't concerned that neither Tracks, Resonate, nor the American Music Library is a fix-all solution that will work for all artists and all listeners, because, given the diversity of music and music-making practice, she doesn't believe such a thing can exist. But she *is* excited about their potential to offer alternatives to the music streaming status quo: "Considered together, all three of these projects really do offer some compelling ideas to think about."[38]

National governments could also help creative workers seeking to extricate themselves from chokepoints by providing the infrastructure necessary to do so. In the UK, for example, publisher and author Dan Hind has called for the creation of a British Digital Cooperative, owned collectively by all citizens and "tasked with developing a surveillance-free platform architecture to enable citizens to interact with one another, provide support for publicly funded journalism, and develop resources for social and political communication." Recognizing the difficulties of individually competing with giants like Apple, Amazon, Google, and Facebook, this proposal would give alternatives the backing of an entire nation. Designed well, such initiatives could support the kind of meaningful alternatives that would let creative producers bust chokepoints wide open.

CHAPTER 19

UNITING AGAINST CHOKEPOINT CAPITALISM

"The purpose of a system is what it does."[1] So what is the point of the systems for commercializing culture that we've examined throughout this book? They're failing creators, but they're not failing *everyone*. They are highly effective at giving corporations power to mediate access between audiences and creators. They do a terrific job of extracting value from culture and of funneling it to those corporations' executives and shareholders.

This isn't an accident—it's by design. Our exploration shows corporations have strategically achieved the conditions they need to take control of creative markets and use them to shake down creators: anticircumvention laws, vertical and horizontal integration, high costs of market entry, captured regulators, opaque accounting, and the power to aggregate copyrights on an industrial scale and wield them against the very people they are ostensibly meant to protect. Combined with antitrust's blinkered focus on consumer welfare and the neoliberal economic dogma that a company's only purpose is to increase profits and maximize shareholder value, the outcome is inevitable: ever bigger corporations squeezing out an ever bigger share. That's why the choice between Big Tech and Big Content is no choice at all. Whomever creators throw their lot in with, they'll get essentially the same deal: the least the industry can get away with, and the promise it will be ratcheted downward whenever it's possible to do so.

Humans have an innate drive to create, and many of us prefer creative labor to other kinds of work. Most of our creations will never find a big enough market to support the costs of making them, and that's okay. While there's a case to be made that the world would be a better place if everyone got to follow their dreams, it's reasonable enough to understand that your neighbor's terrible rapping can't supply him with a full-time living. What's not okay is the current system, which actively facilitates the shakedown of creators, making it harder and harder for even those who have substantial audiences to make a living.

Copyright is a policy that aims to structure the market for creative works. It's a mistake to weigh copyright systems based on the volume of revenue they create—you have to pay attention to where those dollars actually end up. It should allow the greatest variety of creators to make the widest variety of works and apportion the revenues they generate fairly between their progenitors and those who provide the support services necessary for us to access them.

Knowledge and culture are vital to human thriving. Art gives expression to new ideas and movements and cultures. Making and experiencing it can be an act of solidarity or protest; it can succor our traumas and heighten moments of joy. Music, poetry, fiction, memoir, sculpture, painting, and dance are all necessary to making sense of (and bearing!) being human. We *need* people to be able to dedicate their professional lives to these crafts.

Creative workers and producers deserve a better deal—one that delivers them a dignified and fair share of the wealth generated by their work. We've shown some of the key actions that can get them there, like enshrining transparency and interoperability rights, simplifying licensing, facilitating collective action and cooperative ownership, putting time limits on copyright contracts, and mandating minimum wages for creative work. To make such changes a reality, however, we need to unite. We need to recognize that the strip-mining of creative workers is part of a broader project in service of an oligarchy—that it's not just creators and independent producers who are being screwed over, but almost everyone, as wealth keeps being inexorably funneled toward the rich. The death of the middle-class creator is part of the death of the middle class.

In the ongoing war of capital versus labor, between oligarchy and democracy, capital is clearly ascendant. Wages in most developed nations have stagnated over the last forty years, though productivity has risen steeply.[2] At the same time, profit margins in concentrated industries are rising.[3] Anti-competitive flywheels are *everywhere*, locking in users and suppliers, making markets hostile to new entrants, and leveraging that power to force suppliers and workers to accept ever lower prices. We are sharing less in the returns of our work because chokepoints are sapping our ability to bargain for improved conditions and pay.

We have focused on the plight of creative workers, but they're by no means the only ones hurting under chokepoint capitalism. Monopolies and monopsonies have become endemic, squeezing the life out of customers and suppliers. And then there are the uncountable corporations who don't quite meet the extraordinarily high standards required by US antitrust law to earn that label, but which also use their control over chokepoints to siphon away a disproportionate share of value, particularly from other people's labor.

It's not just antitrust that helps companies suck their suppliers dry—there's a whole bestiary of terrible policies that abet vampire capitalists as they drain their victims. Noncompete clauses used to protect businesses by forbidding senior staff from taking confidential information and intellectual property to rivals, but now employers routinely use them to prevent even entry-level workers from moving to better paying jobs. This is endemic in the US fast food industry, where they affect an incredible *80 percent* of workers: if you're a cashier at Taco Bell, you can't take those skills to a rival franchise.[4] Higher-paid workers can be affected too: Apple, Facebook, Google, and other Silicon Valley giants colluded with each other and with media companies (like Pixar) for years, agreeing not to poach each other's highly skilled techies, illegally reducing workers' options, and putting downward pressure on their salaries. This was a no-no even under America's neutered antitrust law—and since high-paid engineers can afford high-paid lawyers, these companies were forced to settle for $415 million after being caught out.[5] Other businesses learned from this, and prefer to engage in tacit collusion instead—what asset management firms coyly call "cooperative behavior," which works best in industries "with few players, rational management, barriers to entry, a lack of exit barriers and noncomplex rules of engagement"—exactly the conditions that are most likely to exist in heavily concentrated markets.[6]

Another popular tactic is to strip power from suppliers and workers via contracts binding them to private arbitration, so that if there's a dispute, they're not allowed to exercise their legal rights in court. As we've discussed, arbitration is a private process, hidden from public scrutiny, usually with caps on the amounts that can be recovered and no right of appeal. Arbitrators have a vested interest in siding with employers, since they're the repeat hirers, so it's not surprising employers win much more in arbitration than in court, and, even when they lose, have to pay out less by way of damages.[7]

Such terms typically also force employees to give up rights to class action lawsuits. If workers can't band together to collectively assert their rights, corporations have a much easier time violating them. This encourages abuses such as wage theft, which in America has become pervasive and routine. Like the record companies that didn't want to hand over to artists even the measly share they were owed, surveys have found 60 percent of nursing homes, 58 percent of onion producers, and 100 percent of poultry plants steal wages.[8] In 2017, the Economic Policy Institute found that 2.4 million workers in the ten most populous states had been cheated out of $3,300 each due to minimum wage violations alone—an amount approaching 25 percent of the wages they actually took home.[9] Some of these thefts are no doubt by companies whose own margins are getting squeezed by large corporations above them, and who then try to make up the difference by taking it from the most atomized and vulnerable people in the supply chain.

Workers who try to unionize—like the Amazon warehouse workers in Bessemer, Alabama, in 2021—face vicious, lawless, anti-union blitzes that trample all over the tattered remains of labor law. The goal—as Alex N. Press explained to the hosts of the techno-critical podcast *This Machine Kills*—is not just to defeat the union drive, but to salt the earth, traumatizing all the workers involved so that they *never join another union drive, ever again.*[10]

Of course, to have a union drive, you must first be entitled to unionize. In the US, worker misclassification—the risible fiction that "gig economy" workers, whose every movement is scripted in fine detail by their employers, are actually "independent contractors"—is the go-to tactic for denying workers the right to form a union in the first place. In California, the fight to enshrine worker misclassification in law hit a peak in 2020, when gig economy companies spent an unprecedented $200 million to pass Proposition 22—outspending nearly all the races for actual seats in the state legislature combined.[11] Predictably, California businesses started firing their "essential" workers within weeks of its passage, replacing them with scabs whose boss was an app.[12] As we go to press, Uber and Lyft are leading a charge to spend $100 million to put a Prop 22–style measure on the ballot in Massachusetts for the 2022 mid-term elections (one spot of good news: a drafting error in California's Prop 22 led to a court's invalidating the measure, though the state Supreme Court was yet to rule on the appeal as we went to press).

Though wages haven't been growing, costs have. Monopolies bear much of the blame for this, too, especially when it comes to education, healthcare, and housing, which have all outpaced wages over the last half century. Over the last forty years, college tuition in the US has risen four times faster than inflation, and eight times faster than household income, leaving forty-five million Americans with $1.5 trillion in debt.[13] This has trickle-down effects: "Balances carried further into mid-life, or taken on later in life to finance further education or a family member's education, impairing economic wellbeing for a widening and diversifying swathe of the population, inhibiting savings, increasing precarity, and draining the very incomes the student debt was supposed to increase."[14]

In health, monopolies are everywhere: emergency care, ambulance rides, kidney dialysis, nursing homes, and even *saline bags*.[15] Health insurance is particularly concentrated, and, for families, premiums average over $20,000 a year—often with high deductibles if they actually have to use it.[16] Employers pick up much of that cost for those in jobs with benefits, but that too is a form of lock-in: leaving an abusive job doesn't just mean losing pay but potentially risks *everything* if someone in your family lives with a chronic illness, falls ill, or has an accident before you find a replacement.

The growing concentration of wealth in the hands of the financial elite has also contributed to massive rises in the cost of housing as they speculatively invest in property as a vehicle for multiplying their money. Private equity is playing a part there too, having bought up hundreds of thousands of single-family homes in the wake of the housing crash. It now rents them out, issuing regular above-inflation increases and extortionate fees and charges that take advantage of high switching costs (think how much it costs to move!) to keep people locked in.[17] The COVID-19 crisis has only exacerbated this, as speculators have driven house prices to double or triple their prices, especially in depressed midwestern cities, making homeownership unaffordable for regular families who end up paying more than a mortgage would cost in rent to offshore investors.[18]

The combination of stagnant wages and increasing costs results in ever less financial safety: 40 percent of Americans don't have $400 to cover an unexpected expense.[19] The evidence is damning: the Chicago School's fixation on the consumer harm standard has failed even on its own narrow terms. By putting the focus so exclusively on consumer prices, it encouraged corporations to squeeze their workers and suppliers, which reduced people's ability to pay for goods and services—exactly the same result as if consumer prices had gone up! The increasing financial precarity that has accompanied these forty years of antitrust neglect is one reason why so many people are desperate and angry, and perhaps also helps explain why they are willing to listen to demagogues promising to blow the system up.

The current system is self-reinforcing: concentrated industries generate big profits for their investors, who, seeing how well their anticompetitive flywheels work, go looking for other industries to which they can apply the same extractive tactics. Its primary beneficiaries are an infinitesimal coterie of the ultra-rich, who spend increasing amounts of time segregated from the rest of society in their gate-guarded mansions. The philosophy that underpins the billionaire class (and the Chicago School generally) is a sort of right-wing Marxism. "They buy the Marxian proposition that the state is an executive committee for rigging the economy in the interest of the ruling class," says Harvard professor Joseph Kalt. "But they think that that is a good thing as long as the ruling class is based on wealth, however previously acquired. All their objections are to those who use some form of societal power other than wealth to try to rig the economy in their interest."[20] This is the pathology of a tiny minority who believe having more money than they could ever conceivably spend is more important than other humans' having access to basic food and shelter.

Things are seriously messed up, and not just for creative workers. Therein lies the possibility for change.

Copyright scholar James Boyle tells a parable about the birth of the ecology movement: before the term *ecology* was coined, there were thousands of issues that weren't obviously part of the same cause. If you cared about endangered owls and I cared about the ozone layer, were we on the same side? Your thing is the charismatic nocturnal avian, and my thing is the chemical composition of upper atmosphere gasses. How are those two related? The coining of the term *ecology* united the thousands of issues into a single movement, with thousands of constituencies working toward a shared goal. You were fighting for endangered owls and I was fighting for the ozone layer but we were also fighting *together* and having each other's backs.[21]

Today, chokepoint capitalism afflicts everyone from chicken farmers to professional wrestlers (a kind of high-risk creative labor that is dominated by just *one* employer, a Trumpist billionaire who bought out all his competition, misclassified his employees as contractors, stripped them of health insurance, and left them to beg on GoFundMe for palliative care as they die young from workplace-related injuries).[22] It afflicts bank tellers—US retail banking is dominated by four firms; the largest, Wells Fargo, long pressured its tellers to defraud customers to meet unrealistic sales quotas and retaliated against those who refused by firing them and then adding them to a do-not-hire list that prevented them from getting other work.[23] When Wells Fargo got caught, it blamed its low-level employees, and summarily fired thousands for fraud, making it almost impossible for them to get new jobs too.[24] Chokepoint capitalism hurts nurses and rideshare drivers and delivery riders and adjunct professors at major universities. It afflicts fast food workers and thoracic surgeons, journalists and auto mechanics and countless more professions. And since big companies force other companies in their supply chains to get big too, even if your part of your industry doesn't look like these labor markets yet, it's only a matter of time if things keep heading in this direction.

There are, in short, thousands of issues waiting to be turned into a movement, and billions of people who stand to benefit from such a coalition. In fact, it's hard to think of a progressive movement this fight *doesn't* touch: worried about racial and gender pay gaps? Well, chokepoint firms preferentially suppress and steal the wages of racialized people and women. Worried about access to healthy food? Chickenizers process food beyond recognition and make it as addictive as possible to weasel themselves between the people who eat it and the farmers who grow it, all to increase their share. Worried about *ecology*? Corporate concentration worsens all of it—the owls, the ozone layer, the climate, microplastics, soil erosion, animal cruelty, the lot. And meanwhile, this tiny minority's ever growing wealth and power are put to work against us in doing what so obviously needs to be done to save the planet.

Creative workers have an audience, a platform—a source of power. But we're just a part of a much larger struggle, one our comrades have already been fighting for a long time. As revolutionary demands go, ours are pretty basic: to attain an equilibrium between workers, suppliers, and businesses that allows everyone to live sustainably, with economic dignity and a fair share of the value their work creates.

SHATTERING CHOKEPOINTS

We've seen it's supremely difficult to maintain the free conditions that are central to capitalism, since markets have such a strong natural tendency toward concentration, extraction, and rent-seeking.[25] That's why ongoing interventions are needed, and why, without them, we've ended up in another robber baron era.

One systematic solution that would provide a continuing check on these abuses is a job guarantee. These can be formulated in any number of different ways, but the kind we're talking about is a federally funded, locally administered job for anyone who wants one, with full benefits, at a socially inclusive wage, doing the kinds of work that needs doing in their communities but that the market fails to achieve.

Guarantee skeptics like to quote the story of Milton Friedman, who, while traveling overseas, once enquired why workers were using shovels instead of bulldozers. When told it was to increase the number of construction jobs, Friedman apparently replied: "Then instead of shovels, why don't you give them spoons and create even more . . . ?"[26]

But of course, nobody's proposing using guaranteed jobs to dole out meaningless labor. Why would they, when there's so much important work we urgently need done and that the market is failing to deliver? Remediating climate change will involve unimaginably labor-intensive tasks, like relocating every coastal city miles inland, building high-speed rail links to replace aviation, caring for hundreds of millions of traumatized, displaced people, and treating runaway zoonotic and insect-borne pandemics. We also need to fill gaps caused by the current system, which under-resources important activities that won't generate enough profit in the market: caring for children and the elderly, repairing crumbling infrastructure, transitioning from our suicidal reliance on fossil fuels, developing communities, building and running libraries and museums, providing quality news journalism, making art, and any number of other activities that support the public good. There are people who need work and work that needs doing, and a job guarantee would unite the two where the market fails to do so.

Providing nonmarket jobs is particularly important for art. Excessively powerful corporations are a huge part of why creators struggle to get paid, but not the only challenge. Another one is "Baumol's cost disease," the phenomenon where labor-intensive work becomes relatively more expensive over time. A performance of Beethoven's Ninth Symphony in 1824, the year it was completed, took about 70 minutes. A performance of the same symphony today, some 200 years later, takes about 70 minutes. In 1824, it required 30 to 40 performers, depending on the size of the chorus. Today it's just the same. With practice, perhaps they could play it twice as fast, or with half as many performers. But not many people would pay to hear that. By contrast, the car that drives you to the symphony, the wine you drink at the intermission, the clothes you wear, and the upholstery on your seat all embody *far* less labor: in 1824, a pair of stockings to wear to the symphony would cost $1 (about $22 in 2020 dollars); today, Amazon will sell you a pair of "No Nonsense Great Shapes All Over Shaping Tights" for $1.99. Automation, material science and other productivity gains have reduced the labor embodied in a pair of tights by about 90 percent. While the musicians who perform the Ninth do benefit from productivity gains (their clothes, instruments, transport, homes, sheet music, and even their training are much cheaper than in 1824), the actual labor in their performance is stubbornly stuck in the forty-five person-hour range. This is cost disease. Music is actually a little cheaper than it was in Beethoven's day, but, relative to most everything else, it is *much* more expensive. The same goes for sculpting, painting, dancing, and writing books. The wage-bill of all these labor-intensive arts just keeps increasing relative to everything else—and it always will. If we leave their funding entirely to the market, eventually they'll no longer be possible, and important parts of human culture will be lost. A job guarantee for creative workers could help prevent that.

There's precedent for this: the US successfully responded to the Great Depression in the 1930s by creating millions of public jobs as part of Roosevelt's New Deal. As Naomi Klein explains, this included meaningful work for "tens of thousands of painters, musicians, photographers, playwrights, filmmakers, actors, authors, and a huge array of craftspeople," generating "an explosion of creativity and a staggering body of work," including live music performances that reached 150 million people.[27]

A job guarantee would mean that the day you lose your employment you could pick up a new, dignified job—including whatever training that requires—until someone in the private sector decides to offer you a better one. With a job guarantee, no one would suffer the paradox of chronic unemployment—when employers won't hire you because you don't have a job—and we'd get done important, socially valuable work that is not valued by the market.

One criticism of job guarantees is that they're too expensive and can't possibly be afforded. That isn't so. For one thing, they're not all that expensive. One 2018 analysis estimated a full guarantee for US workers would cost $543 billion per year, or 3 percent of GDP.[28] In exchange, we'd have everyone who wanted a job but couldn't otherwise get one working to make society better, adding to community stability and purpose. To put that into context, US government spending in response to just the first few months of the coronavirus pandemic in 2020 is estimated at over $6 *trillion*,[29] about twelve times as much, of which substantial portions are going straight into billionaires' pockets via stock buybacks, special dividends, executive bonuses, and service on debt that's held by the company's investors, who borrowed from the company to pay themselves dividends that will worsen inequality at the public's expense.

Even if it cost more than that, we could afford it. One potential revenue source that's increasingly popular with voters is a wealth tax on the richest individuals and corporations. Taxing the rich is a great idea. Indeed, it's absolutely crucial if we want to have a political process where good ideas can be fairly heard. Right now, as we've seen, the richest people use their money and influence to make public policy (like the tax code, labor laws, and antitrust) serve their own economic interests. Those distortions hurt workers and the environment, giving the uberwealthy free rein to shovel an ever greater proportion of collectively generated wealth into their own accounts.

But we don't actually *need* to tax the rich in order to pay for programs. As Stephanie Kelten explains in *The Deficit Myth*, that's not how money works.[30] Money is spent into existence by "monetarily sovereign" national governments and then taxed back out of existence.[31] Governments can't default on debts in their own currency—they can't run out of money. But they *can* issue too much currency: if governments create money to buy things or labor at a rate that exceeds the supply, then there will be a bidding war, which drives prices up, which creates inflation, which is indeed very bad news.

Done carefully, however, governments can buy anything that's available for sale in their currency without creating inflation. In fact, during extraordinary times, governments can even buy stuff the private sector wants to buy without creating inflation. During World War II for example, the US government spent a *lot* of money into existence to pay for war matériel. But it didn't want defense workers and soldiers' families buying up the same stuff they needed, so they convinced those people to stash away their money in "war bonds," which kept their war wages out of circulation and then dribbled them out once production reverted to peacetime goods. Where that wasn't enough, they imposed rationing to limit the amount of key goods and materials the private sector was allowed to buy. If we decide to prioritize full employment in dignified and socially useful work, there are ways to achieve it without blowing the economy up.

Right-wing economists criticize job guarantees by arguing that offering everyone a good job would create "pressure to introduce a higher wage or certain benefits that the private sector doesn't offer."[32] They're *so* close to getting it. A jobs guarantee would indeed increase the share of GDP that goes to labor, because every private sector employer would know its workers could shift into public work if the conditions were better there. That's why a job guarantee is such a powerful response to chokepoint capitalists. The only reason megacorporations can steal wages and divert such a big share of profits to investors is because their workers and suppliers have no other choice. By giving them one, a job guarantee would put a meaningful floor under pay and conditions. As private sector conditions improved, people would move away from guaranteed jobs and back into the market. But the public jobs would always be there, a built-in safeguard to respond when corporations grow *too* abusive.

Of course, a job guarantee is just one potential response to corporate shakedowns. There's a lot more we need to do—and that can feel overwhelming. Confronted with all this concentrated corporate power, interwoven with the power of our captured states, how can we also fight the climate emergency, COVID-19, the other pandemics that will inevitably follow, and racial, gender, and economic inequality—especially when we have ever fewer resources left to us to do so?

The starting point is collectivity. When we were looking for a home for this book, we heard from a reader who loved it, but thought it wouldn't be marketable because its solutions were "systemic, not individual." But that's exactly the point. Individual solutions aren't going to get workers a fair go any more than recycling is going to fix climate change. They might move the dial, but they won't achieve the fundamental change we need to save the world. If we're going to successfully countervail the enormous power of today's robber barons, it will be by collectively combining to do so.

The second thing to recognize is that these systems of monopoly, wage-theft, discrimination, environmental devastation, and exploitation reinforce each other, so any territory we win on one front is an advance on *all* fronts. The one good thing about excessive corporate concentration permeating everything is that there are so many places to fight it. Think of the Medicare for All battle: if healthcare in the USA were guaranteed as a basic human right, it would do much to bring abusive healthcare monopolists to heel—and the hours spent wrestling with our insurers or coping with untreated illnesses or trying to bear abusive working conditions so we don't lose our benefits could be turned to fighting wage theft. End wage theft and big corporations would have less money to devote to lobbying to rig the system even more in their favor and working people could reclaim the hours they spend in line at food banks and free themselves from the mental and emotional burden of juggling bills, creating new capacity to fight for better public funding for early childhood and aged care. Achieve that, and the people (usually women) who are forced to amputate their careers to look after small children or elderly parents will face less career discrimination, have higher-quality time with their families, and more energy to fight for climate justice.

In other words, change is iterative: the only way to eat an elephant is one bite at a time. We need to take action that will open some space for reform, then use that to lever open some more. And of course, once we collectively achieve a few big victories, the proof that real change is possible would itself invigorate us to fight on other fronts—providing the conditions for a new New Deal.

In this book we've focused predominantly on the American legal structures that have enabled corporations to grab so much power. But of course neoliberalism and Chicago School reasoning have been exported far and wide, and chokepoints can be found the world over. The tools we've identified for slowing down anticompetitive flywheels—like transparency rights, minimum wages for creative work, reversion rights, reform of DRM law and creator contracts, collective action, and collective ownership—can all help elsewhere too.

But the wider world has a key role to play in shattering chokepoints beyond this. Today's oligarchs have a great tradition of regulatory arbitrage (obtaining a law that favors them in one jurisdiction, and then using it to ratchet up the protection they get elsewhere). Take copyright term extension, for example, which we've shown disproportionately benefits not the creators who made the works, but the corporate owners who extract their rights. The Berne Convention mandates a minimum copyright term of author's life plus fifty years. That was the term adopted by nearly all European nations, but when the EU harmonized copyright law in 1993, major rights holders successfully lobbied for everyone to have to adopt the German term of life plus seventy—the longest outlier. Within five years, those same corporations had persuaded US legislators to match the European term. Since then, the extended term has been exported widely around the world via trade agreements.

There's potential for similar arbitrage in a way that supports *creators*, as distinct from copyright owners. As it becomes clearer that neither Big Tech nor Big Content will deliver a sustainable creative ecosystem, we are going to see more pro-creator policies implemented around the world. It's already happening—just look at those EU mandates that will empower artists via new rights to fair payment, transparency, and reversion, the proposals in countries like South Africa and Canada to give creators meaningful new rights to reclaim their copyrights, and the increasingly widespread actions (initiated most significantly in South

Korea and Japan) that are preventing Apple and Google from using their app store chokepoints.

Yes, the same powerful corporations that reign in the US are spending big to mitigate these new laws and prevent others from being enacted. Yes, that made the EU mandates less powerful than they could have been, and it's watering down their implementations in each member nation. But the tide is turning, and genuinely pro-creator (as distinct from pro-copyright owner) policies are being implemented around the world. They are hugely powerful levers for change because effective policy is contagious. As it becomes clear that such laws meaningfully help creators, it will feed organization and resistance elsewhere, increasing momentum and the case for further reform.

Even mere *scrutiny* in one nation can force change that affects others. When the Japan Fair Trade Commission investigated Apple's app store monopoly, for example, it forced the giant to agree to allow "reader apps" like Netflix and Spotify, which allow users to access previously purchased or subscribed content, to offer in-app links for account sign-ups that would bypass Apple's vig. Perhaps because it was too complex to limit this to Japan, Apple announced that this change would apply globally.[33] Although this is a relatively small concession, and much more needs to be done, it demonstrates the power of change in one country to influence what happens elsewhere. And of course, pro-creator policies don't have to take the form of regulation. Revolutionary arts funding programs and new investments in collectively owned public infrastructure can be powerfully contagious too.

Corporations rely on the illusion of corporate personhood, using expensively crafted "brand identities" to present themselves to us as having personalities aimed at making us feel an emotional connection—and like we're all in this together. But firms have no intrinsic virtues. They are not our friends. If a corporation is a "person," it's an immortal colony organism that treats human beings as inconvenient gut flora. It doesn't have a personality and it doesn't have ethics. Its sole imperative is to do whatever it can get away with to extract maximum economic value from humans and the planet.

Left to its own devices, Big Tech will never do well by creative workers, not because Big Tech companies are staffed by robotic engineers who don't value art, but because the more they pay artists, the less they can funnel to executives and shareholders. Big Tech treats its techies better than its artists because it has to: there are far more tech jobs than there are qualified technologists to fill them. The instant that changes, those engineers are toast.

We noted in this book that the Big Three recording companies have started playing it much straighter with artists over the last few years, abandoning many of their historic fraud practices. That's not because UMG or Warner are "good" companies: it's because recording artists gained more choices about how they make, disseminate, and earn money from their art. When record companies held the whip hand over artists, they wielded it cruelly. If they ever regain that power, they'll do exactly the same thing again. That's what an unfettered capitalist system is set up to do.

The only one way to make corporations respect their suppliers and workers is to ensure those people have genuine alternatives. Make content companies fear their artists will take their art elsewhere. Make real the risk of legal and economic reprisals for abuse. Demand meaningful rights for workers. Drag corporations to the bargaining table and make them sign union contracts that more fairly balance the interests of capital and labor. Competition isn't about "making the market efficient." It's not even about "choice." It's about self-determination: weakening the power of intermediaries who would otherwise take away our ability to lead our creative and human lives in the way of our choosing, who would—and do—force us to arrange our lives to benefit their shareholders, no matter how badly that works for us.

Creators are told that the solution to their financial woes is more copyright, or internet filters, or stronger digital locks. But that's just like telling Walmart employees the reason they can't survive without food stamps is because people don't buy enough stuff, like telling the employees of the Tyson poultry empire that the reason they need to wear adult diapers on the production line is because people don't eat enough chicken. All three phenomena have the same root cause: that we've organized our societies to make rich people richer at everyone else's expense. If we're going to do something about it, we're going to have to do it together.

ACKNOWLEDGMENTS

Thanks to Alex Adsett, Jake Beaumont-Nesbitt, Jamie Boyle, Alicia Brown, Richard Burgess, Peter Carstensen, Seb Chan, Colleen Cross, Kevin Erickson, Jacob Flynn, Ula Furgal, Daniel Gilbert, Jane C. Ginsburg, Jake Goldenfein, David Goodman, Evan Greer, Amanda Harcourt, Matt Hawn, Gwen Hinze, Justine Hyde, Jennifer Jenkins, Olivia Lanchester, Aurora Lucien, Carl Malamud, Paris Marx, Susan May, Corynne McSherry, Michelle Meagher, James Meese, Rev. Moose, Lisa Morrison, Daniel Olszewski, Lizzie O'Shea, James Parker, Liz Pelly, Palmyre Pessiot, Paola Pessiot, François Petitjean, JP Pomare, Bram Presser, João Pedro Quintais, Mary Rasenberger, Barak Richman, Sam Ricketson, Juliet Rogers, Orna Ross, Tom Ryan, Stefan Rudnicki, Pam Samuelson, Nicholas Shaxson, David Slack, Nicola Solomon, Matt Stoller, Zephyr Teachout, Kay Tucker, Diane Wachtell, Christina Ward, Kim Weatherall, Tim Wu, Joshua Yuvaraj, and Brian Zisk. Not all of them agree with everything we've written in this book, but their experiences and insights have enriched it, each of whom contributed in some way to this book.

We're exceptionally grateful to Joanna Green, Susan Lumenello, Will Morningstar, and the rest of the Beacon Press crew who helped birth this book, as well as our agent for it, Paul Lucas of Janklow & Nesbit Associates. Lauren Kinnard drew the gorgeous illustrations.

Thanks also to the folks we interviewed who needed to remain anonymous for fear of reprisals, to the hundreds of other people we've spoken to about creators' rights and the excessive power of big business over the last decade, and to those we should have mentioned by name here but regrettably forgot—sorry about that!

Rebecca worked on this book from unceded lands of the Wurundjeri people of the Kulin nations. She pays her respects to their elders past and present, including those fighting to reclaim the knowledge, language, and culture Australia's white settlers worked so systematically to destroy. Cory is a special advisor to the Electronic Frontier Foundation, but the views expressed here are his own. The research in this book was partly supported by funding from the Australian Research Council (FT170100011 and LP160100387) and Melbourne Law School.

NOTES

CHAPTER 1: BIG BUSINESS CAPTURED CULTURE

1. Scott Timberg, *Culture Crash: The Killing of the Creative Class* (New Haven, CT: Yale University Press, 2015), 79, 94.

2. Committee on Digital, Culture, Media and Sport, UK House of Commons, *Economics of Music Streaming*, Second Report of Session 2021–22 (London, July 15, 2021), 45, https://committees.parliament.uk/publications/6739/documents /72525/default.

3. William Deresiewicz, *The Death of the Artist: How Creators Are Struggling to Survive in the Age of Billionaires and Big Tech* (New York: Henry Holt, 2020), 42.

4. Deresiewicz, *The Death of the Artist*, 319–20.

5. Orley Ashenfelter, Daniel Hosken, and Matthew Weinberg, "Did Robert Bork Understate the Competitive Impact of Mergers? Evidence from Consummated Mergers," *Journal of Law and Economics* 57, no. S3 (Aug. 2014): S67–S100, https://doi.org/10.1086/675862.

6. Julie Cohen, *Between Truth and Power: The Legal Constructions of Informational Capitalism* (New York: Oxford University Press, 2019), 7.

7. Credit Suisse, "The Incredible Shrinking Universe of Stocks: The Causes and Consequences of Fewer U.S. Equities," http://www.cmgwealth.com/wp -content/uploads/2017/03/document_1072753661.pdf.

8. Ashenfelter, Hosken, and Weinberg, "Did Robert Bork Understate the Competitive Impact of Mergers?" S67–S100; John Kwoka, *Mergers, Merger Control, and Remedies: A Retrospective Analysis of U.S. Policy* (Cambridge, MA: MIT Press, 2014).

9. Edward Wyatt, "F.C.C. Commissioner Leaving to Join Comcast," Media Decoder Blog, *New York Times*, May 11, 2011, https://mediadecoder.blogs .nytimes.com/2011/05/11/f-c-c-commissioner-to-join-comcast/.

10. Matthew Yglesias, "New Federal Reserve Data Shows How the Rich Have Gotten Richer," *Vox*, June 13, 2019, https://www.vox.com/policy-and-politics /2019/6/13/18661837/inequality-wealth-federal-reserve-distributional -financial-accounts.

11. Gustavo Grullon, Yelena Larkin, and Roni Michaely, "Are U.S. Industries Becoming More Concentrated?" Swiss Finance Institute Research Paper no. 19–41 (Aug. 31, 2017), https://ssrn.com/abstract=2612047.

12. Simcha Barkai, "Declining Labor and Capital Shares," *Journal of Finance* 75, no. 5 (2020): 2421–63, https://onlinelibrary.wiley.com/doi/full/10.1111/jofi .12909.
13. Jonathan Tepper and Denise Hearn, *The Myth of Capitalism: Monopolies and the Death of Competition* (Hoboken, NJ: Wiley, 2019), 38.
14. Zephyr Teachout, *Break 'Em Up: Recovering Our Freedom from Big Ag, Big Tech, and Big Money* (New York: All Points Books, 2020), 145.
15. Lina Khan, "The Ideological Roots of America's Market Power Problem," *Yale Law Journal Forum* 127 (2018), https://ssrn.com/abstract=3367602, 961; internal note omitted.
16. Teachout, *Break 'Em Up*, 163.
17. Teachout, *Break 'Em Up*, 14–15.
18. Tepper and Hearn, *The Myth of Capitalism*, 15.
19. Warren Buffett and Carol Loomis, "Mr. Buffett on the Stock Market," *Fortune*, Nov. 22, 1999, https://archive.fortune.com/magazines/fortune/fortune _archive/1999/11/22/269071/index.htm.
20. Adrianne Jeffries, "To Head Off Regulators, Google Makes Certain Words Taboo," *The Markup*, Aug. 7, 2020, https://themarkup.org/google-the-giant /2020/08/07/google-documents-show-taboo-words-antitrust.
21. Jason Del Rey, "The Making of Amazon Prime, the Internet's Most Successful and Devastating Membership Program," *Vox*, May 3, 2019, https://www.vox .com/recode/2019/5/3/18511544/amazon-prime-oral-history-jeff-bezos-one -day-shipping.
22. Tepper and Hearn, *The Myth of Capitalism*, 103.
23. Stacy Mitchell, "Amazon Is a Private Government. Congress Needs to Step Up," *The Atlantic*, Aug. 10, 2020, https://www.theatlantic.com/ideas/archive /2020/08/americans-can-barely-imagine-congress-works/615091.
24. George Anderson, "Is Amazon Undercutting Third-Party Sellers Using Their Own Data?" *Forbes*, Oct. 30, 2014, https://www.forbes.com/sites/retailwire /2014/10/30/is-amazon-undercutting-third-party-sellers-using-their-own-data.
25. Anderson, "Is Amazon Undercutting Third-Party Sellers Using Their Own Data?"
26. Kiri Masters, "89% Of Consumers Are More Likely to Buy Products from Amazon Than Other E-Commerce Sites: Study," *Forbes*, Mar. 20, 2019, https://www .forbes.com/sites/kirimasters/2019/03/20/study-89-of-consumers-are-more -likely-to-buy-products-from-amazon-than-other-e-commerce-sites.
27. Barry C. Lynn, "The Big Tech Extortion Racket," *Harper's Magazine*, Aug. 14, 2020, https://harpers.org/archive/2020/09/the-big-tech-extortion-racket.
28. When several firms control buying, that's technically called an "oligopsony," but, again, the term *monopsony* is colloquially used to refer to both a single firm and a collection of firms with buying power. We use the term *monopsony* to refer to both a pure monopsony and an oligopsony.
29. Deresiewicz, *Death of the Artist*, 168.
30. Peter C. Carstensen, *Competition Policy and the Control of Buyer Power: A Global Issue* (Cheltenham, UK: Edward Elgar, 2017), 15, https://doi.org/10.4337 /9781782540588.
31. Carstensen, *Competition Policy and the Control of Buyer Power*, 10.

32. Carstensen, *Competition Policy and the Control of Buyer Power*, 12.
33. Carstensen, *Competition Policy and the Control of Buyer Power*, 12.
34. Adam Lashinsky, Doris Burke, and J. P. Mangalindan, "Jeff Bezos: The Ultimate Disrupter," *Fortune* 166, no. 9 (Dec. 3, 2012): 100.
35. Nicole Goodkind, "Jeff Bezos Thanks Amazon Workers and Customers After Space Flight: 'You Paid for All of This,'" *Fortune*, July 21, 2021, https://fortune.com/2021/07/20/jeff-bezos-thanks-amazon-workers-and-customers-after-space-flight-you-paid-for-all-of-this.
36. Executive Office of the President [Joseph R. Biden Jr.], Executive Order no. 14036: Executive Order on Promoting Competition in the American Economy, July 9, 2021, https://www.whitehouse.gov/briefing-room/presidential-actions/2021/07/09/executive-order-on-promoting-competition-in-the-american-economy.
37. Christine S. Wilson, "Welfare Standards Underlying Antitrust Enforcement: What You Measure Is What You Get," transcript of keynote speech delivered at George Mason Law Review Antitrust Symposium "Antitrust at the Crossroads?" Arlington, VA, Feb. 15, 2019, https://www.ftc.gov/system/files/documents/public_statements/1455663/welfare_standard_speech_-_cmr-wilson.pdf.
38. Frank H. Easterbrook, "The Limits of Antitrust," *Texas Law Review* 63, no. 1 (Aug. 1984): 2.
39. Astra Taylor, *The People's Platform: Taking Back Power and Culture in the Digital Age* (New York: Picador, 2015), 201.
40. Orla Lynskey, "Regulating 'Platform Power,'" working paper, Jan. 2017, LSE Law, Society and Economy Working Papers, Department of Law, London School of Economics and Political Science, London, UK, 6, http://eprints.lse.ac.uk/73404.
41. Sangeet Paul Choudary, Marshall W. Van Alstyne, and Geoffrey G. Parker, "Network Effects: The Power of the Platform," in *Platform Revolution: How Networked Markets Are Transforming the Economy—and How to Make Them Work for You*, ed. Parker, Van Alstyne, and Choudary (New York: W. W. Norton, 2016).
42. Ruth Towse, *Creativity, Incentive and Reward: An Economic Analysis of Copyright and Culture in the Information Age* (Cheltenham: Edward Elgar, 2001), 58.
43. Eric E. Johnson, "Intellectual Property and the Incentive Fallacy," *Florida State University Law Review* 39 (2012): 668–69.
44. Ruth Towse, "Copyright and Cultural Policy for the Creative Industries," in *Economics, Law and Intellectual Property: Seeking Strategies for Research and Teaching in a Developing Field*, ed. Ove Granstrand (Boston: Kluwer Academic, 2003), 427.
45. Leigh Phillips and Michal Rozworski, *The People's Republic of Walmart: How the World's Biggest Corporations Are Laying the Foundation for Socialism* (London: Verso, 2019), 2.

CHAPTER 2: HOW AMAZON TOOK OVER BOOKS

1. Brad Stone, *The Everything Store: Jeff Bezos and the Age of Amazon* (New York: Little, Brown, 2013), 37.

2. Authors Guild to David Cicilline, Aug. 17, 2020, https://www.authorsguild
.org/wp-content/uploads/2020/08/Joint-Letter-to-Rep-Cicilline-AAP-AG
-ABA-Aug-17-2020-.pdf.

3. Stone, *The Everything Store*, 24.

4. Stone, *The Everything Store*, 243.

5. George Packer, "Cheap Words," *New Yorker*, Feb. 9, 2014, https://www.new
yorker.com/magazine/2014/02/17/cheap-words.

6. Packer, "Cheap Words."

7. Peter C. Carstensen, *Competition Policy and the Control of Buyer Power: A Global
Issue* (Cheltenham, UK: Edward Elgar, 2017), 65, https://doi.org/10.4337
/9781782540588.

8. Packer, "Cheap Words."

9. Carstensen, *Competition Policy and the Control of Buyer Power*, 58.

10. Packer, "Cheap Words."

11. William Deresiewicz, *The Death of the Artist: How Creators Are Struggling to
Survive in the Age of Billionaires and Big Tech* (New York: Henry Holt, 2020),
156.

12. Barry C. Lynn, "The Big Tech Extortion Racket," *Harper's Magazine*, Aug. 14,
2020, https://harpers.org/archive/2020/09/the-big-tech-extortion-racket.

13. Carstensen, *Competition Policy and the Control of Buyer Power*, 4.

14. Stone, *The Everything Store*, 234.

15. Article 11, World Intellectual Property Organization (WIPO) Copyright
Treaty, 1996, https://wipolex.wipo.int/en/text/295166; Article 18, WIPO
Performances and Phonograms Treaty, 1996, https://wipolex.wipo.int/en
/treaties/textdetails/12743.

16. Article 11, WIPO Copyright Treaty, 1996.

17. Dale Clapperton and Stephen Corones, "Technological Tying of the Apple
iPhone: Unlawful in Australia?" *Queensland University of Technology Law and
Justice Journal* 7, no. 2 (2007): 351, http://classic.austlii.edu.au/au/journals
/QUTLawJJl/2007/21.html.

18. Apple, "iTunes Store Tops Two Billion Songs," Jan. 9, 2007, https://news
.cision.com/pilgrim/r/itunes-store-tops-two-billion-songs,c252337.

19. Apple, "iTunes Store Top Music Retailer in the US," Apr. 3, 2008, https://
www.apple.com/newsroom/2008/04/03iTunes-Store-Top-Music-Retailer
-in-the-US.

20. David Kravets, "Like Amazon's DRM-Free Music Downloads? Thank Apple," *Wired*, September 25, 2007, https://www.wired.com/2007/09/drm
-part-one.

21. Cory Doctorow, "Amazon's Anti-DRM Tee," *Boing Boing*, Feb. 1, 2008,
https://boingboing.net/2008/02/01/amazons-antidrm-tee.html.

22. Andrew Savikas, "Over 160 O'Reilly Books Now in Kindle Store (Without
DRM), More on the Way," Tools of Change for Publishing, Apr. 17, 2009,
http://toc.oreilly.com/2009/04/over-160-oreilly-books-now-in-kindle-store
-without-drm-more-on-the-way.html.

23. Stone, *The Everything Store*, 250.

24. Stone, *The Everything Store*, 255.

25. Packer, "Cheap Words."

26. Parker Higgins, "Accepting Amazon's DRM Makes It Impossible to Challenge Its Monopoly," *parker higgins dot net* (blog), May 26, 2014, https://parkerhiggins .net/2014/05/accepting-amazons-drm-makes-it-impossible-to-challenge-its -monopoly.

27. Charlie Stross, "What Amazon's Ebook Strategy Means," *Charlie's Diary* (blog), Apr. 14, 2012, http://www.antipope.org/charlie/blog-static/2012/04 /understanding-amazons-strategy.html.

28. United States v. Apple Inc., 952 F.Supp.2d 638, 649.

29. United States v. Apple Inc., 952 F.Supp.2d 638, 671.

30. Brad Stone and Motoko Rich, "Amazon Removes Macmillan Books," *New York Times*, Jan. 30, 2010, https://www.nytimes.com/2010/01/30/technology /30amazon.html.

31. Heavy Duty Trucking, "FTC Investigates Port Trucker Organizing Efforts," *Trucking Info*, Dec. 2, 1999, https://www.truckinginfo.com/86044/ftc -investigates-port-trucker-organizing-efforts.

32. United States v. Apple Inc., 952 F.Supp.2d 638, 708.

33. Jonathan Tepper and Denise Hearn, *The Myth of Capitalism: Monopolies and the Death of Competition* (Hoboken, NJ: Wiley, 2019), 29.

34. United States v. Apple Inc., 952 F.Supp.2d 638, 686.

35. Matt Day and Jackie Gu, "The Numbers Behind Amazon's Market Reach," *Bloomberg*, Mar. 27, 2019, https://www.bloomberg.com/graphics/2019-amazon -reach-across-markets.

36. Edward W. Robertson, "Self-Publishing's Share of the Kindle Market by Genre," Feb. 15, 2014, http://edwardwrobertson.com/self-publishing/self -publishings-share-of-the-kindle-market-by-genre.

37. Frank Catalano, "Traditional Publishers' Ebook Sales Drop as Indie Authors and Amazon Take Off," GeekWire, May 19, 2018, https://www.geekwire.com/2018 /traditional-publishers-ebook-sales-drop-indie-authors-amazon-take-off.

38. Amazon UK, "Kindle: A Year in Review," *Day One* (blog), Dec. 23, 2019, https://blog.aboutamazon.co.uk/innovation/kindle-a-year-in-review.

39. Rebecca Giblin, "What's Happening to Authors' Earnings? Surveying the Surveys," The Author's Interest, Feb. 20, 2018, https://authorsinterest.org /2018/02/20/whats-happening-to-authors-earnings-surveying-the-surveys.

40. Nina Amir, "Good News for POD World: Amazon Settles Antitrust Lawsuit Filed by BookLocker," *Write Nonfiction NOW!*, Jan. 20, 2010, https://write nonfictionnow.com/good-news-for-pod-world-amazon-settles-antitrust -lawsuit-filed-by-booklocker.

41. Peter Sayer, "Amazon Buys Audible for US$300 Million," *Good Gear Guide*, Feb. 1, 2018, https://www.goodgearguide.com.au/article/205192/amazon _buys_audible_us_300_million.

42. Cory Doctorow, "Random House Audio Abandons Audiobook DRM," *Boing Boing*, Feb. 21, 2008, https://boingboing.net/2008/02/21/random-house-audio -a.html.

43. Cory Doctorow, "Google Launches a DRM-Free Audiobook Store: Finally, a Writer- and Listener-Friendly Audible Alternative!," *Boing Boing*, July 20, 2018, https://boingboing.net/2018/07/20/dont-restrict-me.html.

44. Stone, *The Everything Store*, 48.

45. Matt Stoller, "Could Google Soon Face . . . Competition?" *BIG* (newsletter), Nov. 26, 2020, https://mattstoller.substack.com/p/could-google-soon-face -competition.
46. Alexandra Alter, "Best Sellers Sell the Best Because They're Best Sellers," *New York Times*, September 19, 2020, https://www.nytimes.com/2020/09/19 /books/penguin-random-house-madeline-mcintosh.html.
47. Alter, "Best Sellers Sell the Best Because They're Best Sellers."
48. Packer, "Cheap Words."
49. For more on this, see Cory's 2020 monograph, *How to Destroy Surveillance Capitalism*, from OneZero/Medium, available at https://onezero.medium .com/how-to-destroy-surveillance-capitalism-8135e6744d59.
50. Tim Wu, "What Years of Emails and Texts Reveal About Your Friendly Tech Companies," *New York Times*, Aug. 4, 2020, https://www.nytimes.com/2020 /08/04/opinion/amazon-facebook-congressional-hearings.html.
51. Tepper and Hearn, *The Myth of Capitalism*, 108–9.
52. Ian Hathaway, "Platform Giants and Venture-Backed Startups," Oct. 12, 2018, http://www.ianhathaway.org/blog/2018/10/12/platform-giants-and-venture -backed-startups.
53. James Fallows, "The Boiled-Frog Myth: Stop the Lying Now!" *The Atlantic*, Sept. 16, 2006, https://www.theatlantic.com/technology/archive/2006/09 /the-boiled-frog-myth-stop-the-lying-now/7446.
54. If this horrifies or fascinates you, check out Andrea Matwyshyn's "The Internet of Bodies," which analyzes the way the integrity and functionality of human bodies increasingly relies on the internet and other digital technologies. Andrea M. Matwyshyn, "The Internet of Bodies," *William & Mary Law Review* 61, no. 1 (2019), https://scholarship.law.wm.edu/wmlr/vol61/iss1/3.

CHAPTER 3: HOW NEWS GOT BROKEN

1. Adam Lashinsky, "Burning Sensation," CNN, Dec. 12, 2005, https://money .cnn.com/magazines/fortune/fortune_archive/2005/12/12/8363113/index .htm.
2. Robert Seamans and Feng Zhu, "Responses to Entry in Multi-Sided Markets: The Impact of Craigslist on Local Newspapers," *Management Science* 60, no. 2 (Feb. 2014): 476–93, https://www.hbs.edu/faculty/Pages/item.aspx?num=45143.
3. Pew Research Center, "Newspapers Fact Sheet," July 9, 2019, https://www .journalism.org/fact-sheet/newspapers.
4. Paris Marx, "Big Tech Can't Save Journalism. Democratic Socialism Can," *Jacobin*, September 17, 2020, https://www.jacobinmag.com/2020/09/big-tech -journalism-democratic-socialism-decentralization.
5. Competition and Markets Authority, "Online Platforms and Digital Advertis- ing: Market Study Final Report," July 1, 2020, 20, https://assets.publishing .service.gov.uk/media/5efc57ed3a6f4023d242ed56/Final_report_1_July _2020_.pdf.
6. Josh Marshall, "A Serf on Google's Farm," *Talking Points Memo*, Septem- ber 1, 2017, https://talkingpointsmemo.com/edblog/a-serf-on-googles-farm.
7. Dina Srinivasan, "Why Google Dominates Advertising Markets," *Stanford Technology Law Review* 21, no. 1 (2020): 55–175.

8. Scott Timberg, *Culture Crash: The Killing of the Creative Class* (New Haven, CT: Yale University Press, 2015), 171.

9. David Pidgeon, "Where Did the Money Go? Guardian Buys Its Own Ad Inventory," *Mediatel News*, Oct. 4, 2016, https://mediatel.co.uk/news/2016/10/04/where-did-the-money-go-guardian-buys-its-own-ad-inventory.

10. Eli Pariser, *The Filter Bubble: What the Internet Is Hiding from You* (New York: Penguin, 2011), 49.

11. Competition and Markets Authority, "Online Platforms," 8.

12. Tim Hwang, *Subprime Attention Crisis: Advertising and the Time Bomb at the Heart of the Internet* (New York: Farrar, Straus and Giroux, 2020), 99.

13. Matt Stoller, "Spotify Is Mimicking Google's and Facebook's Strategy: Will It Ruin Podcasting?" *Promarket*, Mar. 6, 2020, https://promarket.org/2020/03/06/spotify-is-mimicking-googles-and-facebooks-strategy-will-it-ruin-podcasting.

14. Pew Research Center, "Newspapers Fact Sheet."

15. Elizabeth Grieco, "U.S. Newspapers Have Shed Half of Their Newsroom Employees Since 2008," Fact Tank, Pew Research Center, Apr. 20, 2020, https://www.pewresearch.org/fact-tank/2020/04/20/u-s-newsroom-employment-has-dropped-by-a-quarter-since-2008.

16. Jaclyn Peiser, "The Rise of the Robot Reporter," *New York Times*, Feb. 5, 2019, https://www.nytimes.com/2019/02/05/business/media/artificial-intelligence-journalism-robots.html.

17. Archie Bland, "Rolling Stone Seeks 'Thought Leaders' Willing to Pay $2,000 to Write for Them," *Guardian*, Jan. 23, 2021, https://www.theguardian.com/media/2021/jan/23/rolling-stone-magazine-culture-council-publication.

18. BrandVoice, *Forbes*, https://www.forbes.com/connect/content-solutions/brandvoice.

19. Timberg, *Culture Crash*, 231.

20. James Meese, "Advertising, Algorithms, and Democratic Risk," unpublished manuscript, 2020, 16.

21. Michael Hiltzkik, "Facebook's Bogus Video Claims Just Cost It $40 Million, But They Caused Much More Damage," *Los Angeles Times*, Oct. 10, 2019, https://www.latimes.com/business/story/2019-10-10/hiltzik-facebooks-bogus-video-claims-40-million.

22. Alex Heath, "Facebook Says It Can Reach 25 Million More People in the US Than Census Data Shows Exist," *Business Insider Australia*, September 7, 2017, https://www.businessinsider.com.au/facebook-tells-advertisers-reaches-25-million-more-people-than-exist-us-census-data-2017-9.

23. Alan Hart and Keven Frisch, "Historic Ad Fraud at Uber with Kevin Frisch," *Marketing Today*, Feb. 12, 2020, https://www.marketingtodaypodcast.com/194-historic-ad-fraud-at-uber-with-kevin-frisch.

24. Hart and Frisch, "Historic Ad Fraud."

25. Hwang, *Subprime Attention Crisis*, 84.

26. Augustine Fou, "When Big Brands Stopped Spending on Digital Ads, Nothing Happened. Why?" *Forbes*, Jan. 2, 2021, https://www.forbes.com/sites/augustinefou/2021/01/02/when-big-brands-stopped-spending-on-digital-ads-nothing-happened-why/?sh=a866d831166d.

27. Hwang, *Subprime Attention Crisis*, 120.

28. Fiona M. Scott Morton and David C. Dinielli, "Roadmap for a Digital Advertising Monopolization Case Against Google," Omidyar Network, May 2020, https://omidyar.com/wp-content/uploads/2020/09/Roadmap-for-a-Case-Against-Google.pdf.

CHAPTER 4: WHY PRINCE CHANGED HIS NAME

1. Jon Pareles, "A Re-Inventor of His World and Himself," *New York Times*, Nov. 17, 1996, https://www.nytimes.com/1996/11/17/arts/a-re-inventor-of-his-world-and-himself.html?searchResultPosition=42.

2. Courtney Love, "Courtney Love Does the Math," *Salon*, June 14, 2000, http://www.salon.com/2000/06/14/love_7.

3. Cliff Jones and Gareth Iwan Jones, "How the Record Industry Cares More About Making Money Than Music," *Financial Times*, Dec. 1, 2017, https://www.ft.com/content/4821c3a2-c92d-11e7-8536-d321d0d897a3.

4. Matt Villmer, "5 Tips Every Artist Must Know Before Signing Their First Record Deal," *Sonicbids* (blog), July 3, 2015, https://blog.sonicbids.com/5-tips-every-artist-must-know-before-signing-their-first-record-deal.

5. Richard James Burgess, *The History of Music Production* (New York: Oxford University Press, 2014), 41.

6. Committee on Digital, Culture, Media and Sport, UK House of Commons, *Economics of Music Streaming,* Second Report of Session 2021–22 (London, July 15, 2021), 29, https://committees.parliament.uk/publications/6739/documents/72525/default.

7. Jason B. Bazinet et al., *Putting the Band Back Together: Remastering the World of Music*, Citi Global Perspectives & Solutions, 2018, 3, https://ir.citi.com/Nhxm HW7xb0tkWiqOOG0NuPDM3pVGJpVzXMw7n%2BZg4AfFFX%2BeFq DYNfND%2B0hUxxXA.

8. Chuck Philips, "Auditors Put New Spin on Revolt Over Royalties," *Los Angeles Times*, Feb. 26, 2002, https://www.latimes.com/archives/la-xpm-2002-feb-26-mn-29955-story.html.

9. Justin Pritchard, "Striking a Chord with Congress," *Los Angeles Times*, Aug. 19, 1998, https://www.latimes.com/archives/la-xpm-1998-aug-19-fi-14460-story.html.

10. Technically, it was a penny per record but only payable on 85 percent of sales; the rest were treated as "promos" or "breakage" for which royalties would never be paid. David Kronemyer, "Deconstructing Pop Culture: The Beatles' Contract History with Capitol Records," *Musewire*, May 15, 2009, https://musewire.com/deconstructing-pop-culture-the-beatles-contract-history-with-capitol-records.

11. House of Commons, *Economics of Music Streaming*, 28.

12. Josh Kun, Twitter post, June 3, 2020, 12:00 a.m., https://twitter.com/JDKun/status/1267818430956101632?s=20.

13. House of Commons, *Economics of Music Streaming*, 29.

14. House of Commons, *Economics of Music Streaming*, 61.

15. House of Commons, *Economics of Music Streaming*, 63.

16. Interview with Jake Beaumont-Nesbitt, 2020.

17. Kembrew McLeod and Peter DiCola, *Creative License: The Law and Culture of Digital Sampling* (Durham, NC: Duke University Press, 2011), 1.
18. In the US, see Bridgeport Music, Inc. v. Dimension Films, 383 F.3d 390 (9th Cir. 2004), though c.f. Newton v. Diamond, 388 F.3d. 1190 (9th Cir. 2004).
19. McLeod and DiCola, *Creative License*, 158.
20. McLeod and DiCola, *Creative License*, 150.
21. McLeod and DiCola, *Creative License*, 162.
22. McLeod and DiCola, *Creative License*, 27.
23. McLeod and DiCola, *Creative License*, 159–60.
24. McLeod and DiCola, *Creative License*, 159.
25. McLeod and DiCola, *Creative License*, 163.
26. McLeod and DiCola, *Creative License*, 164.
27. Brief of 212 Songwriters, Composers, Musicians, and Producers as Amici Curiae in Support of Appellants, Williams v. Gaye, No. 15–56880 (9th Cir. 2018), https://www.scribd.com/document/322595201/Brief-of-Amici-Curiae-212 -Songwriters-Composers-Musicians-And-Produce.
28. Ted Gioia, "Is Old Music Killing New Music?" *The Atlantic*, Jan. 23, 2022, https://www.theatlantic.com/ideas/archive/2022/01/old-music-killing-new -music/621339.

CHAPTER 5: WHY STREAMING DOESN'T PAY

1. Stuart Dredge, "Artist Zoë Keating Reveals Latest Spotify Per-Stream Payouts," *Music Ally*, Nov. 22, 2019, https://musically.com/2019/11/22/artist -zoe-keating-reveals-latest-spotify-per-stream-payouts.
2. Liz Pelly, interview with Holly Herndon and Mat Dryhurst, *Interdependence*, podcast audio, Apr. 12, 2021, https://interdependence.simplecast.com /episodes/interdependence-5-liz-pellyonpatrons-zv055d_C.
3. Roneil Rumberg, Forrest Browning, and Clayton Blaha, interview with Holly Herndon and Mat Dryhurst, "Artist Led Pricing, Scene Ownership and Defecting From Spotify with Audius," *Interdependence*, podcast audio, Feb. 12, 2021, https://open.spotify.com/episode/108mGczQPRD8ZA0otIDmZX?si =-4AUVNL6RhSIXmio2xIFtg&utm_source=native-share-menu.
4. Tim Ingham, "Spotify Dreams of Artists Making a Living. It Probably Won't Come True," *Rolling Stone*, Aug. 3, 2020, https://www.rollingstone.com /pro/features/spotify-million-artists-royalties-1038408.
5. Katia Moskvitch, "YouTube Music Is Great for Record Labels, but Bad for Music Lovers," *Wired UK*, May 23, 2018, https://www.wired.co.uk/article /youtube-music-premium-originals.
6. David Turner, "The False Promise of User-Centric Streaming," *Penny Fractions* (newsletter), Oct. 2, 2019, https://www.getrevue.co/profile/pennyfractions /issues/penny-fractions-the-false-promise-of-user-centric-streaming-201362.
7. Committee on Digital, Culture, Media and Sport, UK House of Commons, *Economics of Music Streaming,* Second Report of Session 2021–22 (London, July 15, 2021), 61, https://committees.parliament.uk/publications/6739/documents /72525/default.

8. House of Commons, *Economics of Music Streaming*, 5.

9. Victor Luckerson, "Is Spotify's Model Wiping Out Music's Middle Class?" *The Ringer*, Jan. 16, 2019, https://www.theringer.com/tech/2019/1/16/18184314 /spotify-music-streaming-service-royalty-payout-model.

10. Simone, "User-Centric Payment System (UCPS)," Deezer Support, 2019, https://support.deezer.com/hc/en-gb/articles/360002471277-User-Centric -Payment-System-UCPS.

11. Turner, "The False Promise of User-Centric Streaming."

12. Turner, "The False Promise of User-Centric Streaming."

13. MusicLinkUp, "How the MMA Could Shift Music's Wealth From Labels to Publishers—and Impact Companies That Own Both," *MusicLinkUp Daily Insight (Global)*, Nov. 5, 2018, https://www.musiclinkup.com/pulse/15689/how -the-mma-could-shift-music%27s-wealth-from-labels-to-publishers——and -impact-companies-that-own-both.

14. Nate Rau, "Nashville's Musical Middle Class Collapses," *Tennessean*, Jan. 4, 2015, https://www.tennessean.com/story/entertainment/music/2015/01/04 /nashville-musical-middle-class-collapses-new-dylans/21236245.

15. Amanda Harcourt and Steve Gordon, "International Digital Music Licensing," in *The Future of the Music Business: How to Succeed with New Digital Technologies*, 4th ed., ed. Steve Gordon (MusicPro Guides, 2015), chapter 8.

16. *Music Licensing Under Title 17, Part Two*, testimony before the Subcommittee on Courts, Intellectual Property and the Internet, House Judiciary Committee (June 25, 2014) (statement of Darius Van Arman, cofounder, Secretly Group), 5–6.

17. Nick Messitte, "Inside The Black Box: A Deep Dive into Music's Monetization Mystery," *Forbes*, Apr. 15, 2015, https://www.forbes.com/sites/nick messitte/2015/04/15/inside-the-black-box-a-deep-dive-into-musics -monetization-mystery/#18eaf6185d4a.

18. Messitte, "Inside The Black Box."

19. Van Arman testimony, *Music Licensing*, 4.

20. Van Arman testimony, *Music Licensing*, 5.

21. Worldwide Independent Network, "Fair Digital Deals Declaration Pledge," https://web.archive.org/web/20200926112858/https://winformusic.org /fair-digital-deals/fair-digital-deals-pledge.

22. Tim Ingham, "Warner Pays Artists Share of Spotify Advances . . . and Has for 6 Years," *Music Business Worldwide*, May 29, 2015, https://www.musicbusiness worldwide.com/warner-pays-artists-a-share-of-spotify-advances-and-has -for-6-years.

23. Rethink Music, "Fair Music: Transparency and Payment Flows in the Music Industry," Berklee Institute for Creative Entrepreneurship, 16, https:// static1.squarespace.com/static/552c0535e4b0afcbed88dc53/t/55d0da1ae 4b06bd4 bea8c86c/1439750682446/rethink_music_fairness_transparency_final.pdf.

24. Charles Caldas, "Merlin CEO Charles Caldas on a Two-Tier Statutory Rate," *Billboard*, Oct. 20, 2015, http://www.billboard.com/articles/news/6746030 /charles-caldas-op-ed-merlin.

25. Zack O'Malley Greenburg, "Revenge of the Record Labels: How the Majors Renewed Their Grip On Music," *Forbes*, May 4, 2015, https://www.forbes .com/sites/zackomalleygreenburg/2015/04/15/revenge-of-the-record-labels -how-the-majors-renewed-their-grip-on-music.

26. Andrew Ross Sorkin and Jeff Leeds, "Music Companies Grab a Share of the YouTube Sale," *New York Times*, Oct. 19, 2006, https://www.nytimes.com /2006/10/19/technology/19net.html.

27. Rethink Music, "Fair Music," 15.

28. *Variety* Staff, "Merlin Sells All of Its Spotify Shares for an Estimated $125 Million-Plus," *Variety*, May 14, 2018, https://variety.com/2018/biz/news /merlin-sells-all-of-its-spotify-shares-for-an-estimated-125-million-plus -1202810275.

29. Tim Ingham, "Here's Exactly How Many Shares the Major Labels and Merlin Bought in Spotify—and What Those Stakes Are Worth Now," *Music Business Worldwide*, May 14, 2018, https://www.musicbusinessworldwide.com/heres -exactly-how-many-shares-the-major-labels-and-merlin-bought-in-spotify -and-what-we-think-those-stakes-are-worth-now.

30. *Variety* Staff, "Sony Has Sold Half of Its Spotify Shares," *Variety*, May 1, 2018, https://variety.com/2018/biz/news/sony-has-sold-half-of-its-spotify-shares -1202794230.

31. Messitte, "Inside The Black Box."

32. Robert Levine, "UMG's Deal With Spotify: How Lucian Grainge and Daniel Ek (Finally) Got It Done," *Billboard*, Apr. 6, 2017, http://www.billboard .com/articles/business/7752318/universal-spotify-deal-streaming-daniel -ek-lucian-grainge.

33. Ben Sisario, "Licensing Accord Eases Spotify's Path to Going Public," *New York Times*, Apr. 4, 2017, https://www.nytimes.com/2017/04/04/business /media/spotify-universal-music-group-licensing.html.

34. Tim Ingham, "Universal: We WILL Share Spotify Money with Artists When We Sell Our Stock in Streaming Platform," *Music Business Worldwide*, Mar. 5, 2018, https://www.musicbusinessworldwide.com/universal-we-will-share -spotify-money-with-artists-when-we-sell-our-stock-in-streaming-platform.

35. Tim Ingham, "Why Spend $4.1BN on A&R? Because New Artists are Accelerating Streaming's Growth," *Music Business Worldwide*, June 6, 2019, https:// www.musicbusinessworldwide.com/why-spend-4-1bn-on-ar-new-artists-are -accelerating-streamings-growth.

36. "The Universal Music Group/EMI Merger and the Future of Online Music," testimony before the Subcommittee on Antitrust, Competition Policy, and Consumer Rights, U.S. Senate Judiciary Committee, June 21, 2012 (statement of Gigi B. Sohn, President, Public Knowledge), 2.

37. Statista, "Digital and Physical Revenue Market Share of the Largest Record Companies Worldwide from 2012 to 2018," May 2019, https://www.statista .com/statistics/422926/record-companies-market-share-worldwide-physical -digital-revenues (accessed Apr. 22, 2021); Worldwide Independent Network, *WINTEL Worldwide Independent Market Report 2018*, 2018, 8, https://winfor music.org/mp-files/wintel-2018.pdf.

38. Merlin Network, *Merlin Impact Report 2018*, 2018, 6, https://merlinnetwork
.org/merlin-10th-anniversary-impact-report-to-celebrate-global-success-of
-its-independent-members.
39. Merlin Network, "Representing the Rights of Independent Record Labels
Worldwide," June 18, 2019, https://web.archive.org/web/20190625143620
/https://merlinnetwork.org/news/post/merlin-reveals-record-revenue
-distributions-in-new-2019-membership-report.
40. Worldwide Independent Network, *WINTEL Worldwide Independent Market
Report 2018*, 8.

CHAPTER 6: WHY SPOTIFY WANTS YOU TO RELY ON PLAYLISTS
1. IFPI, *Global Music Report 2021*, 2021, 13, https://gmr2021.ifpi.org/assets
/GMR2021_State%20of%20the%20Industry.pdf.
2. Dorian Lynskey, "The 'Big Three' Record Labels Are About to Make a Lot
of Noise," *GQ*, Nov. 17, 2018, https://www.gq-magazine.co.uk/article
/major-record-labels.
3. Alexandra Bruell, "Spotify Has Big Ambitions for Ad Business," *Wall Street
Journal*, Aug. 17, 2017, https://www.wsj.com/articles/spotify-has-big
-ambitions-for-ad-business-1502964001.
4. Liz Pelly, "Big Mood Machine," *The Baffler*, June 10, 2019, https://thebaffler
.com/downstream/big-mood-machine-pelly.
5. Committee on Digital, Culture, Media and Sport, UK House of Commons,
Economics of Music Streaming, Second Report of Session 2021–22 (London, July
15, 2021), 22, https://committees.parliament.uk/publications/6739/documents
/72525/default.
6. David Turner, "User-Centric Streaming and Other Radical Streaming Proposals," *Penny Fractions* (newsletter), Feb. 20, 2019, https://www.getrevue.co
/profile/pennyfractions/issues/penny-fractions-user-centric-streaming-and
-other-radical-streaming-proposals-160441.
7. Liz Pelly, "Discover Weakly," *The Baffler*, June 4, 2018, https://thebaffler.com
/latest/discover-weakly-pelly.
8. Dan Kopf, "Is Spotify Killing the Top 40?" *Quartz*, Sept. 5, 2020, https://qz
.com/1899097/is-spotify-killing-the-top-40.
9. Pelly, "Discover Weakly."
10. David Turner, "Do Playlists Dream of Fake Artists?" *Penny Fractions* (newsletter), July 25, 2018, https://www.getrevue.co/profile/pennyfractions/issues
/penny-fractions-issue-38-do-playlists-dream-of-fake-artists-124631.
11. Tim Ingham, "'Fake Artists' Have Billions of Streams on Spotify. Is Sony
Now Playing the Service at Its Own Game?" *Rolling Stone*, May 15, 2019,
https://www.rollingstone.com/pro/features/fake-artists-have-billions-of
-streams-on-spotify-is-sony-now-playing-the-service-at-its-own-game
-834716.
12. Roy Trakin and Jem Aswad, "Spotify Denies Creating 'Fake Artists,' Although
Multiple Sources Claim the Practice Is Real," *Variety*, July 11, 2017, https://
variety.com/2017/biz/news/spotify-denies-creating-fake-artists-although
-multiple-sources-claim-the-practice-is-real-1202492307.

13. Alex Hern, "Spotify to Let Artists Promote Music for Cut in Royalty Rates," *Guardian*, Nov. 4, 2020, https://www.theguardian.com/technology/2020/nov/03/spotify-artists-promote-music-exchange-cut-royalty-rates-payola-algorithm.

14. Tim Ingham, "Streaming Platforms are Keeping More Money From Artists than Ever (and Paying Them More, Too)," *Rolling Stone*, Apr. 9, 2019, https://www.rollingstone.com/music/music-features/streaming-platforms-keeping-more-money-from-artists-than-ever-817925.

15. Goldman Sachs, "The Music in the Air," 2017, https://www.goldmansachs.com/insights/pages/infographics/music-streaming.

16. David George and Alex Immerman, "Moats Before (Gross) Margins," Andreessen Horowitz, May 28, 2020, https://a16z.com/2020/05/28/moats-before-gross-margins.

17. Statista, "Share of Music Streaming Subscribers Worldwide in 2019, by Company," Apr. 2020, https://www.statista.com/statistics/653926/music-streaming-service-subscriber-share.

18. Amanda Harcourt and Steve Gordon, "International Digital Music Licensing," in *The Future of the Music Business: How to Succeed with New Digital Technologies*, 4th ed., ed. Steve Gordon (MusicPro Guides, 2015), chapter 8.

19. Paul Sloan, "The Future of Music, According to Spotify's Daniel Ek," CNET, Apr. 9, 2013, https://www.cnet.com/news/the-future-of-music-according-to-spotifys-daniel-ek.

20. Daniel Ek, "Tencent and Spotify Buy Minority Stakes in Each Other," *Financial Times*, Dec. 9, 2017, https://www.ft.com/content/07ccf3e0-dc28-11e7-a039-c64b1c09b482.

21. House of Commons, *Economics of Music Streaming*, 69.

22. Evan Minsker, "Amazon Music Adding Podcasts, Walk Back Condition That Podcasters Don't Disparage Amazon," *Pitchfork*, Aug. 11, 2020, https://pitchfork.com/news/amazon-music-adding-podcasts-on-the-condition-that-podcasters-dont-disparage-amazon.

23. Aram Sinnreich," Why I Quit Spotify after 13 Years (And Why It Feels Like a Personal Failure)," *Medium*, Jan. 27, 2022, https://medium.com/@aram_87067/why-i-quit-spotify-after-13-years-and-why-it-feels-like-a-personal-failure-9b73bacd3695.

24. Liz Pelly, "Podcast Overlords," *The Baffler*, Nov. 10, 2020, https://thebaffler.com/downstream/podcast-overlords-pelly.

CHAPTER 7: WHAT THE US SHARES WITH RWANDA, IRAN, AND NORTH KOREA

1. Statista, "Radio Station Advertising Revenues in the United States from 2006 to 2019, by Source," June 2020, https://www.statista.com/statistics/253185/radio-station-revenues-in-the-us-by-source.

2. This is courtesy of 17 USC § 114(d)(1)(A), which exempts nonsubscription broadcast transmission from requiring a license to transmit sound recordings. Harcourt and Gordon, "International Digital Music Licensing."

3. Stan J. Liebowitz, "The Elusive Symbiosis: The Impact of Radio on the Record Industry," Social Science Research Network, Mar. 2004, http://www.ssrn.com/abstract=520022.

4. National Association of Broadcasters, "A Performance Tax Threatens Local Jobs National Association of Broadcasters," https://www.nab.org/advocacy /issue.asp?id=1889&issueid=1002.

5. Richard James Burgess, *The History of Music Production* (Oxford University Press, 2014), 157–58.

6. Debbie Weingarten, "America's Rural Radio Stations Are Vanishing—and Taking the Country's Soul with Them," *Guardian*, June 6, 2019, https:// www.theguardian.com/tv-and-radio/2019/jun/06/radio-silence-how-the -disappearance-of-rural-stations-takes-americas-soul-with-them.

7. Peter DiCola, "False Premises, False Promises: A Quantitative History of Ownership Consolidation in the Radio Industry," Future of Music Coalition, Dec. 2006, 5, 13, http://futureofmusic.org/article/research/false-premises -false-promises.

8. Weingarten, "America's Rural Radio Stations."

9. Interview with Richard Burgess, 2020.

10. Paul Krugman, "Channels Of Influence," *New York Times*, Mar. 25, 2003, https://www.nytimes.com/2003/03/25/opinion/channels-of-influence .html.

11. Duncan Stewart, "Radio: Revenue, Reach, and Resilience," Deloitte, Dec. 11, 2018, https://www2.deloitte.com/us/en/insights/industry/technology /technology-media-and-telecom-predictions/radio-revenue.html.

12. Todd Spangler, "iHeartMedia Stock Drops in NASDAQ Debut," *Variety*, July 18, 2019, https://variety.com/2019/music/news/iheartmedia-stock-drops -nasdaq-debut-1203271620.

13. Eileen Appelbaum and Rosemary L. Batt, *Private Equity at Work: When Wall Street Manages Main Street* (New York: Russell Sage Foundation, 2014), 2.

14. Appelbaum and Batt, *Private Equity at Work*, 3.

15. United for Respect, "Pirate Equity: How Wall Street Firms Are Pillaging American Retail," https://united4respect.org/pirateequity.

16. Ludovic Phalippou, "An Inconvenient Fact: Private Equity Returns & The Billionaire Factory," working paper, June 10, 2020, Social Sciences Research Network, https://ssrn.com/abstract=3623820.

17. Joe Rennison, "Private Equity Owners Pile on Leverage to Pay Themselves Dividends," *Financial Times*, Sept. 17, 2020, https://www.ft.com/content /a9ff463b-01d7-4892-82dc-2dbb74941a16.

18. Matthew S. DelNero, "Long Overdue? An Exploration of the Status and Merit of a General Public Performance Right in Sound Recordings," *Vanderbilt Journal of Entertainment Law & Practice* 6 (2004): 181.

19. Future of Music Coalition, "Public Performance Right for Sound Recordings," Mar. 5, 2018, http://www.futureofmusic.org/article/fact-sheet /public-performance-right-sound-recordings.

20. Nick Messitte, "Inside The Black Box: A Deep Dive Into Music's Monetization Mystery," *Forbes*, Apr. 15, 2015, https://www.forbes.com/sites/nick messitte/2015/04/15/inside-the-black-box-a-deep-dive-into-musics -monetization-mystery.

21. David Dayen, *Monopolized! Life in the Age of Corporate Power* (New York: New Press, 2020), chapter 3, ebook.

22. This quote is routinely attributed to John Steinbeck, but it is, in fact, Ronald Wright in *A Short History of Progress* (New York: House of Anansi Press, 2004) paraphrasing Steinbeck's comments in *Esquire* (1960), later republished in *America & Americans* (1966). See account of the misattribution at WikiQuote (https://en.wikiquote.org/wiki/John_Steinbeck#Disputed).

CHAPTER 8: HOW LIVE NATION CHICKENIZED LIVE MUSIC

1. Zephyr Teachout, *Break 'Em Up: Recovering Our Freedom from Big Ag, Big Tech, and Big Money* (New York: All Points Books, 2020), 19–20.
2. Live Nation Entertainment, *Annual Report for the Fiscal Year Ended December 31, 2019*, US Securities and Exchange Commission, https://investors.livenation entertainment.com/sec-filings/annual-reports/content/0001335258-20 -000028/0001335258-20-000028.pdf.
3. Tim Ingham, "Live Nation Companies Now Manage Over 500 Artists World-wide," *Music Business Worldwide*, Feb. 27, 2017, https://www.musicbusiness worldwide.com/live-nation-companies-now-manage-500-artists-worldwide.
4. See the 10-K reports covering the fiscal years of 2012–2019: Live Nation En-tertainment, "Annual Reports," https://investors.livenationentertainment .com/sec-filings/annual-reports.
5. Plaintiff United States' Memorandum in Support of Motion to Modify Final Judgment, United States et al. v. Ticketmaster, Inc., and Live Nation Enter-tainment, Inc., 1:10-cv-00139-RMC (DDC Jan. 25, 2010), at 8, 9.
6. *United States v. Ticketmaster*, at 6.
7. US Government Accountability Office, "Event Ticket Sales: Market Charac-teristics and Consumer Protection Issues," GAO-18-347, Apr. 12, 2018, at 6, 30, https://www.gao.gov/products/gao-18-347.
8. Dave Brooks, "How Live Nation Reached a Settlement with the DOJ in the Con-sent Decree Investigation," *Billboard*, Oct. 1, 2020, https://www.billboard.com /articles/business/8547798/live-nation-doj-settlement-avoid-contempt-charges.
9. Interview with a live music insider, 2020.
10. Jennifer M. Oliver, "DOJ: Event Powerhouse Live Nation Punished Concert Venues for Using Competing Ticketers Despite Bar," *National Law Review*, Mar. 19, 2020, https://www.natlawreview.com/article/doj-event-powerhouse -live-nation-punished-concert-venues-using-competing-ticketers.
11. Uri Gneezy and Aldo Rustichini, "A Fine Is a Price," *Journal of Legal Studies* 29 (Jan. 2000), https://rady.ucsd.edu/faculty/directory/gneezy/pub/docs/fine.pdf.
12. Dave Seglins et al., "'A Public Relations Nightmare': Ticketmaster Recruits Pros for Secret Scalper Program," *CBC News*, Sept. 19, 2018, https://www .cbc.ca/news/business/ticketmaster-resellers-las-vegas-1.4828535.
13. Seglins et al., "A Public Relations Nightmare."
14. Dave Seglins et al., "'I'm Getting Ripped Off': A Look Inside Ticketmaster's Price-Hiking Bag of Tricks," *CBC News*, Sept. 18, 2018, https://www.cbc.ca /news/business/ticketmaster-prices-scalpers-bruno-mars-1.4826914.
15. Jared Smith, "Setting the Record Straight on TradeDesk and Ticketmaster Resale," Ticketmaster (blog), Sept. 24, 2018, https://blog.ticketmaster.com /jared-smith-statement-tradedesk-resale.
16. Interview with a live music insider, 2020.

17. Christine Jurzenski and Avenir Capital, "Live Nation Stock Can More Than Double in 3 Years, Analyst Says," *Barron's Advisor*, Apr. 8, 2020, https://www .barrons.com/articles/live-nation-stock-can-more-than-double-in-three -years-analyst-51586380765.
18. Alex Weprin, "Saudi Arabia Purchases $500 Million Stake in Live Nation," *Billboard*, Apr. 27, 2020, https://www.billboard.com/articles/business /9366439/saudi-arabia-500-million-stake-live-nation-ticketmaster.
19. Martin Gilens and Benjamin I. Page, "Testing Theories of American Politics: Elites, Interest Groups, and Average Citizens," *Perspectives on Politics* 12, no. 3 (2014).
20. Daniel Kreps, "Jimmy Carter: U.S. Is an 'Oligarchy with Unlimited Political Bribery,'" *Rolling Stone*, July 31, 2015, https://www.rollingstone.com/politics /politics-news/jimmy-carter-u-s-is-an-oligarchy-with-unlimited-political -bribery-63262.
21. Interview with a live music insider, 2020.

CHAPTER 9: WHY SEVEN THOUSAND HOLLYWOOD WRITERS FIRED THEIR AGENTS
1. Cynthia Littleton and Matt Donnelly, "WGA Sues Talent Agencies in Battle Against Packaging Fees," *Variety*, Apr. 17, 2019, https://variety.com/2019/biz /news/wga-sues-talent-agencies-1203191199.
2. Krista Vernoff, "'Grey's Anatomy' Boss: Why I Left My Agent, Despite the Sales Pitch (Guest Column)," *Hollywood Reporter*, Apr. 14, 2019, https://www .hollywoodreporter.com/news/krista-vernoff-why-i-left-my-agent-sales -pitch-guest-column-1201920.
3. Correspondence between the authors and David Goodman, 2021.
4. Writers Guild of America West, "'No Conflict, No Interest': How the Major Hollywood Talent Agencies Put Their Interests Ahead of Their Clients' Interests," *The Wrap*, Mar. 12, 2019, https://www.thewrap.com/wp-content /uploads/2019/03/No-Conflict-No-Interest.pdf.
5. Gavin Polone, "Why Everyone in Hollywood Is Paying More for a Manager," *Vulture*, July 11, 2012, https://www.vulture.com/2012/07/polone-why -everyone-pays-more-for-a-manager.html.
6. Polone, "Why Everyone in Hollywood Is Paying More for a Manager."
7. Writers Guild of America, *Annual Financial Report*, June 29, 2019, https://www .wga.org/uploadedfiles/the-guild/annual-report/annualreport19.pdf; John Koblin, "Peak TV Hits a New Peak, with 532 Scripted Shows," *New York Times*, Jan. 9, 2020, https://www.nytimes.com/2020/01/09/business/media /tv-shows-2020.html.
8. Kyle Paoletta, "Why It's Harder Than Ever to Make It in Hollywood," *New Republic*, July 16, 2020, https://newrepublic.com/article/158491/its-harder -ever-make-hollywood.
9. Paoletta, "Why It's Harder Than Ever to Make It in Hollywood."
10. Vernoff, "'Grey's Anatomy' Boss."
11. Interview with David Slack, 2020.
12. Amended Final Award, Twentieth Century Fox Film Corporation et al., v. Wark Entertainment, Inc., JAMS Arbitration Case References No. 1220052735,

"Bones," Feb. 20, 2019, https://www.documentcloud.org/documents/5753328
-Bones-Arbitration.html.

13. Stephen Battaglio and Wendy Lee, "The End of the Backend? Disney Wants to
Limit Profit Participation on Its New TV Shows," *Los Angeles Times*, September 12, 2019, https://www.latimes.com/entertainment-arts/business
/story/2019-09-12/disney-tv-shows-backend-profit-participation-changes.

14. Scott Timberg, *Culture Crash: The Killing of the Creative Class* (New Haven, CT:
Yale University Press, 2015), 246.

15. Nellie Andreeva, "Disney TV Studios Eyes New Profit Participation Model as
Industry Continues to Pull Away From Traditional Backend Deals," *Deadline*,
July 8, 2019, https://deadline.com/2019/07/hollywood-profit-participation
-tv-deals-changes-disney-streaming-services-1202641423.

CHAPTER 10: WHY *FORTNITE* SUED APPLE

1. Claire Cain Miller and Miguel Helft, "Apple Moves to Tighten Control of
App Store," *New York Times*, Feb. 1, 2011, https://www.nytimes.com/2011/02
/01/technology/01apple.html.

2. Chris Cooke, "Spotify and Netflix Both Make Moves to Reduce Payments to
Apple," *Complete Music Update*, Aug. 23, 2018, https://completemusicupdate.com
/article/spotify-and-netflix-both-make-moves-to-reduce-payments-to-apple.

3. Apple Developer, App Store Review Guidelines, https://developer.apple.com
/app-store/review/guidelines, accessed June 7, 2021.

4. David B. Nieborg and Thomas Poell, "The Platformization of Cultural
Production: Theorizing the Contingent Cultural Commodity," *New Media &
Society* 20, no. 11 (2018): 4286, https://doi.org/10.1177/1461444818769694.

5. Sensor Tower, "Top Charts: iPhone—US—All Categories," Apr. 8, 2021, https://
sensortower.com/ios/rankings/top/iphone/us/all-categories?date=2021-04-08.

6. Stephanie Chan, "Global Consumer Spending in Mobile Apps Reached a Record $111 Billion in 2020, Up 30% from 2019," *Sensor Tower Blog*, Jan. 4, 2021,
https://sensortower.com/blog/app-revenue-and-downloads-2020.

7. Tripp Mickle, "Apple Dominates App Store Search Results, Thwarting Competitors," *Wall Street Journal*, July 23, 2019, https://www.wsj.com/articles/apple
-dominates-app-store-search-results-thwarting-competitors-11563897221.

8. Stuart Dredge, "Apple and Google Shift to 15% App-Subscriptions Rev-Share,"
Music Ally, June 9, 2016, https://musically.com/2016/06/09/apple-and-google
-shift-to-15-app-subscriptions-rev-share.

9. Sarah Perez, "Netflix Stops Paying the 'Apple Tax' on Its $853m in Annual
iOS Revenue," *Tech Crunch*, Jan. 1, 2019, https://techcrunch.com/2018/12/31
/netflix-stops-paying-the-apple-tax-on-its-853m-in-annual-ios-revenue.

10. Dieter Bohn, "Why Amazon Got Out of the Apple App Store Tax, and Why
Other Developers Won't," *The Verge*, Apr. 3, 2020, https://www.theverge.com
/2020/4/3/21206400/apple-tax-amazon-tv-prime-30-percent-developers.

11. David Curry, "App Revenue Data (2021)," Business of Apps, Apr. 1, 2021,
https://www.businessofapps.com/data/app-revenues.

12. Nick Statt, "Epic Gives In to Google and Releases Fortnite on the Play Store,"
The Verge, Apr. 21, 2020, https://www.theverge.com/2020/4/21/21229943
/epic-games-fortnite-google-play-store-available-third-party-software.

13. Order Granting in Part and Denying in Part Motion for Preliminary Injunction, Epic Games, Inc. v. Apple Inc., 4:20-cv-05640-YGR, Dkt. No. 61 (N.D. Cal. Oct. 9, 2020), https://cdn.vox-cdn.com/uploads/chorus_asset/file/21949772/gov.uscourts.cand.364265.118.0.pdf.
14. *Epic Games v. Apple.*
15. *Epic Games v. Apple.*
16. John Gruber, "Kara Swisher: 'Is It Finally Hammer Time for Apple and Its App Store?'" *Daring Fireball*, June 19, 2020, https://daringfireball.net/linked/2020/06/19/swisher-app-store-hey; Kara Swisher, "Is It Finally Hammer Time for Apple and Its App Store?" *New York Times*, June 19, 2020, https://www.nytimes.com/2020/06/19/opinion/apple-app-store-hey.html; Ben Thompson, "Hey v. Apple Follow-Up, Shopify and Walmart, Three Follow-Ups," *Stratechery*, June 18, 2020, https://stratechery.com/2020/hey-v-apple-follow-up-shopify-and-walmart-three-follow-ups.
17. Nick Statt, "Apple Will Reduce App Store Cut to 15 Percent for Most Developers Starting January 1st," *The Verge*, Nov. 18, 2020, https://www.theverge.com/2020/11/18/21572302/apple-app-store-small-business-program-commission-cut-15-percent-reduction.
18. Subcommittee on Antitrust, Commercial and Administrative Law of the Committee on the Judiciary, US House of Representatives, "Investigation of Competition in Digital Markets," 2020, at 17, https://judiciary.house.gov/uploadedfiles/competition_in_digital_markets.pdf?utm_campaign=4493–519.
19. Dan Goodin, "Developer of Checkm8 Explains Why iDevice Jailbreak Exploit Is a Game Changer," *Ars Technica*, September 9, 2019, https://arstechnica.com/information-technology/2019/09/developer-of-checkm8-explains-why-idevice-jailbreak-exploit-is-a-game-changer.
20. Cory Doctorow, "Why I Won't Buy an iPad (and Think You Shouldn't, Either)," *Boing Boing*, Apr. 2, 2010, https://boingboing.net/2010/04/02/why-i-wont-buy-an-ipad-and-thi.html.
21. Tim Bradshaw, "Apple Drops Hundreds of VPN Apps at Beijing's Request," *Financial Times*, Nov. 21, 2017, https://www.ft.com/content/ad42e536-cf36-11e7-b781-794ce08b24dc.
22. Rita Liao, "Apple Removes Two RSS Feed Readers From China App Store," *TechCrunch*, September 30, 2020, https://techcrunch.com/2020/09/30/apple-removes-two-rss-feed-readers-from-china-app-store.
23. Bruce Schneier, "Feudal Security," *Schneier on Security* (blog), Dec. 3, 2012, https://www.schneier.com/blog/archives/2012/12/feudal_sec.html.

CHAPTER 11: YOUTUBE: BAKING CHOKEPOINTS IN
1. See, for example, "Children Turn Backs on Traditional Careers in Favour of Internet Fame, Study Finds," *Sun*, May 22, 2017, https://www.thesun.co.uk/news/3617062/children-turn-backs-on-traditional-careers-in-favour-of-internet-fame-study-finds.
2. Jean Burgess and Joshua Green, *YouTube: Online Video and Participatory Culture*, 2nd ed. (London: Polity, 2018), 2.
3. Burgess and Green, *YouTube*, 74.

4. Jefferson Graham, "Video Websites Pop Up, Invite Postings," *USA Today*, Nov. 21, 2005, https://usatoday30.usatoday.com/tech/news/techinnovations /2005-11-21-video-websites_x.htm.

5. Steven Levy, *In the Plex: How Google Thinks, Works, and Shapes Our Lives* (New York: Simon & Schuster, 2011), 247.

6. Levy, *In the Plex*, 248.

7. 17 USC § 512; "Directive on Electronic Commerce," 2000/31/EC, Official Journal L178, European Parliament and the Council of the European Union, June 8, 2020, Articles 12–14, https://eur-lex.europa.eu/legal-content/EN /TXT/HTML/?uri=CELEX:32000L0031&from=EN.

8. Levy, *In the Plex*, 245.

9. Levy, *In the Plex*, 242.

10. Levy, *In the Plex*, 253.

11. Steve Chen, "The State of Our Video ID Tools," *The Official Google Blog*, June 14, 2007, https://web.archive.org/web/20070616154903/https://googleblog .blogspot.com/2007/06/state-of-our-video-id-tools.html.

12. *New York Times* Staff, "YouTube Sets Tests of Video Blocking," *New York Times*, June 12, 2007, https://www.nytimes.com/2007/06/12/technology /12google.html.

13. Zahavah Levine, "Broadcast Yourself," *Google Public Policy Blog*, Mar. 18, 2010, https://publicpolicy.googleblog.com/2010/03/broadcast-yourself.html.

14. Sam Gustin, "YouTube Founders Knew Illegal Content Was Driving Explosive Growth," AOL, Mar. 21, 2010, https://www.aol.com/2010/03/21/youtube -founders-knew-illegal-content-was-driving-explosive-grow; David Kravets, "Accusations Fly in Viacom, YouTube Copyright Fight," *Wired*, Mar. 18, 2018, https://www.wired.com/2010/03/viacom-youtube.

15. Viacom International, Inc. v. YouTube, Inc., No. 07 Civ. 2103 (S.D.N.Y. Jun. 23, 2010), at 16, https://www.docketalarm.com/cases/New_York_Southern _District_Court/1-07-cv-02103/Viacom_International_Inc._et_al_v. _Youtube_Inc._et_al/364.

16. Jonathan Stempel, "Google, Viacom Settle Landmark YouTube Lawsuit," Reuters, Mar. 18, 2014, https://www.reuters.com/article/us-google-viacom -lawsuit-idUSBREA2H11220140318.

17. Erick Schonfeld, "Google Spent $100 Million Defending Against Viacom's $1 Billion Lawsuit," *TechCrunch*, July 16, 2020, https://techcrunch.com/2010/07 /15/google-viacom-100-million-lawsuit.

18. Levy, *In the Plex*, 255.

19. Leena Rao, "YouTube CEO Says There's 'No Timetable' For Profitability," *Fortune*, Oct. 19, 2016, https://fortune.com/2016/10/18/youtube-profits-ceo -susan-wojcicki.

20. Levy, *In the Plex*, 265.

21. Victoriano Darias, "Content ID as a Solution to Address the Value Gap," *Journal of the Music and Entertainment Industry Educators Association* 18, no. 1 (2018): 105, 128.

22. Christophe Muller, "YouTube: 'No Other Platform Gives as Much Money Back to Creators,'" *Guardian*, Apr. 28, 2016, https://www.theguardian.com/music/music blog/2016/apr/28/youtube-no-other-platform-gives-as-much-money-back-to

-creators; Paul Resnikoff, "YouTube: 99.5% of All Infringing Music Videos Resolved by Content ID," *Digital Music News*, Aug. 9, 2016, https://www.digital musicnews.com/2016/08/08/copyright-problems-resolved-content-id.

23. *How Google Fights Piracy*, Google, Nov. 2018, https://www.blog.google /documents/27/How_Google_Fights_Piracy_2018.pdf.

24. Julia Alexander, "Creators Finally Know How Much Money YouTube Makes, and They Want More of It," *The Verge*, Feb. 4, 2020, https://www.theverge.com /2020/2/4/21121370/youtube-advertising-revenue-creators-demonetization -earnings-google; Susan Wojcicki, "YouTube at 15: My Personal Journey and the Road Ahead," *YouTube Official Blog*, Feb. 14, 2020, https://blog.youtube /news-and-events/youtube-at-15-my-personal-journey.

25. Resnikoff, "YouTube."

26. 17 US Code § 107.

27. Chris Baraniuk Cellan-Jones Rory, "White Noise Video Hit by Copyright Claims," *BBC News*, Jan. 5, 2018, https://www.bbc.com/news/technology -42580523.

28. Nancy Messieh, "YouTube's Automated Copyright System Triggered by Chirping Birds," *The Next Web*, Feb. 27, 2012, https://thenextweb.com /google/2012/02/27/a-copyright-claim-on-chirping-birds-highlights-the -flaws-of-youtubes-automated-system.

29. Katharine Trendacosta, "Unfiltered: How YouTube's Content ID Discourages Fair Use and Dictates What We See Online," Electronic Frontier Foundation, Dec. 10, 2020, https://www.eff.org/wp/unfiltered-how-youtubes-content-id -discourages-fair-use-and-dictates-what-we-see-online.

30. Trendacosta, "Unfiltered."

31. Sophie Bishop. "Managing Visibility on YouTube Through Algorithmic Gossip," *New Media & Society* 21, no. 11–12 (2019): 2589.

32. Chris Stokel-Walker, "Why YouTubers are Feeling the Burn," *Guardian*, Aug. 12, 2018, https://www.theguardian.com/technology/2018/aug/12/youtubers -feeling-burn-video-stars-crumbling-under-pressure-of-producing-new-content.

33. Sophie Bishop, "Algorithmic Experts: Selling Algorithmic Lore on YouTube," *Social Media + Society* 6, no. 1 (2020): 8, https://doi.org/10.1177/205630511 9897323.

34. Bishop, "Algorithmic Experts," 3.

35. Stokel-Walker, "Why YouTubers Are Feeling the Burn."

36. Janko Roettgers, "Maker Studios Is Shutting Down Blip Next Month," *Variety*, July 20, 2015, https://variety.com/2015/digital/news/maker-studios-is -shutting-down-blip-next-month-1201544219.

37. US House of Representatives, "Investigation of Competition in Digital Markets," 191.

38. Alex Weprin, "YouTube Ad Revenue Tops $8.6B, Beating Netflix in the Quarter," *Hollywood Reporter*, Feb. 1, 2022, https://www.hollywood reporter.com/business/digital/youtube-ad-revenue-tops-8-6b-beating -netflix-in-the-quarter-1235085391.

39. Hoang Nguyen, "The Most Popular Music Streaming Platforms in Key Markets Globally," YouGov, Mar. 19, 2021, https://yougov.co.uk/topics/media /articles-reports/2021/03/18/services-used-stream-music-poll.

40. Definition (IFPI): "The value gap describes the growing mismatch between the value that user upload services, such as YouTube, extract from music and the revenue returned to the music community—those who are creating and investing in music. The value gap is the biggest threat to the future sustainability of the music industry." IFPI, "Fixing the Value Gap," *Global Music Report*, 2018, https://perma.cc/SGZ3-PLHM.

41. Recording Industry Association of America, "Five Stubborn Truths About YouTube and the Value Gap," *Medium*, Aug. 21, 2017, https://medium .com/@RIAA/five-stubborn-truths-about-youtube-and-value-gap-4faff 133271f.

42. *Bloomberg* Staff, "Why 'Success' on YouTube Still Means a Life of Poverty," *Fortune*, Feb. 28, 2018, https://fortune.com/2018/02/27/youtube-success -poverty-wages.

43. Lyor Cohen, "YouTube Pays Out More Than Spotify for Ad-Supported Streams in the US," *Music Business Worldwide*, Aug. 17, 2017, https://www .musicbusinessworldwide.com/lyor-cohen-youtube-pays-out-more-than -spotify-for-ad-supported-streams-in-the-us.

44. Statista, "Number of YouTube Users"; Statista, "Most Popular Websites Worldwide as of June 2021, by Total Visits (in Billions)," July 2021, https:// www.statista.com/statistics/1201880/most-visited-websites-worldwide.

45. Jonathan Tepper and Denise Hearn, *The Myth of Capitalism: Monopolies and the Death of Competition* (Hoboken, NJ: Wiley, 2019), 15.

46. Aaron Mak, "How Facebook Tried to Make Itself Antitrust-Proof," *Slate*, Dec. 9, 2020, https://slate.com/technology/2020/12/facebook-antitrust-ftc -breakup-whatsapp-instagram-zuckerberg.html.

47. Jasper L. Tran, "The Myth of *Hush-A-Phone v. United States*," *IEEE Annals of the History of Computing* 41, no. 4 (2019): 6n33.

48. Paul Keller, "Article 17, the Year in Review (2021 edition)," *Kluwer Copyright Blog*, Jan. 24, 2022, http://copyrightblog.kluweriplaw.com/2022/01/24/article -17-the-year-in-review-2021-edition.

49. Susan Wojcicki, "YouTube Chief Says EU Copyright Plan Could Lead to Blocked Access," *Financial Times*, Nov. 12, 2018, https://www.ft.com/content /266e6c2a-e42e-11e8-a8a0-99b2e340ffeb.

50. *Economics of Music Streaming*, 89.

CHAPTER 12: IDEAS LYING AROUND

1. Stacy Mitchell, "After Three Decades of Neglect, Antitrust Is Back on the Democratic Platform," Institute for Local Self-Reliance, Aug. 4, 2016, https://ilsr.org /after-three-decades-of-neglect-antitrust-is-back-on-the-democratic-platform.

2. Jake Walter-Warner and William F. Cavanaugh Jr., "The New Brandeis School Manifesto," *Antitrust Update* (blog), Patterson Belknap Webb & Tyler, Feb. 5, 2020, https://www.pbwt.com/antitrust-update-blog/the-new-brandeis-school -manifesto.

3. Aoife White and Stephanie Bodoni, "Amazon Hit by EU Complaint, Faces New Probe Over Sales," *Bloomberg*, Nov. 10, 2020, https://www.bloomberg .com/news/articles/2020-11-10/amazon-set-to-get-eu-antitrust-objections -over-sales-data.

4. Peter C. Carstensen, *Competition Policy and the Control of Buyer Power: A Global Issue* (Cheltenham, UK: Edward Elgar, 2017), 133.

5. Carstensen, *Competition Policy and the Control of Buyer Power*, 118.

6. Carstensen, *Competition Policy and the Control of Buyer Power*, 133.

7. Olivia Perreault, "Antitrust Institute Slams DOJ Missed Opportunity in Live Nation Settlement," *Ticket News*, Feb. 6, 2020, https://www.ticketnews.com /2020/02/antitrust-institute-doj-live-nation-settlement.

8. Zephyr Teachout, *Break 'Em Up: Recovering Our Freedom from Big Ag, Big Tech, and Big Money* (New York: All Points Books, 2020).

9. Tim Wu, *The Curse of Bigness: Antitrust in the New Gilded Age* (New York: Columbia Global Reports, 2018), 87–88.

10. Carstensen, *Competition Policy and the Control of Buyer Power*, 133, 139.

11. Gabriel Winant, "No Going Back: the Power and Limits of the Anti-Monopolist Tradition," *Nation*, Jan. 21, 2021, https://www.thenation.com /article/culture/goliath-monopoly-and-democracy-matt-stoller-review.

12. Carstensen, *Competition Policy and the Control of Buyer Power*, 139.

13. Milton Friedman, *Capitalism and Freedom* (Chicago: University of Chicago Press, 1962).

14. Naomi Klein, *The Shock Doctrine: The Rise of Disaster Capitalism* (New York: Knopf, 2007), 7.

15. Citizens United v. Federal Election Commission, 558 US 310 (2010).

CHAPTER 13: TRANSPARENCY RIGHTS

1. Interview with Susan May, 2021.

2. Interview with Susan May, 2021.

3. The original post has been deleted but is archived at https://web.archive.org /web/20200921135114/https://www.yaplex.com/blog/how-to-rent-books -with-audible.

4. Interview with Susan May, 2021.

5. Interview with Colleen Cross, 2021.

6. Colleen Cross, "How Audiobook Authors and Narrators Are Paid by Audible-ACX. We Think," Alliance of Independent Authors, Feb. 8, 2021, https:// selfpublishingadvice.org/how-audiobook-authors-are-paid-by-audible-acx /?fbclid=IwAR1_F0nAJ4gvYbdjvCn-5Ec8XpMC8ReRFZr9zEdtwdw YJrv68adjDHKzB7g.

7. Interview with Colleen Cross, 2021.

8. Interview with Orna Ross, 2021.

9. Interview with Susan May, 2021.

10. Future of Music Coalition, Twitter post, July 15, 2021, 11:59 p.m., https:// twitter.com/future_of_music/status/1415672344471871488?s=20.

11. Elias Leight, "Fake Streams Could Be Costing Artists $300 Million a Year," *Rolling Stone*, June 18, 2019, https://www.rollingstone.com/pro/features/fake -streams-indie-labels-spotify-tidal-846641.

12. "Digital Forensics Report for Dagens Næringsliv," Norwegian University of Science and Technology, Apr. 10, 2018, https://www.musicbusinessworld wide.com/files/2018/05/NTNU_DigitalForensicsReport_DN_Final _Version.pdf.

13. "The IMMF's Open Letter on Record Label and Music Publisher Deals in the Digital Market," *Complete Music Update*, May 21, 2015, https://completemusic update.com/article/the-immfs-open-letter-on-record-label-and-music -publisher-deals-in-the-digital-market.

14. Committee on Digital, Culture, Media and Sport, UK House of Commons, *Economics of Music Streaming*, Second Report of Session 2021–22 (London, July 15, 2021), 74, https://committees.parliament.uk/publications/6739/documents /72525/default.

15. Molly Crabapple, "Filthy Lucre," *Vice*, June 6, 2013, https://www.vice.com/en /article/mvp8dn/filthy-lucre.

16. Article 19, European Union Directive 2019/790 on copyright and related rights in the digital single market.

17. European Commission, "Remuneration of Authors of Books and Scientific Journals, Translators, Journalists and Visual Artists for the Use of Their Works," Jan. 10, 2017, https://op.europa.eu/en/publication-detail/- /publication/81acd376-d896–11e6-ad7c-01aa75ed71a1.

18. David Turner, "The False Promise of User-Centric Streaming," *Penny Fractions* (newsletter), Oct. 2, 2019, https://www.getrevue.co/profile/pennyfractions /issues/penny-fractions-the-false-promise-of-user-centric-streaming-201362.

19. Chuck Philips, "Auditors Put New Spin on Revolt Over Royalties," *Los Angeles Times*, Feb. 26, 2002, https://www.latimes.com/archives/la-xpm-2002 -feb-26-mn-29955-story.html.

20. House of Commons, *Economics of Music Streaming*, 73.

21. Mike Moffitt, "How a Racist Genius Created Silicon Valley by Being a Terrible Boss," *SFGate*, Aug. 21, 2018, https://www.sfgate.com/tech/article /Silicon-Valley-Shockley-racist-semiconductor-lab-13164228.php.

22. "Record Label Accounting Practices," Joint Hearing of the California State Senate Committee on the Judiciary and State Senate Select Committee on the Entertainment Industry (Senate Publications, 2002), https://catalog.hathitrust .org/Record/100797529.

23. Philips, "Auditors Put New Spin on Revolt Over Royalties."

CHAPTER 14: COLLECTIVE ACTION

1. Mark Egan, Gregor Matvos, and Amit Seru, "Arbitration with Uninformed Consumers," Working Paper no. 3768, Oct. 2018, Stanford Graduate School of Business, https://www.gsb.stanford.edu/faculty-research/working-papers /arbitration-uninformed-consumers.

2. Eamonn Forde, "Taylor Swift: Does Apple's Climbdown Really Demonstrate Her Power?" *Guardian*, June 22, 2015, https://www.theguardian.com/music /musicblog/2015/jun/22/taylor-swift-does-apples-climbdown-really -demonstrate-her-power.

3. Julia Angwin, "The Antitrust Case for Gig Worker Rights," *The Markup*, Nov. 7, 2020, https://www.getrevue.co/profile/themarkup/issues/the-antitrust -case-for-gig-worker-rights-289982.

4. Applicants 1–4 v. Uber BV, C/13/692003/HA RK 20–302 (Court of Amsterdam), Mar. 11, 2021, https://uitspraken.rechtspraak.nl/inziendocument?id =ECLI:NL:RBAMS:2021:1018; Applicants 1–10 v. Uber BV, C/13/687315 /

HA RK 20–207 (Court of Amsterdam), Mar. 11, 2021, https://uitspraken
.rechtspraak.nl/inziendocument?id=ECLI:NL:RBAMS:2021:1020.

5. John B. Kirkwood, "Collusion to Control a Powerful Customer: Amazon,
E-Books, and Antitrust Policy," *Miami Law Review* 69, no. 1 (2014): 51–63.

6. Zachary D. Carter, "The Woman Who Shattered the Myth of the Free Market," *New York Times*, Apr. 24, 2021, https://www.nytimes.com/2021/04/24
/opinion/joan-robinson-economy-monopoly-labor.html.

7. Leo Rosten, *Hollywood: The Movie Colony, the Movie Makers* (New York:
Harcourt Brace, 1941), 307.

8. Catherine L. Fisk, *Writing for Hire: Unions, Hollywood, and Madison Avenue*
(Cambridge, MA: Harvard University Press, 2016), 212–18.

9. Krista Vernoff, "'Grey's Anatomy' Boss: Why I Left My Agent, Despite the
Sales Pitch (Guest Column)," *Hollywood Reporter*, Apr. 14, 2019, https://www
.hollywoodreporter.com/news/krista-vernoff-why-i-left-my-agent-sales
-pitch-guest-column-1201920.

10. David Robb, "WME Signs WGA Franchise Agreement, Giving Guild Historic
Win in Campaign to Reshape Talent Agency Business," *Deadline*, Feb. 5, 2021,
https://deadline.com/2021/02/wme-signs-writers-guild-deal-wga-reshapes
-talent-agency-business-1234688833.

11. Jonathan Handel, "Writers Guild Reveals Studio Deal Details, Says Pandemic
Limited Leverage," *Hollywood Reporter*, July 1, 2020, https://www.hollywood
reporter.com/news/writers-guild-reveals-studio-deal-details-says-pandemic
-limited-leverage-1301488.

12. Wendy Lee, "WGA Aims to Crack Down on Writers Secretly Working with
'Fired' Agents," *Los Angeles Times*, Feb. 16, 2020, https://www.latimes.com
/entertainment-arts/business/story/2020-02-14/wga-aims-to-crack-down
-on-writers-working-with-non-approved-agents.

13. Sanjukta Paul, "Antitrust as Allocator of Coordination Rights," *UCLA Law
Review* 67, no. 2 (2020), https://papers.ssrn.com/sol3/papers.cfm?abstract
_id=3337861.

14. Sandeep Vaheesan, "Gig Workers Need Antitrust Reform," *Dissent*, Dec. 18,
2020, https://www.dissentmagazine.org/online_articles/gig-workers-need
-antitrust-reform.

CHAPTER 15: TIME LIMITS ON COPYRIGHT CONTRACTS

1. Paul Slade, "Superheroes in Court: Continued," http://www.planetslade.com
/superheroes8.html.

2. Richard Harrington, "MCA to Pay Royalties to RB Greats," *Washington Post*,
Dec. 7, 1989, https://www.washingtonpost.com/archive/lifestyle/1989/12/07
/mca-to-pay-royalties-to-rb-greats/63714098-29be-481e-915f-cb43f6bdf07c.

3. Joshua Yuvaraj and Rebecca Giblin, "Are Contracts Enough? An Empirical
Study of Author Rights in Australian Publishing Agreements," *Melbourne University Law Review* 44, no. 1 (2020), https://papers.ssrn.com/sol3/papers.cfm
?abstract_id=3541350.

4. See, for example, Jacob Flynn, Rebecca Giblin, and François Petitjean, "What
Happens When Books Enter the Public Domain?" *University of New South
Wales Law Journal* 42 (2019): 39.

5. For a detailed analysis of the Statute of Anne's origins, how the reversion right evolved and the legal uncertainties that plagued it, see Lionel Bently and Jane C. Ginsburg, "'The Sole Right . . . Shall Return to the Authors': Anglo-American Authors' Reversion Rights from the Statute of Anne to Contemporary U.S. Copyright," *Berkeley Technology Law Journal* 25 (2010): 1475, 1482–1541.

6. Richard B. Sher, *The Enlightenment & the Book: Scottish Authors & Their Publishers in Eighteenth-Century Britain, Ireland & America* (Chicago: University of Chicago Press, 2006), 353–57.

7. Bently and Ginsburg, "The Sole Right."

8. Ronan Deazley, "Commentary on Milton's Contract 1667," in *Primary Sources on Copyright (1450–1900)*, ed. Lionel Bently and Martin Kretschmer (2008), https://www.copyrighthistory.org/cam/tools/request/showRecord.php?id=commentary_uk_1667.

9. Fred Fisher Music Co. v. M. Witmark & Sons, 318 US 643, 656 (1943).

10. Bently and Ginsburg, "The Sole Right," 1563n416.

11. Copyright Law Revision Part 3: Preliminary Draft for Revised US Copyright Law and Discussions and Comments on the Draft (US Government Printing Office, 1964), 287.

12. Phillip W. Hall Jr., "Smells Like Slavery: Unconscionability in Recording Industry Contracts," *Hastings Communications and Entertainment Law Journal* 25, no. 1 (2002): 215.

13. Joshua Yuvaraj, Rebecca Giblin, Daniel Russo-Batterham, and Genevieve Grant, "US Copyright Termination Notices 1977–2020: Introducing New Datasets."

14. Yuvaraj, Giblin, Russo-Batterham, and Grant, "US Copyright Termination Notices 1977–2020."

15. Jacob Flynn, Rebecca Giblin, and François Petitjean, "What Happens When Books Enter the Public Domain? Testing Copyright's Underuse Hypothesis Across Australia, New Zealand, the United States and Canada," *University of New South Wales Law Journal* 42, no. 4 (2019): 1218.

16. Larry Rohter, "Record Industry Braces for Artists' Battles over Song Rights," *New York Times*, Aug. 15, 2011, https://www.nytimes.com/2011/08/16/arts/music/springsteen-and-others-soon-eligible-to-recover-song-rights.html.

17. Eriq Gardner, "Sony Suing Musicians for Allowing Attorney to Use Album Artwork," *Hollywood Reporter*, Oct. 5, 2020, https://www.hollywoodreporter.com/thr-esq/sony-suing-musicians-for-allowing-attorney-to-use-album-artwork.

18. Joshua Yuvaraj and Rebecca Giblin, "Why Were Commonwealth Reversionary Rights Abolished (and What Can We Learn Where They Remain)?" *European Intellectual Property Review* 41, no. 4 (2019): 232.

19. Rian Malan, *ReMastered: The Lion's Share*, dir. Sam Cullman, Netflix, 2019.

20. Committee on Digital, Culture, Media and Sport, UK House of Commons, *Economics of Music Streaming*, Second Report of Session 2021–22 (London, July 15, 2021), 105, https://committees.parliament.uk/publications/6739/documents/72525/default.

21. If you're interested in digging into the detail of how this figure is calculated, see the discussion in Rebecca Giblin, "A New Copyright Bargain? Reclaiming

Lost Culture and Getting Authors Paid," *Columbia Journal of Law & the Arts* 41 (2018): 369.

22. Brief of George A. Akerlof et al. as Amici Curiae in Support of Petitioners, Eldred v. Ashcroft, 537 US 186, 01–618, 2003, at 7.

23. Paul J. Heald, "How Copyright Keeps Works Disappeared," *Journal of Empirical Legal Studies* 11, no. 4 (2013): 829.

24. Jacob Flynn, Rebecca Giblin, and François Petitjean, "What Happens When Books Enter the Public Domain? Testing Copyright's Underuse Hypothesis Across Australia, New Zealand, the United States and Canada," *University of New South Wales Law Journal* 42, no. 4 (2019): 1215.

25. Giblin, "A New Copyright Bargain."

26. Joshua Yuvaraj and Rebecca Giblin, "Are Contracts Enough? An Empirical Study of Author Rights in Australian Publishing Agreements," *Melbourne University Law Review* 44, no. 1 (2020).

27. Jane Weaver, "How to Be an Independent Artist in 2015," *Guardian*, Mar. 30, 2015, https://www.theguardian.com/music/2015/mar/30/jane-weaver-folky -psychedelia.

28. Article 22, European Union Digital Single Market Directive 2019/790.

CHAPTER 16: RADICAL INTEROPERABILITY

1. Marianna Longmire, "5 Surprising Items That Are Cheaper Than Printer Ink," *Choice*, https://www.choice.com.au/electronics-and-technology /computers/scanners-and-printers/articles/5-surprising-items-that-are -cheaper-than-printer-ink.

2. 18 USC § 1030: Fraud and Related Activity in Connection with Computers.

3. Syllabus, Google LLC v. Oracle America, Inc., 593 U.S. 1 (C.A.F.C. Apr. 5, 2021).

4. James Wallace and Jim Erickson, *Hard Drive: Bill Gates and the Making of the Microsoft Empire* (New York: Harper, 1993), 233.

5. Massachusetts House of Representatives, Right to Repair Initiative 11–17 (2012), H. 4362, passed Nov. 6, 2012, http://archive.boston.com/news/special /politics/2012/general/mass-ballot-question-1-election-results-2012.html. To reconcile disparities between the original ballot initiative and the House bill, an additional bill was passed in the following year: H. 3757, 188th Gen. Ct. (Mass. 2013).

6. Cory Doctorow and Christoph Schmon, "The EU's Digital Markets Act: There Is a Lot to Like, but Room for Improvement," Dec. 15, 2020, Electronic Frontier Foundation, https://www.eff.org/deeplinks/2020/12/eus-digital -markets-act-there-lot-room-improvement.

7. UK Competition and Markets Authority, *Online Platforms and Digital Advertising: Market Study Final Report*, July 1, 2020, https://assets.publishing.service .gov.uk/media/5efc57ed3a6f4023d242ed56/Final_report_1_July_2020_.pdf.

8. Associated Press, "South Korea Bans Google, Apple Payment Monopolies," September 1, 2021, https://apnews.com/article/technology-business-south -korea-a8e160fb9b43681557445cfe06f25bc1.

9. Aaron Perzanowski, *The Right to Repair* (New York: Cambridge University Press, 2022), 18.

10. Perzanowski, *The Right to Repair*, 230.
11. Matthew Gault, "Auto Industry TV Ads Claim Right to Repair Benefits 'Sexual Predators,'" *Vice*, Feb. 9, 2020, https://www.vice.com/en/article/qj4ayw/auto-industry-tv-ads-claim-right-to-repair-benefits-sexual-predators.
12. Hiawatha Bray, "Will Carmakers Defeat Question 1 in Court?" *Boston Globe*, May 12, 2021, https://www.bostonglobe.com/2021/05/12/business/will-carmakers-defeat-question-1-court.
13. Van Buren v. United States, 940 F. 3d 1192 (2021).

CHAPTER 17: MINIMUM WAGES FOR CREATIVE WORK

1. Mary Robinette Kowal, "#DisneyMustPay Alan Dean Foster," Science Fiction Writers of America, Nov. 18, 2020, https://www.sfwa.org/2020/11/18/disney-must-pay.
2. Peter C. Carstensen, *Competition Policy and the Control of Buyer Power: A Global Issue* (Cheltenham, UK: Edward Elgar, 2017), 9, https://doi.org/10.4337/9781782540588.
3. Article 18(1), EU Copyright Directive (2019).
4. Raquel Xalabarder, "The Principle of Appropriate and Proportionate Remuneration of ART.18 Digital Single Market Directive: Some Thoughts for Its National Implementation," Social Sciences Research Network, https://www.ssrn.com/abstract=3684375.
5. Jon Burlingame, "Discovery Networks Corners Composers in Music Royalties Battle," *Variety*, Dec. 12, 2019, https://variety.com/2019/music/news/discovery-networks-composers-music-royalties-1203434924.
6. Kathryn Kranhold, "TV and Film Composers Say Netflix, Other Streaming Services Insist on Buying Out Their Music Rights," *Hollywood Reporter*, Dec. 11, 2019, https://www.hollywoodreporter.com/news/tv-film-composers-say-netflix-streaming-services-insist-buying-music-rights-1261940.
7. 17 US Code § 114.
8. SoundExchange, "About Digital Royalties," https://www.soundexchange.com/artist-copyright-owner/digital-royalties.
9. 17 US Code § 114.
10. BMI v. DMX, 683 F.3d 32, at 38.
11. Donald S. Passman, *All You Need to Know About the Music Business*, 8th ed. (New York: Free Press, 2013), 277.
12. Tim Ingham, "Songwriters Are Already Fighting for Better Pay. But in 2021, They Face an Even Bigger Battle," *Rolling Stone*, June 15, 2020, https://www.rollingstone.com/pro/features/songwriters-spotify-amazon-crb-royalties-war-1015116.
13. Ingham, "Songwriters Are Already Fighting for Better Pay."
14. Copyright Act of 1976 § 801(b)(1), 90 Stat. at 2594–95.
15. Mat Dryhurst, Twitter post, Aug. 10, 2020, 10:06 p.m., https://twitter.com/matdryhurst/status/1292794458782740481?s=20.
16. Future of Music Coalition, "FMC Testimony Submitted to House Small Business Committee on Webcasting Rates," June 27, 2007, http://futureofmusic.org/filing/fmc-testimony-submitted-house-small-business-committee-webcasting-rates.

17. Committee on Digital, Culture, Media and Sport, UK House of Commons, *Economics of Music Streaming,* Second Report of Session 2021–22 (London, July 15, 2021), 29, https://committees.parliament.uk/publications/6739/documents /72525/default.
18. Harcourt and Gordon, "International Digital Music Licensing."
19. Article 3, European Union Directive 2006/116/EC.
20. House of Commons, *Economics of Music Streaming*, 29.
21. Carstensen, *Competition Policy*, 67n66.
22. Pelly, interview, *Interdependence* podcast.
23. 17 USC § 115.
24. Á. Semprún and J. Romera, "El Auditor Eleva a 87 Millones el Dinero que la SGAE Desvió a la Red de Neri" [The auditor raises the money that the SGAE diverted to the Neri Network to 87 million], *El Economista* [The Economist], Nov. 29, 2011, https://www.eleconomista.es/empresas-finanzas/noticias /3566939/11/11/El-auditor-eleva-a-87-millones-el-dinero-que-la-SGAE -desvio-a-la-red-de-Neri.html.
25. David Turner, "The False Promise of User-Centric Streaming," *Penny Fractions* (newsletter), Oct. 2, 2019, https://www.getrevue.co/profile/pennyfractions /issues/penny-fractions-the-false-promise-of-user-centric-streaming-201362.
26. Rethink Music, "Fair Music: Transparency and Payment Flows in the Music Industry," Berklee Institute for Creative Entrepreneurship, 21, https://static1 .squarespace.com/static/552c0535e4b0afcbed88dc53/t/55d0da1ae4b06bd4 bea8c86c/1439750682446/rethink_music_fairness_transparency_final.pdf.
27. Becky Brook, "A Blanket License for Online Music featuring Cory Doctorow," *Music Ally*, ep. 7, podcast audio, June 11, 2020, https://podcasts.google .com/feed/aHR0cHM6Ly9hbmNob3IuZm0vcy8xZDAxZjM1Yy9wb2Rj YXN0L3Jzcw/episode/YjY0MmYwNWEtNzhkZS00MjA0LTg3ZjYtMjI 5ZGFlODBjZDVl?sa=X&ved=0CAUQkfYCahcKEwiQrvSx7p3wAh UAAAAAHQAAAAQiAE.
28. Ben Sisario, "Going to the Ends of the Earth to Get the Most Out of Music," *New York Times*, June 8, 2015, https://www.nytimes.com/2015/06/08 /business/media/going-to-the-ends-of-the-earth-to-get-the-most-out-of -music.html.
29. Rethink Music, "Fair Music." https://static1.squarespace.com/static/552c 0535e4b0afcbed88dc53/t/55d0da1ae4b06bd4bea8c86c/1439750682446 /rethink_music_fairness_transparency_final.pdf.
30. Mechanical Licensing Collective, "The Mechanical Licensing Collective Receives $424 Million in Historical Unmatched Royalties from Digital Service Providers," Feb. 16, 2021, https://www.themlc.com/press/mechanical-licensing -collective-receives-424-million-historical-unmatched-royalties-digital.
31. Annabella Coldrick, "Where Are the Missing Song Royalties?" *Music Business Worldwide*, July 16, 2019, https://www.musicbusinessworldwide.com/where -are-the-missing-song-royalties-2.
32. Klementina Milosic, "GRD's Failure," *Music Business Journal*, Aug. 31, 2018, http://www.thembj.org/2015/08/grds-failure.
33. Nick Messitte, "Inside The Black Box: A Deep Dive into Music's Monetization Mystery," *Forbes*, Apr. 15, 2015, https://www.forbes.com/sites/nick

messitte/2015/04/15/inside-the-black-box-a-deep-dive-into-musics-
monetization-mystery/#18eaf6185d4a.
34. Rethink Music, "Fair Music," 16.
35. House of Commons, *Economics of Music Streaming*, 51–52.
36. Brook, "A Blanket License."

CHAPTER 18: COLLECTIVE OWNERSHIP
 1. Astra Taylor, *The People's Platform: Taking Back Power and Culture in the Digital Age* (New York: Picador, 2015), 175.
 2. Peter Walsh, Michael Peck, and Ibon Zugasti, "Why the U.S. Needs More Worker-Owned Companies," *Harvard Business Review*, Aug. 8, 2018, https://hbr.org/2018/08/why-the-u-s-needs-more-worker-owned-companies; Rhokeun Park, Douglas Kruse, and James Sesil, "Does Employee Owner-ship Enhance Firm Survival?" in *Employee Participation, Firm Performance and Survival*, 8, ed. Virginie Perotin and Andrew Robinson (Bingley, UK: Emerald Publishing, 2004), 3–33, https://web.archive.org/web/20191008040837/https://smlr.rutgers.edu/sites/default/files/documents/faculty_staff_docs/does%20employee%20ownership%20enhance%20firm%20survival.pdf.
 3. Park, Kruse, and Sesil, "Does Employee Ownership Enhance Firm Survival?" 25.
 4. Park, Kruse, and Sesil, "Does Employee Ownership Enhance Firm Survival?" 22.
 5. Nick Srnicek, *Platform Capitalism* (Cambridge: Polity Press, 2017), 70, https://mudancatecnologicaedinamicacapitalista.files.wordpress.com/2019/02/platform-capitalism.pdf, accessed Apr. 28, 2021.
 6. Gilad Edelman, "Can Killing Cookies Save Journalism?" *Wired*, Aug. 5, 2020, https://www.wired.com/story/can-killing-cookies-save-journalism.
 7. James Meese, "Advertising, Algorithms, and Democratic Risk," unpublished manuscript, 2020, 16.
 8. Meese, "Advertising, Algorithms, and Democratic Risk," 34.
 9. Jeanine Poggi, "Vice Calls on Brands to Rethink Keyword Blocklists Associ-ated with Racism," *AdAge*, June 24, 2020, https://adage.com/article/special-report-newfronts/vice-calls-brands-rethink-keyword-blocklists-associated-racism/2263781.
10. Nathan J. Robinson, "The Truth Is Paywalled But the Lies Are Free," *Current Affairs*, Aug. 2, 2020, https://www.currentaffairs.org/2020/08/the-truth-is-paywalled-but-the-lies-are-free.
11. Article 15, European Union Digital Single Market Directive 2019/790.
12. Nicolas Jaimes and Marjolaine Tasset, "Droit voisin pour la presse: les éditeurs français plient devant Google" [Neighboring rights for the press: French publishers bow to Google]," *Le Journal du Net* [Net Newspaper], Oct. 24, 2019, https://www.journaldunet.com/media/publishers/1459188-droit-voisin-pour-la-presse-les-editeurs-francais-plient-devant-google.
13. Société Google LLC et al. v. Le Syndicat Des Éditeurs de la Presse Magazine et al. [Google v. Magazine Press Publishers Union], RG No. 20/08071 (Cour d'appel de Paris [Paris Court of Appeal], Oct. 8, 2020), https://www.autoritedela concurrence.fr/sites/default/files/appealsd/2020-10/ca_20mc01_oct20.pdf.

14. Treasury Laws Amendment (News Media and Digital Platforms Mandatory Bargaining Code) Act 2021, no. 21 (Parliament of Australia, Mar. 2, 2021), https://www.legislation.gov.au/Details/C2021A00021.

15. Alan Kohler, "The News Bargaining Code Is Dead. Long Live the News Bargaining Chip," *New Daily*, Mar. 17, 2021, https://thenewdaily.com.au/news/2021/03/17/alan-kohler-news-bargaining-code-dead.

16. Harold Feld, "America Needs a Public Interest Approach to Solving Big Tech Harms to News," *Public Knowledge* (blog), Feb. 9, 2021, https://www.public knowledge.org/blog/america-needs-a-public-interest-approach-to-solving -big-tech-harms-to-news.

17. New Jersey Civic Information Consortium, "About the Consortium," https:// njcivicinfo.org/about.

18. Rasmus Kleis Nielsen, Robert Gorwa, and Madeleine de Cock Buning, "What Can Be Done? Digital Media Policy Options for Europe (and Beyond)," Reuters Institute, University of Oxford, Nov. 25, 2019, https://reutersinstitute .politics.ox.ac.uk/what-can-be-done-digital-media-policy-options-europe -and-beyond.

19. Will Oremus, "There's a Smarter Way to Make Tech Pay for News," *Pattern Matching* (newsletter), OneZero, *Medium*, Feb. 21, 2021, https://onezero .medium.com/a-smarter-way-to-make-tech-pay-for-news-9255e3b8dccb.

20. Trebor Scholz, "Platform Cooperativism: Challenging the Corporate Sharing Economy," Rosa Luxemburg Stiftung New York, 2016, 26, https://rosalux .nyc/wp-content/uploads/2020/11/RLS-NYC_platformcoop.pdf.

21. Liz Pelly, "Protest Platforms: Streaming Co-Op Restores Agency to Artists," *Shadowproof*, Nov. 1, 2017, https://shadowproof.com/2017/11/01/protest -platforms-resonate-streaming-co-op-agency-to-artists.

22. Resonate, "Manifesto," https://resonate.is/manifesto.

23. Liz Pelly, "Alternative Streaming Models," *Montez Press Radio*, podcast audio, Jan. 27, 2021, https://radio.montezpress.com/#/archive/1755.

24. Resonate, Stream2own, https://resonate.is/stream2own.

25. Mat Dryhurst, "Band Together: Why Musicians Must Strike a Collective Chord to Survive," *Guardian*, Apr. 9, 2019, https://www.theguardian.com /music/2019/apr/09/experimental-musicians-must-strike-a-collective -chord-red-bull-music-academy-closing.

26. Paris Max, "Toxic Workplaces Are Driving Video Game Developers to Unionize," OneZero, *Medium*, Nov. 12, 2019, https://onezero.medium.com/toxic -workplaces-are-driving-video-game-developers-to-unionize-cda5c8b73317.

27. Alex Calvin, "Dead Cells Has Sold 730k Copies Since Its Early Access Launch," *PC Games Insider*, May 1, 2018, https://www.pcgamesinsider.biz /news/66984/dead-cells-has-sold-730k-copies-since-early-access-launch.

28. Nathan Grayson, "Game Studio With No Bosses Pays Everyone the Same," *Kotaku*, July 25, 2018, https://kotaku.com/game-studio-with-no-bosses-pays -everyone-the-same-1827872972.

29. Grayson, "Game Studio."

30. Musicat, "Rabble," https://musicat.co/rabble.

31. Songtrust, "What Is the Pay Rate for Spotify Streams?" https://help.songtrust .com/knowledge/what-is-the-pay-rate-for-spotify-streams.

32. Pelly, "Alternative Streaming Models."
33. State Library of New South Wales: "Indyreads: eBook and eAudio Platform for NSW Public Libraries," https://www.sl.nsw.gov.au/public-library-services /services/indyreads.
34. Interview with Alicia Brown, 2021.
35. Chris O'Falt, "As Kanopy's Popularity Grows, Can Your Library Continue to Afford It?" *IndieWire*, June 26, 2019, https://www.indiewire.com/2019/06 /new-york-public-library-drops-kanopy-netflix-alternative-too-expensive -1202153550.
36. Liz Pelly, "Socialized Streaming: A Case for Universal Music Access," *Real Life Magazine*, Feb. 16, 2021, https://reallifemag.com/socialized-streaming.
37. Henderson Cole, "The American Music Library," https://docs.google.com /document/d/14Wu_2B8fOZAPSpRpiNujrURd94plCzGXVFKLQb8vHeU /edit, accessed June 7, 2021.
38. Pelly, "Alternative Streaming Models."

CHAPTER 19: UNITING AGAINST CHOKEPOINT CAPITALISM

1. Stafford Beer, "What Is Cybernetics?" *Kybernetes* 31, no. 2 (2002): 209–19, 217, https://doi.org/10.1108/03684920210417283.
2. Zephyr Teachout, *Break 'Em Up: Recovering Our Freedom from Big Ag, Big Tech, and Big Money* (New York: All Points Books, 2020), 145.
3. Gustavo Grullon, Yelena Larkin, and Roni Michaely, "Are U.S. Industries Becoming More Concentrated?" *Review of Finance* 23, no. 4 (2019).
4. Mike Pomranz, "Some States Are Questioning Fast Food Chains' Non-Compete Agreements: Here's What We Know So Far," *Food & Wine*, July 10, 2018, https:// www.foodandwine.com/news/fast-food-non-compete-agreement-inquiry.
5. Lance Whitney, "Apple, Google, Others Settle Antipoaching Lawsuit for $415 Million," CNET, Sept. 3, 2015, https://www.cnet.com/news/apple-google -others-settle-anti-poaching-lawsuit-for-415-million.
6. Edward Chancellor, ed., *Capital Returns: Investing Through the Capital Cycle: A Money Manager's Reports 2002–15* (Palgrave Macmillan, 2015), 27.
7. Teachout, *Break 'Em Up*, 87–92.
8. Kim Bobo, *Wage Theft in America: Why Millions of Working Americans Are Not Getting Paid* (New York: New Press, 2011), 8–9.
9. David Cooper and Teresa Kroeger, "Employers Steal Billions from Workers' Paychecks Each Year: Survey Data Show Millions of Workers Are Paid Less than the Minimum Wage, at Significant Cost to Taxpayers and State Econo-mies," Economic Policy Institute, May 10, 2017, https://www.epi.org /publication/employers-steal-billions-from-workers-paychecks-each-year.
10. Alex N. Press, "Amazon, Vanguard of Class War," *This Machine Kills*, ep. 62, podcast audio, Apr. 21, 2021, https://soundcloud.com/thismachinekillspod /62-amazon-vanguard-of-class-war-ft-alex-n-press.
11. George Skelton, "It's No Wonder Hundreds of Millions Have Been Spent on Prop. 22. A Lot Is at Stake," *Los Angeles Times*, Oct. 16, 2020, https://www .latimes.com/california/story/2020-10-16/skelton-proposition-22-uber-lyft -independent-contractors.

12. Mike Dickerson, "Vons, Pavilions to Fire 'Essential Workers,' Replace Drivers with Independent Contractors," *Knock LA*, Jan. 4, 2021, https://knock-la.com /vons-fires-delivery-drivers-prop-22-e899ee24ffd0.

13. Board of Governors of the Federal Reserve System, "Report on the Economic Well-Being of U.S. Households in 2017," May 2018, https://www.federal reserve.gov/publications/files/2017-report-economic-well-being-us-households -201805.pdf.

14. Marshall Steinbaum, "The Student Debt Crisis Is a Crisis of Non-Repayment," *Phenomenal World*, Nov. 18, 2020, https://phenomenalworld.org/analysis/crisis -of-non-repayment.

15. For a great analysis of how such monopolies are affecting your day-to-day life, see David Dayen, *Monopolized! Life in the Age of Corporate Power* (New York: New Press, 2020), ebook.

16. Amy Fontinelle, "How Much Does Health Insurance Cost?" Investopedia, Mar 13, 2021, https://www.investopedia.com/how-much-does-health -insurance-cost-4774184.

17. Alana Semuels, "When Wall Street Is Your Landlord," *Atlantic*, Feb. 13, 2019, https://www.theatlantic.com/technology/archive/2019/02/single-family -landlords-wall-street/582394.

18. Konrad Putzier, "That Suburban Home Buyer Could Be a Foreign Government," *Wall Street Journal*, Apr. 13, 2021, https://www.wsj.com/articles/that -suburban-home-buyer-could-be-a-foreign-government-11618306380.

19. Board of Governors, "Report on the Economic Well-Being."

20. Brad DeLong, "Rhetorical Question: Why Do Economists Ignore the Greatest of All Market Failures?" *Grasping Reality* (newsletter), Apr. 25, 2021, https:// braddelong.substack.com/p/why-do-economists-ignore-the-greatest-1d7.

21. James Boyle, "A Politics of Intellectual Property: Environmentalism for the Net?" *Duke Law Journal* 47 (1997): 87–116, https://scholarship.law.duke.edu /dlj/vol47/iss1/2.

22. Ryan Reed, "John Oliver Examines World Wrestling Entertainment's Long History of Mistreating Wrestlers," *Rolling Stone*, Apr. 1, 2019, https://www .rollingstone.com/tv/tv-news/john-oliver-wwe-last-week-tonight-vince -mcmahon-815912.

23. "Bad Form, Wells Fargo," *Planet Money*, ep. 732, podcast audio, Oct. 28, 2016, https://www.npr.org/sections/money/2016/10/28/499805238/episode-732 -bad-form-wells-fargo.

24. Rachel Louise Ensign, "No One Wants to Hire the Fired Wells Fargo Branch Staffers," *Wall Street Journal*, Sept. 14, 2019, https://www.wsj.com/articles /no-one-wants-to-hire-the-fired-wells-fargo-branch-staffers-11568453400.

25. Julie Cohen, *Between Truth and Power: The Legal Constructions of Informational Capitalism* (New York: Oxford University Press, 2019), 7.

26. Bradley Thomas, "Why Bernie Sanders's Universal Job Guarantee Is Fool's Gold," Foundation for Economic Education, Oct. 25, 2019, https://fee.org /articles/why-universal-job-guarantees-are-fool-s-gold.

27. Naomi Klein, *On Fire: The Burning Case for a Green New Deal* (New York: Penguin, 2019).

28. Mark Paul, William Darity Jr., and Darrick Hamilton, "The Federal Job Guar-
    antee—A Policy to Achieve Permanent Full Employment," Center on Budget
    and Policy Priorities, Mar. 9, 2018, https://www.cbpp.org/research/full
    -employment/the-federal-job-guarantee-a-policy-to-achieve-permanent
    -full-employment.
29. Andrew Van Dam, "The U.S. Has Thrown More Than $6 Trillion at the
    Coronavirus Crisis. That Number Could Grow," *Washington Post*, Apr. 16,
    2020, https://www.washingtonpost.com/business/2020/04/15/coronavirus
    -economy-6-trillion.
30. Stephanie Kelten, *The Deficit Myth: Modern Monetary Theory and the Birth of the
    People's Economy* (New York: Public Affairs, 2020).
31. A country has "monetary sovereignty" if it (a) issues its own currency and (b)
    borrows primarily in that currency. The US, Japan, Canada, Australia, and the
    UK (among others) are monetarily sovereign. The Eurozone countries are not
    (their currency is issued by the European Central Bank, not the EU member
    states' banks). Venezuela is not (it primarily owes its debts in US dollars, so
    issuing more of its own currency can't help it pay down those debts).
32. Dylan Matthews, "4 Big Questions about Job Guarantees," *Vox*, Apr. 27, 2018,
    https://www.vox.com/2018/4/27/17281676/job-guarantee-design-bad-jobs
    -labor-market-federal-reserve.
33. Apple, "Japan Fair Trade Commission Closes App Store Investigation," Apple
    Newsroom, September 2, 2021, https://www.apple.com/au/newsroom
    /2021/09/japan-fair-trade-commission-closes-app-store-investigation.

INDEX